CONQUERING
CLOUDS

RUTH E WILSON

This book is for:
My sons, Mark and Grant, who have understood and accepted that their mother
followed her own passion in a time when it was not the norm and allowed her to do so.
To Penny and Sharlene, daughters-in-law I have loved from day one.
Finally, to my gorgeous grandchildren Tyler and Josie Wilson - Noona loves you!

PREFACE

Italy or France? Choosing either country as a target would present huge personal and physical challenges.

The first, Italy – to transverse 15,000-foot snow covered Swiss and Italian Alps standing in an open wicker basket with a hydrogen-filled balloon above for over 400-kilometres - just as a start. The alternative, France, variable wind speed and direction that could shatter my flight plan through French territory. Not to mention the French Air Traffic Controllers' demands to be met. "Call or you may be forced to land".

I delayed my final flight decision to continue race preparations for the 2018 Gordon Bennett Gas Balloon Race due to launch that night from Switzerland's capital, the city of Bern. The Race Flight Director Markus Haggeney called a final pilots' briefing at 6pm. The Swiss night vibrated around me.

"Who's going to Italy?" Markus asked the assembled mix of international aviators.

"We are," was my answer. My decision was made. Only two other pilots spoke up. The Russian and the other, an Austrian. The remaining seventeen had plans to fly anywhere but over the Alps to Italy. The majority were heading west towards the south of France. I eagerly checked the final advice from the Italian Air Traffic Controllers. The Padova Airspace north of Milan and Venice looked like a cobweb of varying heights for flight altitudes. I thought of venomous spiders. Had only one reaction. Horror!

"We're not going there," I said with great authority to my co-pilot, Tanys McCarron, standing quietly beside me. The instructions were even more complicated than those received from the French. I now faced my main insecurity about our flight. Working with the myriad of Air Traffic Controllers throughout Europe. Last light was fading. My thoughts danced around inside my brain. Should I have chosen the French direction? What if the projected weather changed over the Alps? What if we found ourselves flying through the demanding Italian Padova air space?

On schedule, *Bernadette* was airborne into the night sky with the city lights of Bern twinkling below us. The notes of the Australian national anthem danced across the night sky beside us. Our balloon climbed towards her destiny as the Australian team in the Gordon Bennett Gas Balloon Race, aviation's most prestigious air race, first launched from Paris in 1906 on a simple principle. Each team to launch from the same location with the same quantity of gas. The team whose balloon landed furthest from the starting point after days of uninterrupted flight won.

While Tanys made sure our night lights were hanging clearly from our basket, I called Bern Air Traffic Control on our aircraft radio. In response, Bern ATC cleared us to 16,000 feet. We were then channel switched to Zurich Air Traffic Control. Our balloon settled into equilibrium above the Alps at a height of 14,800 feet, moving in a constant westerly wind at 33kph towards the East. I had used 20 bags of sand from our total ballast of only 42 bags at launch.

My whole body was humming with excitement. I leaned over the basket edge to peer into blackness below. Once my eyes had adjusted to the dark, I could make out the jagged edges of the mountains straining up to grab us. There was no sign of any other living thing or person. Just two Australian gals alone in their gas balloon,

Bernadette, carrying radios, transponder, instruments, map board, iPads with digital maps of Europe, paper maps, immersion suits in case of overwater flight, food for a couple of days of uninterrupted flight, toilet facility, all positioned inside or around the outside of our basket. We took only the necessities with us, as we needed all the spare weight for extra sandbags. The little comforts that we both had wanted to take were laid aside into their own rejected pile prior to flight - a book, a bugle, my flying teddy bear, extra sunglasses, my favourite small pillow, my makeup bag and hairbrush. A small comb would have to suffice. We did add two small folding stools for sitting.

While an incandescent moon attempted to dodge the heavy clouds, I glanced at Tanys sitting diagonally from me on her tiny chair. She was totally focused on our iPad, our trusty navigation aid throwing images from Sky Demon, checking the height of the oncoming mountaintops, plus the speed we had reached - 35kph at this point. She was wearing five layers of clothing to ward off any cold she had imagined. Her two fears for the flight were cold and flying over large expanses of water. Meanwhile, I scooped tablespoons of sand to spread over the mountains below to ensure level flight.

Around midnight, I reached for my thermos of hot coffee my granddaughter Josie had made for me. The temperature continued to drop. Water froze in the water bottles. Much of the remaining sand froze also. We needed soft, loose sand for our ballast. The small hammer I had brought from my kitchen drawer would be used by Tanys to break up the frozen sand. My job was to concentrate on keeping the balloon flying level to conserve our precious limited sand plus our hydrogen gas, to get us off the Alps and over open ground. There was nowhere safe to go if the balloon developed any problem. Balloon and two pilots would crash into mountainous snow-covered territory. The thought terrified me. Enough that I prayed to my angels for protection. The all-important count of our sandbags continued. The all-important check on our essential oxygen supply for our alpine ballooning challenge was a must.

Three layers of clothing plus my purple sleeping bag wrapped around my shoulders, my red woollen Gordon Bennett blanket over my knees could not hold off my physical reaction to the freezing cold in the wicker basket. My body shuddered and shook, my teeth chattered non-stop. There was nothing I could do but bear the overwhelming discomfort. I had never flown at such a height or with the cold I now encountered. The height did not concern me greatly, but I could do no more than I was doing about the cold that attacked my bones.

The cold felt indeterminable, dominating the eerily quiet of gas ballooning. Both Tanys and I continued to scan the horizon, anxious for the sun to rise, to feel a touch of warmth in our basket. As the first light of dawn spread across the sky, the temperature began to climb from below freezing. After a while, I noticed my teeth had stopped chattering, my shoulders were less hunched. I swear I could feel the blood running through my veins begin to defrost. My mind had found focus again around our flight direction. We were still faced with a final two mountain ranges to cross. With a wind change, our balloon was headed into the belly of the Padova Air Space. My nerves began chattering. Reluctantly I called Italian Air Traffic Control. Briefly the interchange went like this:

"Delta Oscar Whiskey Mike Lima. Permission to transverse airspace at 14,000 feet."

"Delta Oscar Whiskey Mike Lima. Negative. Descend to 9000 feet to be out of controlled airspace."

They did not want us in their controlled airspace. Not what we wanted to hear. I vented a small amount of gas till *Bernadette* settled at the approved 9000 feet. Our speed dropped dramatically. I had now been awake for 23 hours with little food or water. In that final valley to cross, surrounded by the Italian Dolomites, Tanys and I found hell.

I was forced to ask myself, "What am I doing? How did I get here? Will Tanys and I survive this? What drove me to take on such a challenge?" And to remind myself, "Ruth, you are 75 years old."

CHAPTER 1

I was a World War II baby, born in 1943.

Joyce, my mother, was 20 years old, blond, blue-eyed, strong willed, and very unmarried when she gave birth to me at the Salvation Army Home in Rockhampton, on the Tropic of Capricorn in Queensland. "Ruth Evelyn Thorne, a healthy and strong child", the doctor wrote on my birth file.

I was an audacious little thing. By the age of two, I was already reaching for the sky. I climbed whatever I could to its highest point and grabbed anything in reach to loft myself higher. The results were not always pleasant. Once, I pulled a hot iron onto my hand, leaving deep, scarring burns that remain visible to this day. Once, I managed to scald myself by grabbing a cup of boiling water and dumping it onto my chest. And once, I nearly stabbed myself in the heart by running away from my mother with a sharp knife in my hand. I stumbled and fell onto the blade, which narrowly missed that vital organ. Long before I even knew what the word 'adventurous' meant, I was already pushing at its boundaries.

I spent those early years living with my mother's parents in a neat, well-organised house near the Rockhampton Gardens. When mother Joyce became pregnant with her second illegitimate child, a son she named Gene Owen, she moved out.

In Australia, the post-war years were an era driven by class divides and social expectations. A person born into the working class expected to remain there for life. A person born a bastard remained labelled as such forever. Illegitimacy was frowned upon by society and especially by my grandparents. Their daughter had brought disgrace upon the family not once, but twice. My mother moved to a small flat with two of her girlfriends. Initially, she found work as a waitress, then moved to a job at the Rockhampton Meatworks. My brother and I were both declared wards of the state. But while baby Gene was sent into foster homes, I was assigned into my grandparents' care.

My brief stay with them was a soft time. I loved my grandfather. He was one of 15 children and a veteran of the First World War. While serving, he'd lost his left eye at the young age of eighteen. By the time I came into his life, Bill Thorne, as his neighbours knew him, was a tall man with dark brown hair and one hazel-coloured eye who showered me with love and affection. My grandmother, Lillian Thorne, was a petite Scottish woman, just over 5ft tall, but strong minded, capable and quick to correct. She bustled everywhere, setting things to rights as she went. The housekeeper who came regularly to clean did her employer's bidding without question. Grandmother would curl my hair, dress me in a little white dress with my favourite tiny shoes and white socks on my feet, a gold bracelet around my wrist and take me with her to lawn bowls where I was welcomed with much fuss and attention.

Meanwhile, my brother Gene was not so lucky. He was shuffled from foster family to foster family, where little or no affection was shown to him. He was often starved for food and protection.

When I was three years old, my mother returned to her parents' home to collect me. She was accompanied by her new husband, George Edward Lawson, otherwise known as Ted. Ted had come into my mother's life some months before while she happened to be visiting me in my grandparent's home. He'd shown up to take my mother's younger sister Thelma, to the movies. He'd banged loudly on the door expecting Thelma, but it was my mother Joyce who answered his determined knock. She pulled back the door and there was Ted, standing on the stoop. After that first encounter, Ted only had eyes for my mother. He chased her all over, determined to make her his wife. Five months after their initial meeting, they were engaged. They married soon after and showed up at my grandparents to collect me. Now that my mother was married, she and Ted legally adopted both Gene and me, a fact unknown to me until my adult life. As if to erase those awful first years of abandonment, they changed Gene's name to Ronald.

Our little family of four moved to Collinsville, a coal-mining town in North Queensland, to set up a new life. Our family lived in a compact mining house on a street lined with identical buildings. We had only the bare essentials for daily living. My mother's sister Thelma, with her husband Bill Trathen and their three children Colin, Leslie and Heather, also lived locally. They would be my only relatives I knew throughout my childhood. During those initial days in Collinsville, I cried incessantly. I barely knew my mother. I didn't know Ted at all. Who were these strangers who'd stolen me away from my orderly little world? I missed my grandparents and yearned for their tidy house in which I had been adored. I cried and fretted until I made myself ill. In an attempt to help me adjust, my beloved grandparents journeyed to our plain little home in North Queensland, hoping a short visit would calm me. But then they departed just as suddenly as they had arrived. I was three. All I understood was my grandparents were gone and my favourite grandfather had left me. A sense of abandonment settled over my small world.

But as the months passed, I slowly became drawn to Ted. This new man in my life, my father, was not tall. He had a strong wiry physique and a left leg that curved outward at his knee. In his younger days, he'd been a drover tasked with herding a small number of cattle from his boss's property down the stock route to the nearest railhead for transport. His job included riding back and forth behind the animals to keep them on the track, often through dust, haze and heat. It was an isolated life, with barely any time for much else. He spoke little about the accident that had maimed him and would only share that his horse fell on and broke his leg. Injured and alone, it was days before he was found. By then, his wound had become infected.

The doctors managed to save his leg, but it remained deformed. He covered his injury with long pants. Although he remained a quiet man, his clear blue eyes and facial expressions often reflected his troubled thoughts - some of which, I'm sure, were the result of his relationship with his new wife. My mother was born into a generation where the woman's role was to nurture and please her husband and to accept the duties of home as an essential part of her life. This role never sat well with such a spirited, naturally blond, pretty woman. She had a firm figure and an outgoing and social personality, both of which she liked to display. My mother was a woman before her time, they might say today. A rebellious soul. But by the age of twenty-five, she'd stumbled into a traditional, difficult life as housewife to a poor miner and mother of two children with a third on the way.

Daily life in our mining community was a struggle for both my mother and Ted. They were young. Neither had the skills to communicate their feelings, fears or desires. My father had shifted from working at the Rockhampton Meatworks to the hard labour of underground mining at the Collinsville Coal Mine. There he risked hazards such as suffocation, gas poisoning, roof collapse, rock bursts, gas and firedamp explosions. The latter could potentially trigger coal dust explosions that could engulf a pit, burning the entire crew alive.

As a six-year-old, I would watch my father return home from work with his face blackened and his shoulders stooped. I imagined him under the earth in the grimy, dim light while he hacked at the coal-filled earth. I was terrified he would not return. In my imagination, I often felt as if I were trapped underground labouring in a hot, air-less space alongside my hard-working father. The Below - under the ground, under the earth, under the water, was a place I swore to myself I would never go when I grew up.

Not that home was less oppressive. Fights between my parents over the lack of money had become a regular occurrence. Each time their arguments filled our house, I'd retreat outdoors and find calm under the wide and inviting sky. My usual hiding spot was near the outside water tank, where it was cool and quiet.

Wiping away the tears from my face, I would stare at the sky watching the clouds dance. I could sit for hours taking in their shapes and movements. The act of looking up at the sky opened my chest. I stopped bowing my head, I stopped looking down at the ground and I stopped my crying. The sky became my playground and everything in it was at my command.

I just wanted the wind to pick me up, to carry me back to live in Rockhampton with my grandparents, where I'd felt loved and protected. Life at home felt unstable, unfriendly, fractured even. And that was before a bomb blew our fragile existence apart.

One night, by the light of the moon, a man moved stealthily towards the mining home where my family slept ignorant of the approaching danger. At the time, the Miners Federation was heavily influenced by the Communist Party of Australia (CPA). The Party appeared to be challenging Labor reformism by fuelling a class conflict amongst working miners to promote their leadership and platform. The miners had been fighting for a 35-hour week, 30 shillings increase in wages and the inclusion of long service as a normal condition of employment.

The bomb was meant for our neighbour's house-a known and unpopular communist miner who lived alone. But the man who'd carried it through the dark made an error and blew up our home instead, leaving much in rubble. The explosion ripped through the night. Windows smashed and walls caved in as we ran from the warmth and security of our beds. Other neighbours ran into the street towards the wreckage. As they gathered, my little family stood in the back garden, the fragile peace of our small world having shattered. We formed a sad picture that night: my father, my mother holding tiny Glenda, my new little sister, my brother, a four-year-old frightened boy and me, a six-year-old girl, with curly brown hair and hazel eyes. I tried desperately not to sob.

In the months that followed, our already fragile family unit struggled to recover. We children were too fearful to sleep at night. Fights between my parents over limited money escalated. We didn't even have enough for food and essentials. What little joy there'd been in our house flickered and died. "Love flies out the window when there is no money coming in the door," my mother liked to drum into my little brain as she moved around our kitchen. "Remember that Ruth."

Then the Miners' Strike hit in the summer of 1949. It lasted eight long weeks. Two days after the strike commenced, the Labor government passed legislation that made it illegal to give financial support to strikers and their families, including credit from shops. Prime Minister Ben Chifley was prepared to concede to certain demands, but the CPA directed any offer from Chifley be rejected. Chifley chose to use military force and sent the troops in to work the open cut coal mines. It was the only time in Australia's history that troops were called to put down a union strike during peacetime.

Food was scarce for mining families in Collinsville. Often, our family went hungry. Disagreements over whether or not to return to work between men my father deemed friends, grew louder and more regular. Dad was not a fighter. He rarely spoke in anger, even when my mother screamed at him. Finally, he made the decision to move our family away from the ugliness of the mining community to Bowen, 88 kilometres to the east, along the Australian coast.

He secured a six-month lease on a house on Queens Beach that overlooked the ocean and a golf-course. My mother became an active member of the Country Women's Association (CWA); they assisted my family with some payment towards the temporary rental of this property until my father was able to buy a block of land five kilometres outside of Bowen, still at Queens Beach. Our small family of five moved into a tent on the newly purchased land and survived there for several months until my father completed a two-room dwelling for us to shelter in.

Our new home was built of fibrolite, a mixture of asbestos and cement.

Its two windows pushed outward on either side of the front door between the kitchen and the boys' bedroom space. No other windows existed. My father's original intention for the building was that it should serve as a double garage and workshop once a proper family home was built. We were only supposed to have camped in the garage for a couple of years while Dad built us a real house next to it. My father, however, did not believe in borrowing money from the bank. He would not accept the concept of debt. Didn't matter how hard my mother battled with him to change his thinking. He refused to borrow enough for us to buy the materials necessary to commence building. By the time I left home eleven years later, the long-promised family-home was no more than concrete stumps marking the footprint of the 'new' house and the beginnings of a timber skeleton.

Inside the garage, we divided the space in half. One side was sectioned off for my parents' bedroom, the other a bedroom for Glenda and me. The opposite side housed a kitchen area with a wood-burning stove, a table with two long pews. At the other end of the space was Ron's bed and somewhere in the middle was a freezer box to store food. The floor throughout was bare concrete and cold in winter. There was no running hot water. A windmill in the backyard fed water into a tank atop a concrete room with a cold-water shower, which became the family's bathroom. During the winter months, my mother bucketed hot water from the copper stove into a tub so baths could be taken. The dunny was further up the backyard. During the snake season, we made sure there were strong batteries in our torches for any night visits. In winter, or if it was raining heavily, we used chamber pots for nocturnal peeing. It was my job to check three pots each morning and to empty if required.

Snakes were part of our daily life, especially during summer and spring when our cat deposited them at the entrance to the house. The rural countryside surrounding our home was relatively untouched by humans. A scattering of houses dotted the landscape, but not close to each other. Long, untamed grasses grew into wild swaths where we could expect to find any species of snake soaking up the heat of the day, from the coastal taipan, common and northern death adders, to black whip and red-bellied black snakes which, though less venomous than other Australian elapids would bite you all the same. Still, it was the King Brown we were most afraid of - we believed its bite would kill us and we were likely right.

Almost more terrifying than the snakes were the cane toads with their brown warty skin and bony heads. Their poisonous glands hid on each shoulder behind their eardrums. Their hind feet had leathery webbing between the toes while their front feet were unwebbed. Measuring 10-15 cm long and weighing up to 1.3kg, they sat upright, their bellies pale with dark mottling as they moved in short rapid hops.

"Don't look at them or they will spit in your eye and you will go blind," my mother told us. On my journeys to our backyard toilet, I darted past cane toads daily. Each time I managed to arrive, I'd heave a huge sigh of relief. It was quite an achievement to notch another odyssey to the loo into my belt without suffering blindness or death by fang.

My school was a 20 to 25-minute bike ride along virgin bush tracks that wound through a mixture of gum trees, Australian eucalypts and the occasional brush box growing out of long grasses. Bowerbirds, magpies, willie wagtails, the black flying foxes all made their homes in the local trees. Often, as I stomped on the pedals of my bike, keeping a sharp lookout for poisonous critters, I'd catch sight of a swamp wallaby ahead of me on the track staring at the impudent intruder - me.

Where the flora grew thickest, I kept my eyes peeled as I rattled along on my bike. I remembered snakes could not see but reacted only to vibration. Unless they felt themselves under duress, they would slither away for their own safety rather than attack a person. I often saw the green and brown tree snakes prevalent throughout the bush. They were harmless. But still sparked enough fear in me that I searched the bike track thoroughly.

Fortunately, nobody in the family was ever bitten. But once, out of nowhere, as I was cycling to school, a magpie swooped at my head. The bird attacked my face, pecking my forehead. Its dark, powerful wings beat the air, blocking my view and knocking me from my bike. I crashed down upon a large rock. When I tried to stand and re-mount my bike, I found blood dripping from a hole in my right knee. I swung a leg over my bike and attempted to re-launch towards school. But the magpie had me fixed in its sights. She circled, swooped and attacked again and again. I dropped my bike, limped slowly to a nearby tree and broke off a branch to use as a protective weapon.

By the time I arrived at school, I knew I was tardy. Blood ran down my right leg, a large bruise was developing on my forehead between my eyes. I was frightened of what punishment my strict teacher would impose on me. As I hobbled through the door of the school room, all eyes turned upon me. From the rows of shocked faces, I heard: "Look at Ruth's knee!" My teacher sent me to the Principal's office, but not as punishment. Someone called an ambulance. I didn't get into trouble. But for weeks after when I rode through my bush track to and from school, I waved a large leafy tree branch above my head until I was clear of magpie territory. That was the thing about being earthbound—there was always something to be wary of.

My second brother Keith Edward, was born when I was nine years old. Now we were six, crowded into the two dim rooms of our "temporary" garage-house. The presence of the new baby was hardly a treat for me. His arrival brought more jobs and responsibilities. I was called on to help with feeding and whatever else my mother needed. By the time I celebrated my 10th birthday, my mother was completely reliant on me. My days started early. I had to iron my father's clothes before he left to catch the bus to the Meatworks where he worked. Then I made my bed, ate breakfast, washed and dressed for school. It was also now my job to ensure the baby's nappy was clean - and to hose off the dirty nappies in the backyard, then wash and hang them on the clothesline. How I hated changing and washing those soiled pants.

When I arrived home after school, my mother was often in bed with a headache, or complaining of not feeling well. "Make me a cuppa tea, Ruth. You need to peel the potatoes and prepare food for tonight's meal. Don't forget the hot water". The early part of my evenings was spent collecting wood and lighting the fire under the outside copper stove that stood near the windmill so the family would have hot water for cooking and dishes and to wash our bodies. Then I'd have to prepare dinner. For standard meals: three vegetables plus meat: mashed potatoes, pumpkin, peas with lamb chops or mince rissoles or corn beef. In the winter months, stews and soups. On special holiday celebrations, we had jelly and ice cream for dessert.

With each passing week as my brother grew, it seemed like more work fell to me. Helping with the baby's needs, feeding him his bottle of milk, then solid baby food became my jobs too. The grim reality of our household darkened my world. Our dinner table had become a parental war zone. More often than not, heated words flew between my mother and father over one issue or another. Exhausted from my chores and the family evening tensions, I would take off my clothes in the dark in the corner of my bedroom, change into my pyjamas, then sit at the kitchen table to do any homework assigned for that day. A medium size aluminium bowl sat on a small table under the cold water tap near the stove. There I would clean my teeth, emptying and cleaning the bowl after use to leave for another.

Privacy was a rare commodity in our cramped surroundings. The room my sister Glenda and I shared with our parents was around 12ft wide by 40ft, nominally divided by two old-fashioned wardrobes—one facing towards my side of the room, the other opening in the opposite direction.

My parents slept in a double bed behind one wardrobe, while Glenda and I slept in two single beds behind the other. An old, framed picture of a young girl nestling the head of a younger girl, both dressed in 19th century clothing, was positioned above my bed. I would stare at this image nightly. It was the only art in the home. When my parents came to bed, I'd thrust myself under my bed clothes so I could not hear them talking or worse, having sex. Though I had no picture in my head of what was actually going on, I hated and was embarrassed by their sounds and movements. It created an intense shyness in me regarding what went on between adults.

My grandparents visited our crude little house outside of Bowen just a couple of times during my childhood. Each time, I ran to the gate to meet them, my face alight with glee.

"How's my little princess?" Grandfather would say as he bent to kiss my cheek.

"Have you been good?" were my grandmother's first words. She wore a black dress with a white lace collar and her black-rimmed eyeglasses.

"Your grandma has the second sight and knows all," said my mother while sitting at the wooden table pouring tea made from the kettle boiled on the wood-burning stove.

"Can she tell us when we will get our new home built?" came the serious question from a skinny, inquisitive eleven-year-old standing at the door of her two-room fibrolite home. The truth is, I grew up ashamed of our home. Sad that we could not have a normal nice house. Whenever I asked why we were living in a garage, Mum would say 'it's only temporary'. Even now I still think of it that way, despite the decade plus I spent living there. As if my father's promise to build us a real home was still solid and true.

There was little affection in that dark, gritty little abode and less between my parents and grandparents. They were not close. Nor were my parents with me. Touch as an expression of love was a mystery to me. We had no intimate discussions. We never hugged or snuggled each other. I never saw my parents kiss or embrace or hold hands-not once did they ever pause to physically comfort me when I was hurt or feeling down.

The happiest moments of my childhood were Easter and Christmas. As the oldest child, I was allowed to be the Easter Bunny and Santa Claus. Each Easter, I would build a small nest made from sticks and straw to place one at the end of each of my siblings' beds. Once they were asleep, I'd put a small Easter egg into each nest to find next morning. On Christmas Eve, as soon as the other youngsters were asleep, I helped my mother wrap gifts, placing each parcel at the end of the bed of the rightful recipient. But for most of the year, life felt grim and sad.

Since Keith's birth, my mother had remained submerged in post-natal depression that stranded her in a mental, emotional no-man's-land. At only 10 years old, most of the responsibility for bottle feeding, bathing and changing the dirty nappies of my baby brother continued to fall onto me. My mother could not be roused into action. At any hour of the day, I might find her sitting listlessly on the back steps, still in her dressing gown, hair unbrushed, her eyes dead, her mouth sunken because she left her false teeth in the glass of water on her bedside table. She was only in her early 30s. I could not understand why she would not want to look prettier.

"Pop will be home soon, Mum. Why don't I brush your hair and get your teeth so you can look pretty for him?"

"He wouldn't notice if I did," she replied and then disappeared again, sinking into her dark emotional world, hiding any real understanding from her daughter.

In an effort to bring harmony to the household, I worked harder and harder. I kept the house clean, prepared our evening meals, managed the baby, did my homework and awoke each morning to help my father prepare for work and get my siblings off to school. As my mother and I drifted further apart, I developed a closer bond with my father. He liked to go fishing and would often take me with him to help with the dragnet. Knee-deep in the saltwater, I held one end while he stalked into the sea until he was submerged to his shoulders. Dragging the fishing net with him, he would circle around back to shore. Then together, the two of us would haul the net onto the sand, searching for any ensnared fish. There were days when the catch was good, and we'd haul a good amount of flathead fish ashore and there were days when we had little success. I was happy to be out in the open, under the wide blue of the sky and to have a partner to share the task. It was less lonely that way.

Life often felt unfair as I compared my home routine to other kids. Responsibility settled heavily into my bones and though I never shirked, I did resent it. I wanted to study, to finish homework, to be the best. I loved school, for it took me away from home. Despite the lack of time for study, I excelled as a student. I longed to be part of the smart girl group, the four girls who dominated the school, all of whom had proper homes with gardens, fences, hot water, indoor bathrooms with toilets and mothers who were not always unhappy and sick. They ignored my approaches, sometimes laughing at me. I built increasingly high walls around my heart to protect me from the hurt and shame I felt daily.

But if socialising at school was difficult for me, it was much worse for little Ronnie. He was a dreamer. He'd spend more time staring out the window than paying attention to his teacher. He struggled with the schoolwork and developed few friendships. He was not interested in school sports. Still only eleven, Ronnie was not good at sticking up for himself. All these made him a prime target. The larger boys in his class, having taken a dislike to him, lost no time in bullying him. As his older sister, I felt the need to protect him. When I found the older boys shoving Ronnie back and forth between them, I rushed to his defence. The leader of the group usually stood by, laughing and egging them on. Ronnie looked ready to burst into tears. I ran straight at the bullies, pummelling them as I went. I pushed. I hit. I rained blows down upon their bodies relentlessly in a blind fury against their cruelty until they ran away. "Jimmy Carruthers the second," they yelled as I stood glaring at the kids gathering to watch the commotion. It didn't help much.

As a young teen, Ronnie grew increasingly introverted. His main interest was collecting blue mountain parrots that he kept in a huge aviary built at the back of our property. Together we would lay traps. Then we'd hunker down for ages under the scalding summer sun till finally an unsuspecting bird swooped in to eat the seed. A quick pull of the string, the trap fell and Ron had another pet on which to dote. At this time, though I felt attuned to his sensitivities and hurts, I had no knowledge of his early years of abuse in foster homes. Nor was I old enough to understand the impact it had on him. But that aside, it was no surprise he was growing into a fearful young teenager who collected and nurtured soft, hungry beings. He could not control his bed-wetting problem. The punishments issued by our father for this offence didn't help. One day, I found Ronnie standing in the corner, his face to the wall with his hands bound above his head. How this would stop his bed wetting I could not imagine. When he was punished, I was the one who screamed and cried. Ron would just look at our father with hate-filled eyes. I took on all his agony for him. Any belting with the iron cord received, I felt on my own skin. The more he refused to cry, the louder I wailed, till all was quiet and we sunk back into the uneasy gloom of waiting for the next time. He seemed to be the only child out of the four of us who drew such violent attention and I never understood why.

Me, on the other hand, my fearlessness and reliability were starting to be noted. By the time I reached high school, I was chosen as School Captain. I excelled at all sports and finished my exams in the top two or three places. I was still excluded from the smart girls' group, but as I grew stronger and more independent, I found I needed less acceptance from others. My achievements helped to dim the shame I carried within me.

With maturity, I began to judge my mother more harshly. She'd become the example of everything I didn't want to become.

"There's no milk, Joyce," I heard my father say one Sunday afternoon as he poked around in the fridge.

"Send Ruth with the billycan to buy some from the corner shop," my mother replied.

Coins in hand, I launched on my errand with a sense of purpose. The whole exercise should have taken 15 minutes, there and back. But on the way home, I stopped to watch a golfer who managed to lose his golf ball in the bushes. As he slashed the grass with his club, I came over to help him.

"You hit it behind those bushes near the road," I called to him.

Together, we walked towards the place where I'd seen the ball vanish. I kept glancing at the huge stomach inside his blue and white striped sporting shirt. He wore baggy pants and strange navy and white coloured shoes. Eventually, I found the ball for him.

"Thanks, Little One," he said. In gratitude, he reached into his bag and pulled out some coins for me. Back to the shop to buy some chocolate, I went. Then dawdled home to allow time to eat all the spoils. When I walked into the kitchen and handed the billycan of milk to my mother, she shouted at me for not buying the correct amount and for taking so long. I did not see the billycan as she swung it through the air at my head. But I soon saw the blood trickle hotly down my face from the wound. I was 13.

My mother would never raise her hand to me again, but my relationship with her was broken, never to improve.

Not long after my 15th birthday, a raging cyclone had devastated my hometown. The storm set upon the town one April night with little warning. The wind rose to a shriek. "We need to evacuate the house," yelled my father against the noise of the howling winds. Our neighbour had a brick house and he instructed us to run there. As I raced through the soaking rain, tin sheeting from a nearby building and other bits of twisted material torn up by the storm hurled past. Around me the wind flung its full rage as it tore at roofs and trees and my body. I never made it to the sanctuary of the brick house. Upon arriving there, my father did a head count of his children and discovered one missing. He found me lying unconscious amongst the rubble. I had been struck in the head by a sizable log. He lifted me in his arms and carried me into the safety of Mrs. Edward's living room, along with the log that had knocked me out.

For months after the cyclone, I began to experience spasmodic paranormal activities. At times, my dreams foretold future events. Nothing important enough for the world to hear. The premonitions circled small things within the family or my sporting activities. Was this the sixth sense gift genetically handed down from my grandmother? I often wondered as I tried to fall asleep, and if so, would it ever be of any use to me?

At 16, the dam around my suppressed rage burst. There seemed no escape from the endless parental fights over money. The inability of both parents to communicate their needs and feelings, the way they took their frustrations out physically on their children, especially Ronnie, my endless household chores, cooking and washing for all family members stretched my nerves to breaking point. One day, standing in the kitchen during a heated fight with Ronnie, I picked up a large carving knife and threw it at him, just missing his head. I ran outside sobbing. He withdrew to his birds. Our parents never knew.

As the family gathered around the dinner table for the meals I prepared, grievances aired and resentments escalated. I yearned to see less fighting between my mother and father. I often took my father's side.

I felt a wife should be more loving and supportive of her husband. A real woman should take care of herself, her children and her husband. If I could manage, so could she. Once I began yelling at her, I couldn't stop. Crying and demanding to know why she married my father if she did not love him. I hurled accusations at her. Was I even her child? Why did I look so different from my blond, blue-eyed siblings? She fought me and I threatened to run-away from her and her rotten home. Our fight ended with me packing a bag. Then I realised I had no idea where to go. So, I unpacked my things and resumed my role.

My father remained quiet during this particularly outrageous fight. A few evenings later, he took me outside. Tears appeared in his eyes. He said, "Ruth, I love your mother, but life can be hard. Try to be more patient with her and not fight. A man wants only three things in life. A cook in the kitchen, a lady in the living room and a whore in the bedroom."

I had no idea what a 'whore' was. I was so touched by our first one-on-one adult conversation that I tearfully promised him I would try to be a better daughter. I doubled down on my efforts to complete the household chores. I now washed loads of dirty clothes over a copper fire each Sunday, then pushed garments through a hand wringer, pegging all the wet clothes on the clothesline in the backyard. On the weekends, when all six family members crowded in our dark small garage-cave, I felt suffocated. I had little or no space of my own. On a Sunday, I would find the comic section of the paper and retire to my bed to try to relax and read. Invariably, this drew disapproval from my father, who always found a job I could be doing instead of 'wasting my time'. Ronnie would often disappear in search of lost golf balls at the local golf club. Glenda was a gentle child, five years younger than me, seemingly happy to play alone with her few toys. As the baby of the family, Keith was noticed only when he was about to do something that might endanger him.

My place of solace became the large mango tree in the corner of our back yard where I would retreat to study the white tufts of clouds in the cobalt sky. Uninhibited, they chased each other towards the horizon. I sensed their freedom as they drifted above me. And I longed for the same.

CHAPTER 2

Just shy of my 17th birthday, I collapsed and was rushed to hospital with appendicitis and tethering on the edge of a nervous breakdown. As I dozed lightly in my bed, I overheard the doctor explaining to my parents the burden of domestic responsibility their daughter carried was not healthy. Hearing this adult speak up on my behalf brought tears to my eyes. I sobbed quietly into my hospital pillow. Now, I hoped, maybe life would get easier.

Five months later on July 9th, my new baby brother Jeffrey Wayne Lawson was born. A change-of-life baby, my mother told me. Our small two roomed dwelling now had seven people living within its fibro walls - two adults plus five children.

Ron was now spending all his spare time at the Queens Beach Golf Club. He graduated from caddy to owning his own limited set of clubs. He was a natural. At 16 years of age, he was playing off a handicap of five. Word of his achievement soon spread around the other clubs, attracting an offer, a large offer — to become a professional player! Ron and I hugged, jumped up and down. But our excitement was short lived- crushed by our father. He refused to allow Ron permission to move to Townsville to take the offer, forcing my brother to reject this life-altering and hard-won opportunity. "'Playing golf is not a job," Dad insisted. Instead, he had Ron take on an apprenticeship as a house painter. The brother I loved so much did not last six months in the job. As soon as he was old enough, he left to join the Army. He had endured physical punishment after physical punishment - for his bedwetting, for his lateness home from school, for his inability to finish any job in a way that met with our father's approval and even the thwarting of his future as a professional golfer. Finally, he had escaped.

My own chance at freedom came soon after.

When the local Lions Club ran the inaugural 1960 Queen of the Coral Coast contest at Horseshoe Bay, my decision to enter was my first step towards emancipation. I stood 160 centimetres tall, weighed 56 kilos and had nicely developed breasts, a small waist and hips that owned my tanned legs. I was blessed with healthy, wavy dark brown hair that fell to the tip of my shoulders. I could put a sparkle into my hazel eyes when required.

Still, I had doubts. Could I really see myself standing in a line of 10 or 12 girls, all in swimsuits, being judged by the local doctor, the dentist and the mayor? The panel judges were all males, of course and I wasn't sure how I felt about that - about *men*, not to mention an entire audience of summer revellers and beachgoers gawping at me in nothing but a swimsuit. But I knew if I was to find a way to change my life, I'd have to squash my body-shyness. I convinced myself I'd just be one of many young females chasing their dreams and while I desperately wanted to win; I didn't think I had much of a chance. Nevertheless, I felt confident the judges would be scoring points not only on body shape, looks and attitude but also for a female who showed intelligence. I holed up under my favourite mango tree and rehearsed intelligent answers to the questions I thought they might ask.

Question: "What are your ambitions?"

Answer: "To be a teacher or a journalist and to travel the world, then marry and settle down with two children."

In my world I rationalised, teachers were shown respect and I enjoyed working with younger children. Every Friday afternoon, I was tasked with being the current instructor for the Under 12s Marching Girls, a responsibility I took seriously. And just recently, journalists had invaded Bowen to report on a local murder. Everyone around town was abuzz with talk of these newsmen from down south. I imagined they must live exciting lives, travelling around the country covering media stories. I wanted to do that too. Frankly, I wanted to do anything that would allow me to leave.

As for marrying and having children - well, they were just expected of a young woman of my generation and I was keen not to seem like too much of a renegade.

Still, however cautious I might be with my answers, I knew I'd have to be willing to take some risk. I secretly bought a red backless bathing suit, so outrageous in 1960 as to be almost considered an act of social resistance. I told no one of my plan, not even my sister and certainly not my parents.

The contest day dawned bright and hot. A bundle of nerves twisted in my stomach. How could I escape the house without Dad asking where I was going? I spent the morning tidying the kitchen, sweeping the rooms, making sure all my chores were completed. My mother was in hospital again, so I prayed my father would attend the afternoon visiting hours. Pacing frantically, I watched the clock tick away. Still, my father showed no sign of leaving. If I asked permission to leave, he'd demand the reason and I knew he would refuse me, just as he had Ronnie. All my silent planning was fading to nothing. I calculated the minutes I needed to reach the beach in time for judging.

Just when I was about to give into despair, my prayers were answered. To my great relief, my father left for his hospital visit. I grabbed my bicycle and rode towards the beach as if the wind were carrying me. It was a magnificent tropical afternoon on Horseshoe Bay Beach, North Queensland. Gentle waves rolled onto the sugar-white sand. A large crowd stood around the raised stage where a group of swimsuit-clad girls between 17 and 21 years of age posed, clutching their individual numbers. I hurried to change, collected my number seven and joined the line.

Most of the other contestants were taller than me. I sneaked a quick look down the line. Only one other girl was shorter. They were all pretty. I wondered who the judges would deem the winning beauty. My nerves made it hard to stand still as I waited to be interviewed. "You can do this, Ruth Lawson," I whispered.

My turn. I stood before the judges in my fire engine red swimsuit, suddenly feeling naked with only the adornments of a watch and a gold bangle on my arm. I fought an inclination to turn and flee, meld into the crowd and disappear forever. It felt surreal to me that I was standing talking with three men, my legs bare from hip to toe. But when I looked into their eyes and saw kindness, my fear slipped away.

Whether it was those well-planned blander than bland answers or my saucy backless suit, I'll never know, but to my intense surprise and delight, I was crowned 1960 Queen of the Coral Coast. Later, riding high on my victory, I rode my bike to the hospital to visit my mother. My father, I anticipated, would still be there and as I neared the building, reality hit. There were going to be questions I'd not rehearsed answers for. I'd never imagined winning or the consequences of winning. As I stood by the bed in my mother's hospital room, wondering if there was any way I could avoid owning up to my afternoon exploits, the doctor, who'd judged me in the contest, suddenly walked into the room.

My heart accelerated. I kept my eyes focused on the hospital floor. I had spent years doing the right thing so as not to disappoint my father or attract punishment. Now my behaviour suddenly seemed completely outrageous. I could hear the doctor talking but could not absorb the back-and-forth between the three adults around the hospital bed. Slowly, I raised my eyes to meet my father's. His gaze revealed nothing at all. I turned my head to look at the doctor.

"Congratulations Mr. & Mrs. Lawson," he was saying. "You have a beautiful, intelligent daughter. Ruth was the only entrant who answered our questions without hesitation and with confidence. She will make a fine Queen of the Coral Coast."

Receiving such acclaim from our town's respected doctor made my father stand taller, my mother smile wider. I opened my mouth to thank the doctor, but he had already turned to continue his rounds through the ward. There was nothing else to say on the matter.

CHAPTER 3

Six months later, I was standing at the bow of a boat that ferried me towards Hayman Island. My prize for winning the contest. To allay parental concern of a young daughter going off on her own to the most exclusive island in Australia, the Lions Club, who'd sponsored the competition, had provided me with a chaperone who now stood a few paces behind me on the ferry.

As the island grew closer, apprehension spread through my body. What would I find? Would the clothes I brought with me be suitable for such an elegant, expensive place? What kind of food would they serve? Definitely not the kind I'd eaten at my home, I suspected. Would there be dancing and, if so, would a man invite me to dance with him? What about swimming, a pastime not allowed by my parents in previous years? They'd forbidden me to go anywhere near the beach. "It is dangerous to swim in the ocean. You could drown, be taken by the current," they'd said. It seemed to me having any fun was incomprehensible to my parents. Going to the beach, taking a holiday-only other people I knew did some of those things. But now I was one of those other people.

The boat docked alongside a long pier that jutted into the aqua blue water. As the passengers stepped off, the island manager directed the guests onto a tiny train as the staff loaded luggage. By 6pm I'd arrived at the main reception. I stood in awe of the decor of my surroundings and tried not to feel out of place. I was three months short of my 18th birthday and had no knowledge of life outside my limited world. A strange mixture of fear and excitement surged through me as I headed for our accommodation, myself in one hut, my chaperone, Fay in the hut adjacent.

After settling into my bungalow, I changed into a pale pink linen sheath dress, brushed my hair and headed to the lounge. Fay was not ready to mingle, so she stayed in her hut, leaving me deliciously unchaperoned for the evening.

A group of holidaymakers, mostly from Sydney and Melbourne, were sitting around the pool and called to me to join them. I sat down. The man on my right side introduced himself as Kevin Wilson. He was tall, with a full head of brown curly hair and blue eyes. A guy named Tony sat to my left. He was lank-haired with sharp features and was deep in conversation with a tanned brunette with bright orange lipstick. Eventually she smiled at me, but it was as plastic as the Coca-Cola straw she was sucking. Across the other side of the table, a woman named Jan raised her glass, letting her shell pink silk wrap slip further down, exposing more of her sizable breasts. This older, sophisticated city group was foreign territory for me. I smoothed my simple linen dress, fretting. If they could see where I lived, how poor my family was, they would not talk with me. The conversation swirled around me. No one addressed me, so I sat quietly, trying to look more elegant and intelligent than I felt.

"What would you like to drink?" Kevin asked.

I didn't know the names of any alcoholic drinks, let alone the fancy cocktails my companions sipped at. "I'll have the same as Jan," I replied. A gin and tonic appeared in front of me, which I downed as if it were a soft drink. It sent my head spinning. Kevin realised I was out of my depth, so he made sure I reached my cabin that evening without being seduced by any of the interested males. Once I was safely delivered, he disappeared.

On my second day on the island, new faces appeared at dinner. One of those was Joyce Meagher from Sydney, who was seated beside me in the tropical restaurant.

We immediately began swapping stories. I listened with interest as Joyce talked about her family and her job working in an office in the centre of Sydney. It all sounded so exciting and glamorous.

At the hotel dance that second night, I introduced Joyce to Kevin and some of the city group. Around midnight, Kevin suggested he walk me back to my bungalow. This time, when he delivered me on my doorstep, he took me into his arms and kissed me goodnight several times. As he held me close, a beautiful warmth spread throughout my body. It was the first time anyone had hugged me closely. I remembered the warning talk my mother had given me earlier in the year, just after my 17th birthday.

"Do not come home pregnant at any time. Your grandfather will never love you again. Men only want one thing from a woman." Though, that one thing was never fully explained. As I stood in Kevin's arms, I felt a sense of belonging to somebody, a real man, a man from Sydney. Surely, he must care for me to hold and kiss me so. I felt a tingle of excitement and surety. This feeling must be love, I thought. But what next? He pulled away from me, smiled and then bid me a good night and said he hoped to see me tomorrow. I opened the door and floated inside, feeling like a very grown-up woman.

Each night, for the remainder of my time on the island, Kevin did the same thing. He walked me to my bungalow, gave me a hug and kiss outside my door and then disappeared. The thought of any sexual activity never entered my mind. Sex education at school in those days did not exist. The subject was never raised between my mother and myself. Even to mention the word 'sex' to any person was thought shocking. Sex was something that happened once a woman was married to a man and I was a long way from that scenario.

Kevin left the island on a Friday, but we had agreed to write to each other. Joyce was due to leave four days later, suggesting I visit her in Sydney. I packed my things and I left the five-star elegance of the resort Saturday morning to return to the small, dreary world of my Queens Beach home. My Hayman Island experience had shone a light on my home life, exposing the incredible contrast of how people live their lives. I thought of the two Hayman bungalows Fay and I had occupied and recognised the footprint of my home was smaller than the two huts put together. I could not begin to share my experience with my parents as I believed they could not possibly understand or appreciate the recent magnificence I had seen. I felt sorrow for the hardship and bleakness of their lives, but had no concept at all how I could bring change to their world.

My thoughts were full of Kevin - was he in love with me? And of Joyce and her invitation to visit her in Sydney. My life had been turned upside down, but I had no person to share my news with who would understand. I went back to my narrow bed in the dark room I shared with my sister and parents and back to my job at the meatpacking factory. I lasted two months. Nine weeks after my Hayman Island experience, I took up Joyce's invitation and flew south to Sydney for what I intended to be a short vacation. After the first week, I recognised I could not and would not return home.

For the first time in my young life, I found myself living in a normal family house where there were no raised voices, people were kind to each other and shared laughter together. In the first days of my visit, I woke ready to face any tension from fights throughout the household. As the week wore on, I found myself surrounded by kindness and laughter. I could feel myself consciously begin to relax, tension began to fade from my body. I had a true friend in Joyce. We went to the movies and to parties together. Joyce's younger sisters Pam and Robyn also readily accepted me into their lives and introduced me to city life in 1961 Sydney. The day loomed for my return to my parents' home. I definitely did not want to go. When Mr. & Mrs. Meagher agreed to my staying in their home, I started job hunting, very quickly securing work as the Personal Assistant to the Managing Director of one of Australia's largest printing companies.

I wrote to my parents to tell them of my decision and to my boss in Bowen, the Managing Director of the Merinda Meatworks, to give my one week's notice. I expect my decision seemed a fait accompli to my parents. The only comment made to me came from my mother. "Your father does not want you going out with too many men, but we expect letters from you with what you are doing." For days afterwards, I felt like a bundle of nerves. I had acted so decisively. The enormous change I had just grabbed left me in a state of confusion. But then I'd look about and I'd remember what living with my parents and what life in Bowen offered in comparison and I'd breathe easily once more. I'd made the right choice.

By the time I received my first pay cheque from my new job, I realised that at 18, I was earning more money than my father. I began sending funds home every week to help my family.

Glenda was 13 years old, taking on my old responsibilities around the family household, helping with baby Jeffrey, establishing her own relationship with our parents. I hoped her role and bond with them were different from mine. But imagined she had her hands full. Keith had grown into a robust 10-year-old. My brother Ron was now with the Australian Army in the Borneo jungle. We had little or no communication from him and knew only that Borneo was overseas. His army life was a mystery to me. I confided my worries about my sister and family to Kevin, who also lived in Sydney. He encouraged me to let go of my guilt about abandoning them. By way of distraction, he took me for dinners at restaurants and long drives to the mountains, all the while acting more like an uncle than a lover. Maybe that was because he was also seeing one of the elegant city-ladies he had met on Hayman Island. At first, I felt jealous that another woman was stealing his time away from me. But as I began making new friends, going dancing at clubs and enjoying my independence and freedom as a young woman without the burden of heavy household responsibilities, my romantic dreams around a potential future with Kevin faded away.

I bought a green star trumpet. Music had been part of my teenage life as a member of the Bowen Brass Band. At 16, I had played the Last Post with my cornet on Anzac Day at the cenotaph in front of the town's citizens. When the popular Sydney singer Col Joye heard about a female trumpet player, he invited me to East Hills and the Joye Boys' bunker to play music.

I had been living in Sydney for a year when I received the phone call. My mother was in hospital. When he called to tell me, I heard the gentle pleading in my father's voice, "She is very ill, Ruth. We are worried about her and I think you should come home." How could I ignore his need? I felt a huge wave of guilt for the selfishness of my choices; I had left my family behind to live my own life. I had no idea how long I would remain in Bowen, so reluctantly I handed in my resignation at my work at the printing company and flew to Proserpine, then took the bus to my hometown. My father met me at the bus stop.

"How serious is it?" I asked my father as we bounced over the old familiar roads towards our Queen's Beach home.

"Her blood pressure is very high; kidneys are a worry," He looked stressed.

The atmosphere between my father and me was quiet and restrained. He rarely communicated easily and I readily accepted this was his way. He never questioned me about my Sydney lifestyle, but he seemed more at ease now that I returned home.

Together we drove to the hospital and stood beside my mother's bedside, quietly showing our support to the best of our abilities. Though I'd cared for my mother frequently in times past, I no longer felt like the same unhappy teenager. Sydney had changed me, matured me, given me confidence and hope that happiness was possible. As I hovered at my mother's beside once again, I felt grown up, an adult navigating my return to my previous life, a capable daughter who would help her mother through her final hours.

But 10 days after my return, the doctor sent my mother home.

I had moved back thinking my mother would die in that hospital, that my father and my siblings needed my support. Now mother was home. I began to feel cheated out of my city life, angry with myself for acting in so drastic a manner and resigning from my job. Within no time, my life settled into its old routines. Tensions between my mother and me raised their ugly heads often. I thought I had concrete walls around my heart where my mother was concerned- but she managed to get to me every time.

In Sydney I had tasted freedom and happiness. Now I found myself back in the cauldron of poverty, drudgery and acrimonious dinner conversations that I'd thought I'd escaped. I questioned my surroundings, my parental relationship. After six weeks, I found myself wanting to cry all the time and the familiar restraint of tears frightened me. This could not be my life. I spent many sleepless nights trying to find the courage to move away a second time. The opportunity came when I was invited to stay with a girlfriend who had moved to live in Surfers Paradise on the Gold Coast. I thought long and hard about this next move, about my mother and father and my siblings and the guilt of leaving them again. But I knew in my heart I had to go. I had to create my own world.

Finally, granting myself permission to leave was made easier because I had the security of a friend and an apartment to travel towards. I'd have my own bedroom. And, whatever it took, I would find a job. Becoming a champion hot-air balloon pilot had not even registered on my radar. I stayed in Surfers Paradise for six months working as a bookkeeper at the only five-star hotel around.

One weekend, sunning myself on the Surfers Paradise beach, I looked up to see Kevin Wilson sitting on the sand nearby. It had been a year and a half since our first meeting on Hayman Island and eight months since our last date in Sydney. We made plans to get together, but that never eventuated. I did not understand my feelings towards him. I felt we had a connection and he was special in my life, even though a strong romantic relationship had not happened in Sydney. I liked him but was not passionately yearning for him at all. I wondered when and how might we come together in the future.

The answer came sooner than expected. A few days after that brief meeting with Kevin, Joyce Meagher called. "I am getting married in Sydney and would like you to be my bridesmaid." I felt unsure about returning to Sydney. I was only 19 years old and finding my feet, building confidence in myself, was yet to happen. I felt insecure about finding my own place to live; on my first foray into city life, the Meagher family had been more than generous housing me. Would I be accepted and embraced by the city folk I'd once called my friends? Or would they turn me away? Despite my uncertainty, I boarded a bus bound for Sydney. And when I arrived, I called Kevin's office to tell him I was back.

CHAPTER 4

In the 1960s Australians marched and demonstrated against the Vietnam War, John Lennon married Yoko Ono and Kevin proposed to me.

I was more than surprised. We had been dating a while, going to live theatre, movies, to restaurants. All the while, he'd remained a confirmed bachelor. On this evening we had been to dinner at a Sydney restaurant, then parked under the Sydney Harbour Bridge. He kissed me once and then he kissed me twice and then he asked: "Will you marry me?"

Thoughts raced through my head - someone loves me enough to spend his life with me. I felt elated, but these were the words that came from my mouth, "I am only 20. I want to travel the world before I marry."

"I promise you we will travel the world and life will be wonderful, Ruth."

We were married August 31 that same year and honeymooned in the snow of Perisher Valley. There were many firsts for me over that period. I was a virgin when I stepped into Kevin's arms on my wedding night. I had little knowledge of what my first time might bring. I had imagined.... Instead, it brought bleeding and a distinct shock of disappointment on my part. Afterwards, I smiled and kissed my new husband goodnight and fell asleep wondering if that was all sex was. It took me years to realise the intense intimacy I was missing.

In addition, I hated the snow. It was cold and I could not master skis. Kevin shushed down the hill side, leaving me crumpled at the top of the slope. All in all, it was a disappointing start to married life.

Over the next couple of years, the daily routines of a young married couple filled my days and nights. Kevin held his accountancy job at his company while I worked as a secretary at Pepsi-Cola. Together we squirrelled away our funds for the deposit on our first home, a pale brick house that shone with '70s decor inside. I loved my new home. I loved the white walls and purple carpet and robust green plants in white pots. I often recalled my childhood home. The entirety of that dark, concrete-floored, two-room shack could have fitted inside my new living room and kitchen. My new home brought me much joy.

When we'd been married four years, we decided to start a family. Two weeks before the due date of our first child, I dreamed he would be a boy and his name would be Mark Gregory. My grandmother's 'sixth sense' had kicked in. Our son Mark was born right on schedule, August 3, 1967 and with his arrival came the joy of motherhood. My home life was pleasant, even comfortable. Kevin and I supported each other in our new-found roles as parents of a young baby. There was no long discussion on whether or not we would have a second child. Kevin was adamant the world of an only child was not a happy one. Mark needed a sibling. Not long after that conversation, I became pregnant once more.

Mark's brother, Grant Edward, was born two weeks early, on February 24, 1970. As the nurse lowered him into my arms, I wept with gratitude that he was healthy... and so beautiful.

After the boys were born, there was no more talk of my working. I had accepted my role as a wife and mother and discarded any dreams of becoming a journalist or teacher. Kevin was the breadwinner. I had two little boys to mother, plus a home to keep clean. I wanted our house to be a special place for Kevin to return to after his daily work pressures. Despite our relative privilege, I realised as a married mother I had many of the same domestic responsibilities I'd tried to escape from by leaving Bowen. Food shopping, preparing meals, looking after young children. Some days it felt like there was little difference between my two lives. Except, instead of caring for my father, I was caring for a husband. But this was my own family and I needed all of us to feel loved and wanted.

Five months after Grant's birth, I was woken in the middle of the night by a presence. I snapped upright in bed. In the room, moving towards me, was a ghostly vision of my father. He extended his right hand and said, *"Come, I need you".* Our home telephone rang about 7am. "It's your mother," Dad said. "They have rushed her to Townsville hospital. Can you come I need you?"

My mother lay on her hospital bed with cords coming out of her body. They led to a bottle on the floor that was collecting fluid. Everything in that room felt brittle. I sat on a hard chair, with my feet on a hard-tiled floor, stroking my mother's dry hair. Despite all that had passed between us, I needed to comb it for her-needed to bring dignity to her. But even then, my mother's eyes held no light. She was only 47 years old but looked closer to 70- battered and exhausted from a life of discontent, living in poverty under the bruising tropical North Queensland sun. She stared at me in utter defeat.

"Why does she have all those tubes in her?" I asked the nurse, who was hurrying in and out of the room.

"Her kidneys have collapsed," the nurse replied, then she disappeared down the hospital corridor, the implications left unsaid.

For the next ten hours, my mother clung to life. I recalled the days when she stumbled through the house unkempt and uncaring. After so many years of illnesses that I'd often pushed aside with frustration, she had always just … lived through it, whatever *it* was. This time, she lost her battle.

I was 27, just 20 years her junior. Contrasting feelings roiled inside me. I could not cry for her. Instead, I promised myself I would live my life differently than she had. I would not surrender to a life that lacked passion. I would not surrender to a life of defeat.

Our relationship had never been easy. Now suddenly she was no longer in my life. I couldn't have known at the time that a day would come when emotional walls around my mother/daughter relationship would crumble. But come it did and with a vengeance.

It took a marlin fishing boat accident and me looking my own death in the eye. During those agonising hours in the sea off the Ballina bar, I thought of my mother a lot. I thought of all the anger that had passed between us, how I'd judged her for the lack of affection between my father and herself. In my desperate struggle against the unmatchable force of the sea, I questioned if I could have related to her in a better way. Surely, she too had once been a girl who'd had hopes and dreams. Surely, she too had floundered, had been overwhelmed by forces larger than her.

I had been in the water then for over two hours, 35 minutes. I could feel my strength ebbing-felt a weakness, a temptation to give in, let go. I closed my eyes, let my head rest in the water. It would be so easy to give up. Was that what my mother had told herself while her life dripped away all those decades? Were those depressive years her final memories in her hospital bed? Or of a time when she'd yearned for a better, happier life? Had I been a disappointment as a daughter? Suddenly, I wished I had talked with her, asked her about her younger life, asked her what was missing and what had gone wrong.

"I am so sorry, Mum," I cried out loud as the waves bashed my body. "I don't want to die here in the ocean. There is so much more life I need to live. I haven't fully loved."

I opened my eyes-raw with salt- and threw my head back far enough to take in the full expanse of sky. It seemed so far away. Memories of my first hot-air balloon inflation 13 years earlier flooded my thoughts; the excitement I'd felt when the burner spat flame into the balloon's belly, the power of the fire, the intensity of the heat thrown from the flame, the potential for danger. I tried to remember how I had controlled that flight. How adrenaline had rushed through my body as the basket rose from the frost- covered grass. How the ground had fallen away as we drifted higher and higher, leaving all my earthly struggles behind.

As I looked up at the sky from the water, I remembered how the land had looked from the air. How the landscape below me fitted together in a stunning synchronicity that I'd never felt before. The river dotted with trees along its banks curved its way through green pastures towards the distant hills. Standing in the balloon's wicker basket, I had absorbed the power of this new and magical playground. My balloon and I had become one with the wind, one of the millions of particles being swept through the sky. Released from gravity's grip and floating towards the heavens, I'd felt light, like air, like the clouds I'd watched hastening across the sky as a girl back in Bowen. It was a privilege I would respect and enjoy as long as I remained alive.

Alive! The word beat like a drum in my head. As the chill of the water crashed against me, all thoughts of mother, my ballooning adventures faded away. Below me was a darkness. *Under the earth, under the ground.* The place I feared the most. I needed to fight both the ocean's swell and the terror that gripped my body. I needed to survive.

CHAPTER 5

By the mid-70s, I was married with two small sons. I had left the poverty and unhappiness of my childhood behind for a better life, one with a bright home, two beautiful children and a husband who provided well. I should have been happy, but I couldn't shake the gnawing feeling something was missing.

In the 1970s, the sex-role attitudes began to shift in favour of women entering the workforce. Even women who had children. Ideals of liberal feminism also became more prominent; women began publicly arguing they were capable of doing anything men could do.

So, when Kevin came home one night from work and informed me we were moving to live in America, I was enthused and excited. Kevin expressed concerns about such a drastic move, but I strongly supported the plan. I hoped a major life- change would squash the feelings of emptiness that sometimes took hold of me, often at unexpected hours of the day or night. I was ready to embrace a new challenge and to have the promise of excitement disrupt our normal lives. We put the home we had designed and had built up for sale. Told each other it would quickly be bought. After all, we had ten months before our departure. In retrospect, it was a risky decision. The stress of waiting caused me to contract shingles which broke out painfully around my waist. Fortunately, at the eleventh hour, we found a buyer and contracts were finally exchanged five weeks before our departure date.

In February 1971, we left Australia to spend a couple of weeks on an island in Fiji en route to the USA, Kevin was 40, Mark, 3 and Grant just one-year-old. I celebrated my 28th birthday on the plane.

We spent our first six months in America in a sweet rental home in New Jersey while I searched for a new family home for us. This I found in Madison, a leafy quiet suburb in New Jersey. Our new suburban home was a charming two-level house, painted a two-tone pale green and white on the outside with classic detailing, hardwood floors, high ceilings, and a huge, finished basement inside. I marvelled over it. I'd never lived in a house with a basement before.

A week after we moved in, I answered a knock at my front door. A representative of a local community organisation service called the *Welcome Wagon,* introduced herself. I invited her into our living room. She handed me a list of services we might need: doctors, dentists, pharmacies, babysitters and so on. In addition, I received a large envelope with discount vouchers from local merchants to help me find my way with my shopping.

"There is a group aligned with WW called the Newcomers Club, open for new residents to join," she explained. "Membership lasts just 12 months. Then you graduate." As soon as it was practical to do so, I joined their monthly meetings. The group offered a myriad of activities; golf, trips to New York to take in shows, chess, cooking classes and so on. I left the first meeting having set up my own group, a gathering opportunity for other newly- arrived women in the area. It drew 15 to 20 new locals to my home every Monday night.

Kevin and I experienced the rush and bustle of New York, the theatre, the New Hampshire autumn colours, the historic images and energy of Jamestown and the nation's capital, Washington DC. Along the way, we formed many great friendships. Our boys were happy with their young American friends. Loved it when I allowed them to eat their favourite all-American snack: peanut butter sandwiches smothered in a gooey white marshmallow spread. Me, I loved it all. I loved being foreign. I loved the newness and challenge of navigating a country other than that of my birth. Each day became its own adventure.

I played the part of the corporate wife excellently. Hosting Kevin's boss and wife, plus other company couples, to our home gave me another challenge to embrace. Our days at home were busy building new friendships and learning to take an interest in politics, in life in America. During this time, I began my real social education; it was strange to learn things were acceptable and what were frowned upon in the States. We joined the Country Club, but my first time in its swimming pool, my tiny bikini drew shocked comments from other wives. My wardrobe was full of miniskirts and knee-high boots which were also frowned upon. It was the early 1970s, I'd presumed all things would be more liberal than back home.

Some of our friends were staunch Republicans; others passionate

Democrats. It was an eye- opening experience for both Kevin and me to listen to the various political discussions that took place over casual drinks. I found such talk and commitment to a cause stimulating, coming from a country where it was not accepted to speak of or discuss politics or religion. Politics was never a part of my growing up, but a vague memory of my father supporting the Unions and Labor Party tried to move into my discussions with my Democrat friends.

Nightly news polls claimed 60% of Americans were against the Vietnam War. Anti-war activists were often arrested, at times by both police and military units.

A popular topic of conversation with our friends focussed on the Watergate scandal and President Nixon - with varying views depending on which party they supported. When the Supreme Court ruled the death penalty was unconstitutional, not one of our friends disagreed with the finding. The Walt Disney World Resort opened in Florida. I added that to the list as a possible future vacation destination for my family.

When Greenpeace was established in 1971 by a small group of concerned individuals, it became a hot topic oft- discussed over drinks, or at any BBQ we attended. The group sailed in an old fishing boat named *The Greenpeace* to Amchitka Island off the coast of Alaska to try to stop a US nuclear weapons test. Such audacity excited me. I was certain I would join this group and try to save the world. But that dream was soon quelled when Kevin told me the company was considering sending him to work in Japan.

On the day I was invited to become the first non-American President of the Newcomers Club, Kevin announced he had accepted the promotion. We would be moving to Japan. As his wife and mother of his two sons, I knew it was my job to support him in this new endeavour. But I was not happy about it. I loved my American home, my friends, my various outside interests. Did I really have to leave my life behind?

While I'd found our move to America to be exciting and liberating, I had huge reservations about moving to a culture where the gender roles remained more traditional. A husband was expected to be the breadwinner. A wife was expected to be submissive. I wrestled through sleeplessness and unsettled dreams until I found a way to turn this decision over which I had no control, into a positive. As a girl, I had learned to accept that thought was the only thing a person had total control over in life: thought. If I could channel mine towards the positive, my feelings would follow. I'd found such happiness in moving to America. Wasn't the same sense of adventure possible in Japan? Each day I told myself that it was until I believed it.

CHAPTER 6

We were approaching Tokyo's airport when the aircraft's fuselage shuddered and screamed. Would we make it safely through the typhoon raging outside? Inside, passengers grabbed for paper bags. My husband, Kevin and two sons Mark, 4 and Grant, 2, huddled close to me. We had left Los Angeles 25 hours earlier. Fatigue hung over us like a wet umbrella.

A sea of foreign faces bustled through the crowded terminal. Our command of the Japanese language was absolutely nil. Unable to communicate, our little ones tired and hungry, a typhoon raging in the darkness – this was our welcome to our new life in Japan. We were shown to the hotel bus. A local gentleman offered our boys candy and patted their blond hair. That small gesture lifted my heart. I felt then that our new life would be fine. The following day we flew to Osaka, took a car to the Oriental Hotel in Kobe situated at the eastern end of the Inland Sea on Ōsaka Bay, about 35 kilometres west of Ōsaka, 506 kilometres southwest of Tokyo. The city is sandwiched between the Rokkō Mountains to the north and the sea to the south.

Along the drive from Osaka to Kobe sat crowded grey concrete buildings with neon signs in Kanji. Through Amagasaki, dirty, heavily polluted, tiny wooden houses merged into one another, each sprouting at least one television antenna. Past Sumiyoshi, where the houses stood on tiny blocks of land with some breathing space. Trees and greenery more prevalent as we sped along the highway. Mikage, Rokko. Obviously, the more affluent areas with beautiful homes were half hidden behind high fences and gardens. These scenes were my first taste of Japan. I was hungry for more.

My initial challenge to living in Kobe was finding a home where my very tall husband could walk through the door without knocking his head. By the time I'd toured six houses, I was almost in despair. In general, Japanese homes had small rooms and simple kitchens. I did not want to appear difficult to impress, but my mind would not allow me to settle for what felt like a step backwards. When I first viewed the Mikage home in Kobe, the house that was to become our home for nearly five years, I was shocked. The paint was peeling off the walls, the tiny kitchen was filthy with an ancient stove and sink. How was it that this house was even offered for viewing? But quickly I was taken in by the Japanese style gate and path leading to the front door. Upon entering, I found a large living room that could hold our furniture and walls suitable for our art. The home was on two levels; with a living-room, kitchen and maid's quarters on the ground-floor and three bedrooms and bath areas upstairs. I felt immediately at home in this space. When the owners agreed the inside of the house would be painted and a new kitchen installed, I took a deep breath and signed the contract.

After a brief trip back to Australia, I walked into the Mikage home with a huge sense of pride. It had been totally painted inside and a new kitchen installed. All our belongings fit perfectly. Home established, I was ready to hurl myself into the next adventure - *Japan!* And towards the new person it would teach me to become.

Just as I had in America, I tried to make friends. Though no local Welcome Wagon members appeared on our doorstep, our landlord's wife did serve me tea in delicate china cups. She was resplendent in her orange, green and gold kimono. As I sipped, I began to absorb my new Oriental life. We bowed low to each other in courteous farewell.

Every bit of our home was a beautiful mystery. I was intrigued by the old-fashioned Japanese bathtub made of wood from the *suginoki* tree and the small bucket and pail finished with a light layer of wax that leaned against the wall in the corner of the room. I quickly accepted the bathing process, cleaning my body outside the bathtub, using the bucket of water to rinse off dirt and soap before climbing into the warm water to soak and relax.

As my circle of female ex-pat friends slowly grew, I learned from our intimate discussions many found the adjustment to life in Japan daunting. No longer could they drive to a large shopping- mall for supplies or find kitchens with all the latest gadgets, especially the large refrigerators they'd used back in the States. We understood Japanese housewives were careful shoppers. They did not buy things in large quantities like Americans, partly because they didn't have room in their relatively small houses for a lot of stuff and partly because cooking with fresh ingredients was preferred. My European friends often shared their disappointment that they could not find their favourite foods. I listened. I sympathised with them, but I remained determined to embrace this new culture.

Kevin worked as Finance Director for an American pharmaceutical company responsible for the Far East that required him to travel to Hong Kong and Tokyo with the occasional trip back to the company's head office in New Jersey. Monday to Friday his days were spent at the office. On weekends, he went to play sports at the Club to relax.

Both our sons attended school; Mark at the Canadian Academy, a private international school approved by the Japanese Ministry of Education. Grant started at a Japanese school, the lone snowy haired foreign child surrounded by local children. He was embraced by his new little friends and seemed very happy. Despite having uprooted them twice in their short lives, I was determined to give them the security and warmth my childhood home had lacked. I noticed my sons' confidence with their new surroundings appeared stronger when Kevin and I displayed close and warm interactions. I knew it was our responsibility as parents to surround our sons with a loving home.

While they were at school, I got on with the business of fitting in.

But in Japan in the 1970s, foreigners and locals rarely mixed socially. Not long after our arrival, Kevin and I joined two clubs where we could meet and mingle with other foreigners. The club culture dominated our lifestyle. Nearly every day of the week found us at one or the other; we passed all our social hours and every Sunday dinner there. Or Kevin and I would have a chance to compete on our respective squash teams, a common interest that bonded us. The club's swimming pool was a favourite destination after school and on the weekends. I settled easily into the social atmosphere with other wives around the pool while our children played and swam together.

Outside the club environment, it was a different story. Not speaking the local language made shopping for groceries difficult. As foreigners, we were continually stared at, often pointed to by locals while they moved away from us, laughing. I couldn't read public signage being unfamiliar with the language. I couldn't communicate my needs in any of the shops I entered. Mostly, my method of selecting fresh fruit and vegetables from the wayside vendors relied on lots of pointing fingers, nodding of head and smiles. There were days when I embraced the 'Japanese challenge' fully and there were other days when I felt conspicuously different, embarrassed I could not communicate, frustrated with the isolation it brought.

Once I travelled by train to Kobe Centre in order to meet my husband and friends at the Kobe Club. I was late and hurried. After exiting the train station, I paused momentarily. No taxis were available and my concern at being late provoked irrational decisions. Navigating the city was difficult for me as I couldn't cipher the street signs. But I could see the Kobe Club standing like a sentinel at the top of the hill on Tor Road, away from the noise of Sannomiya and Motomachi below. "I'll walk," I decided, heading into the dark, winding bar area. I quickly lost my bearings and then my way amongst the footpaths. Now thoroughly desperate, I stared at sign after sign on the buildings, understanding not one word. I began to cry. I hadn't felt so helpless since my days of hiding under the mango tree in the yard back in Bowen.

"Please, where am I?" I pleaded with passing locals. But they hurried on with lowered heads so as not to be embarrassed by the distressed *gaijin* lady crying and stumbling along. My desperation became more obvious when I ran into the middle of traffic on a busy causeway to try to stop a taxi. I had not yet learned the local custom, that taxis only pick up passengers at taxi ranks and they would not stop- especially not for a *gaijin*. After two hours of walking, I finally recognised an intersection. One that was a very long distance from my original destination. Luckily, I was rescued by an American couple who happened to stop at the traffic lights. As I wiped the tears from my drawn face, they drove me to the club and a relieved Kevin.

I decided it was imperative I study the local language so I would never again feel so impotent. Nor would I be unable to communicate with the people of the country I now called home. Chizo Yakamoto was my teacher (sensei). Her parents were diplomats who had lived in many countries, so she had been exposed to lifestyles other than those of her homeland. She came three days each week to my home and her role in our relationship slowly changed from sensei to friend. After lessons over afternoon drinks, she educated me on many facets of life in Japan. In the evenings, wrapped in my *yukata,* I walked to sit down at the dining table, removing the Geisha doll dressed in an orange and gold kimono with purple obi as well as the orange, gold and pink Saji Japanese plate to the end of the table. The antique wall clock ticked loudly in the quiet of the night as I began studying my Nihongo lesson.

Life began to settle in a daily smooth routine. Kevin left home around 7am each morning, walked to the local station and took the train to his office. I breakfasted with my boys, drove them to their respective schools, then returned home to face my daily agenda - either studying Ikebana, the art of flower arrangements, lessons for Nihongo, or coaching squash at the club.

I could not have lived this lifestyle without the support of our live-in helper, Youko.

Her main role was to tend to our boys when Kevin and I were not at home. Household duties, including cleaning the kitchen and bath areas, fell on her shoulders. We often cooked meals together and in a short time period, Youko became one of the family. While the tradition was for such live-in help to receive one day each week off, I insisted Youko take two for her own personal pleasure. This did not make me popular with some of the Club wives.

Youko had her own *tatami* room- with its own entrance on the ground level adjacent to the kitchen. Her space was a traditional Japanese room with *tatami* (mats) on the floor with an alcove called a *tokonoma*, where she placed her personal effects: some pottery and the occasional *ikebana* arrangement I had made for her.

And so, our days and weeks passed. Until our calm routines were disrupted by the unthinkable.

On New Year's Eve afternoon 1972, I left my home to drive to Kobe to get my hair done. Kevin and I were attending the party at the Kobe Club that evening. Kobe roads are only wide enough for one and half cars, with section mirrors placed so cars could pull over to allow other cars to pass. I drove up to a mirror and stopped my car, glancing to my right. A man and woman stood on the footpath with a small boy of about eight years old beside them. The boy was carrying a bag of oranges against his chest. Another adult male was hurrying down the hill towards the stationary threesome. As I started to slowly move my car forward, the youngster ran across the road, hit the front righthand side of my car and fell. On impact, the oranges rolled in every direction. I felt shock zip through me as I looked at the scattering oranges. Where was the boy? Under my car? On the road? Bizarrely, the couple walked away in the opposite direction. The older man accelerated down the hill screaming abuse until he reached my car. He had scuffed, dirty shoes. But on his left pinkie finger, he wore a huge diamond ring. Even in my shocked state, my intuition was clear. My confronter was a 'yakuza'– a 'stand over man', a gangster.

Kevin and I had been warned by other foreign contacts to be careful of the Yakuza. They were known as the Japanese mafia. Their men would knock down the stall of any vendor who failed to pay the protection fees to their stand-over members. The Yakuza also followed a Japanese ritual of amputating portions of one's own little finger to atone for offenses to another. It sounded all very Hollywood movie stuff to me…until suddenly I became part of the drama. Bumping into cars owned by foreigners was a method of getting money. It was common knowledge the Yakuza ran such scams.

I turned to my right. The old man with the ring had arrived at my car and was still screaming at me. A light bulb went off in my brain. The scam I had been told about a few times was actually happening to me. I was out of my depth, but also frightened about what the authorities would do when they arrived. The old man kept hurling abuse at me, his ring glinting in the light. I was certain he was Mafia.

In a short period of time, the police arrived at the accident scene and took me to the station. It was almost 11am. My Japanese neighbour came to act as an interpreter. When Kevin arrived at the police station, the interpreter strongly suggested to him he pay the distress funds demanded by the boy's "uncle" and not to argue. Kevin refused. Negotiations came to a standstill. The police sent us home close to 7pm. We were emotionally drained, Kevin still furious at the injustice of the occasion, me still in shock.

The boy had been taken to the hospital and released later in good condition. My Japanese neighbour explained the local tradition of apology. We would be expected to visit the youngster at his home and to bring the required gifts. She implored me to do so.

I followed her advice, but not without angst and a mixture of emotions. Kevin drove me to the family home and waited in the car while I approached the front door. The child's father acknowledged my presence and bowed. I bowed back, then accepted his invitation to enter. The family sat on cushions on the floor around the accident victim. I kneeled, leaning forward to offer my gifts - Japanese candy and fruit. I was met with lots of wailing I could not understand. Despite all my lessons, I was impotent once again. After 10 minutes I stood, bowed with an apology once more and offered my *sayonara*. I sat in our car, feeling drained and humiliated. The demands for financial compensation for having caused the family distress on the day of a New Year's Eve celebration kept coming. These further requests for money from the uncle of the boy were denied by Kevin. The family renewed their demands. And the figure kept increasing. There were mornings I felt angry when I woke at the unfairness of the situation. Kevin showed a stubbornness that I had not seen before. A crack formed between us.

While Kevin stewed with anger, I found myself gripped by fear. I would not open our front door by myself. I'd wait until our street was clear of any person before I walked down the hill to the train station. I grew suspicious of any male not dressed in a suit and tie. I was overprotective of Mark and Grant, whereas previously I had felt comfortable with them roaming our sweet neighbourhood. How quickly life can change. How fast contentment dissipates.

I began to blame my husband for his stubbornness, for putting our lives under such a huge strain by not paying the initial financial demand as advised by the police.

Three months after the incident, Kevin began receiving threats at his office. When those threats began to include mention of someone tracking the movements of me and the boys and that the things might accidentally befall us, Kevin finally agreed to meet their demands- a sum way higher than originally demanded. In our attempt to move on as quickly as possible, we fell into a pattern of not discussing our feelings with each other, of putting shields over our emotions. That precious, invisible bridge between man and wife was crumbling. It took an enormous effort to consciously re-embrace the alien culture.

But there were things I loved about Japan....

Cherry blossoms graced our neighbourhood every spring for a couple of weeks. Their fragile petals falling to the ground when any wind touched their branches. There were clothes which I loved - the yukata worn primarily by males. My eyes feasted on the gorgeous kimonos the Japanese women wore. The more I grasped the language, the more I understood the people and the more swept up I became in the country's traditions. We became sumo fans attending many sumo matches. Japan's history fascinated me. I read and studied early Japanese history of the Shoguns, the warrior codes and attended many festivals.

I was particularly fascinated by the Tanabata Festival, held on the seventh night of the seventh moon or July 7. The fable behind the festival is well known by young females in Japan. Emperor Tentei decided to punish the young couple, Princess Shokujo and Kengyu, for neglecting their duties, positioning them on either side of the river where there was no bridge. So, the couple relied on magpies to flock together on this night to form a path so Shokujo could walk over to meet her husband. If it rained, the Milky Way would become flooded and the two stars would not be able to meet for another year. In current times, it is believed Shokujo is Vega, the Princess Star, and Kengyu is Altair, the Prince Star. One time each year, these two stars cross paths so they are recognised as the star-crossed lovers. How romantic to come up with such a story then create an annual festival around it.

I blossomed personally. Exposed to living in a country with a history more ancient than that of my birthplace, I grew more curious. Studied the indigenous religion of Japan. Shinto, an optimistic faith with the belief that humans are fundamentally good. Buddhism – achieving enlightenment—a state of inner peace and wisdom to experience nirvana. All concepts I found attractive, as I lived with the ideology that each person was doing the best they could. Living in a foreign land, with foreign attitudes and behaviour, fed my soul as well.

We travelled widely. Our experiences were many. Koya-san, birthplace of Buddhism in Japan; Ise, home of the Shinto religion; Tachikui, a rural settlement famous for its pottery; Toba, birthplace of the Japanese pearl industry; Nara, ancient capital city from the Nara Period (710 – 781); Kurashiki, attracting tourists and local artists. Kyoto, capital from 794 through to 1868, when Emperor Meiji moved the capital to Edo (Tokyo). Kyoto was my favourite city with its many temples, shrines, gardens and the Imperial Palace.

Somewhat out of the blue, I was invited to write for an English newspaper that served Kyoto, Kobe and Osaka. The editor was looking for someone to interview interesting people for his publication. My name had apparently been given to him by a number of people and before I knew it, I was offered an amazing opportunity to fill an entire page with content and photos. I called my page 'The Word'. I could scarcely believe my luck. My journalistic career had commenced. I never ceased to be amazed at the inscrutable industrious, polite manner the Japanese people emanated – in their homes, their business and work and with the local friends we made, even during their relaxation.

As high-profile Australians living in Japan in the early 70s, Kevin and I were on all social invitation lists. Parties amongst the foreign community sprung up spontaneously every weekend. Kevin travelled often throughout the East. My sons were healthy and I enjoyed being a mother, but the people who shared my days and nights in Kobe were not of my spiritual tribe. They filled the space in my life, but I was aware of wanting to meet or be with different people.

However, I was getting better at embracing the expatriate lifestyle of saying goodbye to friends, making new friends and losing them back to their respective countries in a short number of years. So, life went on, with its parties, alcohol, lessons and writing. Despite the kids and my new-found love of journalism, it all felt superficial. I felt restless for something I had not yet identified.

CHAPTER 7

And then my grandfather, my beloved grandfather, died. And a piece of my heart was torn asunder with news his death brought.

I had lost my grandmother while we were living in America and had missed her funeral. There was no way I was missing my grandfather's final send-off. I flew to Australia, towards unsuspecting pain borne of shock. I moved through the funeral in a daze, tired from the long plane flight from Kobe to Rockhampton via Sydney and Brisbane. My father and sister did not attend. I found this odd and wondered why?

The Oxford dictionary shows the meaning of *grief* as *intense sorrow*. It was not sorrow that flowed through my body, but a strong physical pain, pulsing in my muscles and causing the bones to ache further. My beloved grandfather, who had played with me as a child, the person I had adored from afar during my adult life, was now gone. A huge black hole engulfed me as his coffin was pushed through the dark curtains into the fire. My mother and both my grandparents were dead. I remember thinking if it hadn't been for the fact that I still had my father, my siblings, Ron, Glenda, Keith and Jeffrey, I would have felt completely unmoored.

Nine hours after my arrival in Rockhampton, I boarded a coach to travel north to my hometown, Bowen. It was dark when the coach rolled out of its depot with its gaudy advertising signs colouring my bleak mood. Early the following day, after a restless night, I stepped off the coach into the bright sunshine of Far North Queensland for the first time in many years.

Glenda was waiting at the bus stop. "Hi sis," I greeted my younger sister with a hug. Similar in height, with her light brown hair cut short and curled around her face, I marvelled at how grown-up she was. The five-year difference in age meant we had little in common and little in contact after I'd left the family home. I had gone off to marry, moved overseas and was now far removed from Glenda's life. We exchanged birthday cards with each other but with telephone calls expensive and letter writing the only other method of sharing news, neither one of us chose to call or write. We lacked that sister-closeness I saw in other siblings. Which is perhaps why I missed seeing the conflict in her eyes.

Once we arrived at my sister's home, I washed my face in the bathroom, then sought her out in the kitchen. I sat down on a white painted chair at the orange Formica table, watching Glenda pour boiling water into the teapot. Framed family photographs were spread around the room.

"I've got something to tell you," Glenda said.

I had something to say to her, too. I wanted to know why she hadn't come to the funeral. But I never got the words out.

"Pop Lawson, Ted, is not your real father."

My initial reaction was one of confusion. Was I hearing correctly? What had she just said?

"What did you just say?" I asked out loud.

"You are not Pop Lawson's daughter. I found out when I got my birth certificate for my wedding. You were already three years old when Mum and Dad married," she said. "He is my father though and Keith and Jeffrey's. I confronted Mum with my birth certificate. She was very distressed when she explained that you and Ron were little when she met Pop. They married and he adopted both of you. She made me promise never to tell either of you the truth."

"Why are you telling me now?" my response was scarcely a whisper.

She reached for the milk and laced her tea. "Well, with both Grandma, Mum and now Granddad gone, I thought you should know," she replied.

In one sentence, she had taken away the man I had loved and believed was my biological father, the template of a man that life had given me, now shattered and removed. I was too overwrought at the news to wonder at my sister's real motivation in giving me this shock. Later, I'd suspect it was a secret she no longer wished to hold on to personally.

Glenda continued. "Apparently both Grandad and Grandma disapproved of Mum's marriage and your adoption. That's why they were not close and why Dad chose not to go to the funeral. I just did not feel like going either."

Blindsided. Utterly stunned. Felt like I had been stabbed. More than once.

My body began to shake. Sobs wracked through me, filling my sister's small, bright kitchen. My heart wept rivers of tears. I felt orphaned. I had just lost both my beloved grandfather and father within days. Glenda sat across the table, wiping tears from her eyes. That she was my half-sister did not compute. She was still my every-day, baby sister.

Later that afternoon, I finally slept. On waking, my thoughts turned back to my parentage. Who was my real father? Why hadn't my mother told me? I was too emotionally exhausted and drained to feel angry.

When my father arrived at Glenda's home for dinner that night, my feelings towards him were mixed-up– gratitude that he had parented me as my biological father when he was not, followed by intense sadness that he really was not my "real" father. While my sense of loss was overwhelming, I could not bring myself to tell him what I knew. Instead, I decided to continue our father/daughter relationship as usual. Glenda accepted my decision to protect him from the painful emotions of 'losing his daughter'. I held my father a little longer than normal as we hugged farewell. I was leaving the next morning to begin my long journey back to my own family in Kobe and I was not ready to let go of my father-template.

On the return plane trip to Japan, memories of conversations between my mother and me during my teenage years flooded back.

"Why am I so different from the others?" I asked, eyeing my younger siblings. "I have brown hair and hazel eyes, while my brothers and sister are blond with blue eyes." I was stating the obvious. But no one had seemed disturbed by it except me.

"You take after your grandfather, Ruth."

"If you are so unhappy, why did you ever marry Pop? Were you pregnant with me?"

"No. We were married on Boxing Day in December and you were born in February. Do I look pregnant in my wedding dress?" was her reply.

I had to agree, she did not.

So, mother and daughter had soldiered on until the next confrontation. My mother hiding a secret about our connection while I had no knowledge of the complex dynamics between my parents.

After my return to my life in Japan, I often felt fragmented, lost in a sea of mental anguish. When I tried to talk about the loss I was feeling, Kevin would discourage me with the words 'just accept it'. I felt totally unsupported and started to withdraw further from our relationship. There was now an even larger crack in my feelings. There were days when I felt I was drowning and could not see the sky through the black clouds that covered me.

But our time in Japan was coming to an end.

After nearly five years in Kobe and a round of farewell parties, we headed towards Kevin's new corporate position in New Zealand. I did not want to go. It had taken so much work to establish a life in the Land of the Rising Sun. I often expressed my unhappy thoughts to Kevin, but I was a corporate wife and my opinion appeared to have no relevance. In the end, I thought my life would inevitably be governed by wherever he chose to accept his next promotion.

Little did I know....

CHAPTER 8

On the journey to Auckland, we made a stopover in Sydney, where I had to undergo major surgery. I'd been experiencing continual female health issues during my entire time in Japan, but was too embarrassed to visit a local doctor. Now I was at an appointment with my gynaecologist, who had delivered my elder son, Mark.

He did not hesitate with his diagnosis: second stage prolapse brought on by the birth earlier of two whopping 10lb babies. He ordered a hysterectomy and a bladder repair and booked me in for immediate surgery with a recovery period of two weeks.

"You will be able to ride a horse in six weeks," he assured me. He was horribly wrong.

Kevin continued on to Auckland, to his new job responsibilities. Our boys stayed with Kevin's mother in Ryde.

During my convalescence, I wrote about the experience and sent it to Cleo Magazine, a recently launched 1975 ladies' magazine that had featured a male nude centrefold in its debut edition. The editor phoned just prior to my departure for Auckland. "I like your writing style. Would you look for interesting men to interview in New Zealand?" There was no mention of the requirement for a nude centrefold, so I agreed.

Upon our arrival in Auckland in June of 1975 and for the first month or so, I felt I had stepped off the bottom of the earth. After my full social life in Kobe, I had to adjust to a very different lifestyle. Had to start all over again. There were numerous periods of loneliness. I missed my life in Japan where, against the odds, I had established a strong sense of identity. My boys were at school. Kevin was adjusting to the responsibilities of senior management. And I was completely lost.

I kept my feelings to myself. The silences between us grew longer and longer. I had never witnessed open, honest communication between my parents, never seen my father take my mother in his arms or kiss her, or my mother sing or smile as she went about her daily homemaking. I lacked the wisdom of how to commence the expression of my concerns in a partnership. So, I said nothing at all. I continued to flounder under thoughts of loss of my previous lifestyle in Japan, loss that eroded the small amount of self-esteem I carried within myself. From Kevin, there was no comment at all.

I had propelled my husband into the power position in our relationship, *the* authority figure. He never spoke of the strain of his new work responsibilities and I never asked. I was struggling to learn to take responsibility for all my needs and fears. The energy required to connect on the same level with my husband was diminished by my inward search for my own power. The power to find the self-esteem I had felt while living in Kobe.

When I was first introduced to Jim Greig, I knew I had found a possible magazine story. He was a prominent potter whose work had been displayed in galleries in Kyoto that I'd frequented. I felt a profound connection to this artist, so I arranged a time to interview him. When I arrived, I found a slight, quietly spoken, deeply spiritual man, who spoke easily about his passions. Jim was busy preparing to leave for the United States. "I'm actually a balloonist," he told me and went on to explain he intended to compete at the 1975 World Hot-Air Balloon Championships in Albuquerque, New Mexico.

"What's a balloonist?" I said.

Who knew that my life would be changed by one casual question?

We spent the afternoon together looking at photos of his red and white *Bernia* hot-air balloon, while I listened to stories of his flights and his plans to compete in the World Championships. I felt I had made a new friend. As we parted, I asked him if he could take me for a flight in his balloon when he returned to New Zealand.

The 27 days until Jim's return passed as slowly as any I can remember. Each week-day Kevin left for work early. The boys both went to the local school while I tried to climb out of my grief for my grandfather, for the loss of my father, for the loss of my old life.

My New Zealand days were full of nothing. I was desperately unhappy, claustrophobic, depressed. I found it hard to breathe. I had lost my inner smile. I often laid the blame for my misery at Kevin's feet for having taken me away from the life I'd built in Japan. For the first time in a long time, I was back to feeling that unhappy girl from Bowen who had watched clouds escaping across the sky. I ached for something to lift me so I could follow them. While I looked forward to pursuing my Jim Grieg ballooning magazine piece, I could not find the motivation to 'look for interesting men' for any further Cleo articles. I was drifting through my empty days.

Sometimes I glimpsed a stronger me, a woman in her own right, someone who was not just Kevin's wife and mother to my boys. When I'd visited Jim, he'd told me he was a follower of Rudolf Steiner. I'd left his place with Steiner's books, *The Philosophy of Freedom & Theosophy* and *Intuitive Thinking as a Spiritual Path* on the back seat of my car. Over the long weeks that followed, I read both volumes. It was something I told myself, to fill the emptiness of my days until Jim returned.

But when the call came, it wasn't quite what I expected.

"Hello, Ruth. It's Jim here. Just back in Auckland. How are you?"

I assured him I was well. Quickly, I referred to our proposed flight.

"My balloon is damaged. I had a fast landing and ended up dragging into a barbed wire fence. I have ripped eight of the 12 vertical panels. It's a huge repair and I will need help once we start the project next week."

I didn't hesitate. "I don't have much happening during the day. Let me help. Let me know where and when." Jim agreed, and Kevin had no sooner walked in the front door from work when I burst with my new-found excitement. He seemed pleased that I was smiling and had a new focus.

When I saw Jim's balloon for the first time, I was shocked. Hundreds of meters of red ripstop nylon lay tattered and torn on the floor of a sail maker's loft 20 minutes from my home. Vividly, I recalled the elegant curvilinear form I had admired in all Jim's photos. I had identified with the balloon's spirit and playfulness. Now I was overcome with dismay at her mangled state.

"Where do I start?" I asked Jim.

"All the damaged panels have to be unpicked stitch by stitch," he said, 'then each totally replaced with new material. I suggest you start with the unstitching… thanks, Ruth." He added gratefully.

And so I began. For hours, I sat and unpicked the threads that held the panels in place. The light, silky cloth felt slippery and cool in my hands, but quickly took the heat of my fingers, bonding me with *Bernia*. I marvelled at the millions of stitches and the strength of these seemingly flimsy materials. But were they strong enough to bet my life upon? There were many moments when my eyes sought the Auckland sky through the large glass windows, visualising hopping from cloud to cloud in *Bernia*'s basket.

Once the damaged panels had been discarded, I happily assisted the sailmaker's machinist as she sewed the new material, panel by panel, in the machine. Two hundred man-hours later, the re-built red *Bernia* balloon was ready to fly.

And so was I.

"Meet me tomorrow at 6am at Bayswater," Jim said.

That night I tucked myself into bed, determined to have a good sleep, but my mind went skyward. How would I feel standing in an open basket? Would I be frightened of the heights? How dangerous was ballooning and how safe a pilot was Jim? After all, he had just destroyed his balloon flying in New Mexico. What if we crashed? What if I died? Who would look after my darling boys? The bedside clock showed close to 1am. I woke again at 4am, dressed and then drove to the Auckland suburb where I'd agreed to meet Jim. The lights of a car rounded the corner and drove slowly onto the park. The first thing I noticed was the large wicker basket on the trailer attached to the car. Wicker.... Not metal, not plastic, not solid like a ship's hull or an airplane cabin, just a woven, porous vessel-the kind you'd fill with berries or flowers. "How romantic," I thought.

As the rays of first light spread across the sky, a crowd of interested spectators gathered to watch us prepare the red balloon for inflation. The wicker basket was lowered to one side. The crew took the stainless-steel wires attached to the deflated red balloon, checked to ensure no twists existed, then hooked all four karabiners to each corner of the burner frame. Once the balloon and basket were secured, Jim and his crew moved along the deflated balloon, pulling the material out across the grass to ready the envelope for inflation and bring the balloon to life. I stood close by as Jim opened the burner taps and flame poured into the opening of the balloon, heating the inside air. *Bernia* rose majestically from the damp, dewy grass to stand upright. The red and white cloth I'd stitched for days now towered several stories over my head. I took a breath. *Bernia* was a stunningly beautiful vessel.

"Hop in, Ruth," said Jim. I swung my legs over the side of the basket before Jim had finished his invitation.

Jim pulled on the burners and threw another plume of flame upward. Moments later, *Bernia* gently lifted from the ground.

And finally, after 30 years of yearning, I cut ties with the earth.

I felt an overwhelming joy surge through my body. The ground retreated and with it all my anxieties and despair. Below me, the shrinking landscape became organised and manageable. Beauteous. I had found home. Despite the cramped conditions of the tiny basket and the lack of guardrails between me and the long fall to earth, I felt no fear. What I felt was power. The heat of the burner overhead, the dance between pilot, flame, cloth and wind. The wicker of the basket creaked when I shifted my weight but felt completely stable. I was lost in the wonder of being airborne in what was little more than a laundry basket when Jim's words to hold on to the rope handles, filtered through my dreamlike trance. He was taking the balloon back towards earth.

"We're restricted with our flying area, Ruth, so I must land. I'm pleased with the balloon's repairs."

Twenty minutes only. But the joy felt during those 20 minutes fizzed through me. I knew immediately I had found my place. It wasn't in the world, but above it. From now on I would belong to the air. I would become a pilot.

And I wouldn't just fly. I would soar.

CHAPTER 9

And the following night I did soar, though not to the heavens in a balloon basket. I found myself soaring through parallel universes. I slept soundly until the early hours of the morning when my spirit left my body, then floated above. I remained acutely aware of the bright orange and gold Mediterranean patterns of the curtains and bedspread in the room and that my other self, Ruth E Wilson, remained in a deep sleep.

I found myself in Egypt, an officer in a Pharaoh's army leading a large number of soldiers, home from battle. The campaign had been successful. Crowds thronged the streets, shouting and acclaiming their heroes' return. I rode within three metres of the Sphinx, climbed down from my horse, then took a few steps forward. Standing on the left side of the Sphinx was a holy man with a shaven head, dressed in a neutral hessian type wrap over one shoulder, his left. A rope belt adorned his middle. He wore sandals on his feet. His eyes were almost black and held mine powerfully.

He reached into a phial of holy water, sprinkled some of that water on my forehead as a blessing. From my left appeared a strikingly beautiful woman with long black curly hair and deep, deep blue eyes, followed by her maidservant whose hair was fair. At that point I woke, my body physically shaking, continuing to do so for what seemed like minutes.

The intensity of the experience remained with me for hours as I struggled to understand, to accept the many questions assailing me. I knew very little of Egypt, the Sphinx, and Pharaohs. My most profound knowing was that this experience was not a dream. What I began to accept was that I was a spirit who had lived other lifetimes, who lived on after my previous earthly body or bodies had been shed, who was living this lifetime as Ruth.

My fear of death was diminished greatly with this experience.

CHAPTER 10

Forget planes – flying began with balloons. It was the French nobility who conquered the race to put man into the air. The first manned balloon launched on 19 September, 1783 before King Louis XVI and his Queen, Marie Antoinette. Monsieur Pilatre de Rozier and Major d'Arlandes rose into the sky from the grounds of the Chateau la Muette in an aerostat designed by Joseph and Etienne Montgolfier. The 78-foot-tall balloon drifted over the Paris rooftops at about 500 feet for 25 minutes before landing safely five and a half miles away on the Butte-aux-Cailles.

A couple of months earlier, the Montgolfier brothers had launched their first test balloon. Made of rag paper reinforced with linen and paired with a wicker basket, it carried not men but a duck, a sheep and a cockerel. No one was sure what would happen to the balloon once in the air. Suspended over a fire of old shoes, wet kindling, straw and rotten meat, the balloon sucked in the smoke and rose into the sky, floating away for eight minutes, landing one and a half miles from the launch site at the Chateau de Versailles. The animals suffered no ill effects from the experience. The sheep was rewarded by being installed in the Queen's private zoo. But what happened to the duck and the cockerel, no one knows.

"It's the sport of the Gods," declared a delighted Marie Antoinette. Though the same Parisian mob that had cheered along with her and shared in her excitement of that first balloon fight would behead her a few years later. Enthusiastic journalists of the day reported that "journeys by air will be so speedy, so convenient and so low in cost that we shall even see women visiting the four corners of the earth."

CHAPTER 11

And I was committed to becoming one of those women. I just had to find a pilot to teach me and a way to get my own hot-air balloon. No balloons were being manufactured in Australia. Only three or four balloons purchased from the United Kingdom existed around my home country. In New Zealand in 1975, Jim Greig was one of two pilots with their own balloons. The other New Zealander was Laurie Soffe, the dealer for the British balloon manufacturer, Thunder Balloons. Laurie lived in Auckland, not far from my home. I contacted him to arrange to meet and asked, "If I buy a balloon through you, will you teach me how to fly it?"

"Of course," he replied.

It did not occur to me where I would find the funds to purchase any balloon. I was blinded by my vision of standing in a balloon basket, controlling the fire above my head, to float above all below. I walked away from our meeting with the strongest conviction I was on a course and had to find a way to continue.

At my first ballooning lesson, I was numb with cold rather than excitement. Dressed in jeans, an old striped shirt and heavy navy sweater, I would have been more comfortable in a heavy parka and fur-lined weather-resistant boots as I waded through frosty grass at a farmhouse in Ngatea to meet my instructor, Laurie Soffe.

I was about to step into a wicker basket that reached just above my waist to float to 3500 feet, to pilot a hot-air balloon. The New Zealand early morning sky was clear except for an occasional low-flying cloud and a couple of high-flying birds.

These were truly pioneering days of hot-air balloon flight with no regulations. The equipment was minimal; a basket with three tanks of LPG gas, a burner and envelope above my head. The balloon carried no instruments or radios. Mobile phones had not been invented. I had spent the previous afternoon at Laurie's home while he went through the theory and physics of how a balloon worked. For me, it was important to understand the equipment I was to take to the sky.

The basket made from wicker cane had two footholds cut into one side to allow easier access to climb over the top. Inside the basket in each corner stood a gas cylinder with LPG gas. Black hoses were attached to each gas tank at one end, the other screwed tightly to the burner above my head. Two small pilot lights were lit in the middle of the burner. Once the tap on the gas tank was opened, gas moved through the hoses to hit the pilot light. Flame roared overhead, aimed towards the balloon envelope. The heat from the flame warmed the air inside the envelope to cause the complete balloon to rise. To descend, it was a matter of not turning on the gas taps, no flame, so the inside air would cool.

I felt comfortable I could control the flame. Was eager to be airborne.

With such minimal instruction, I was ready, confident and eager to start my journey of flight. I guess I thought at the time this was a fun adventure, something to tell the kids about. Little did I know my life was about to change forever.

Laurie watched as the balloon was laid out with the basket on its side on the ground, ready for inflation. My left knee took my weight, my right knee touched the burner frame edge as my fingers reached to open the burner tap. Short, evenly spaced bursts of flame shot into the mouth of the balloon's envelope, causing the rip stop nylon material to unravel, as the air inside the belly of the balloon grew hotter. At a certain point during the inflation, longer bursts of heat became necessary to cause the balloon to rise to her peak. Flame shot forward from the burner, imitating a flamethrower.

I felt the power of fire, the intensity of heat thrown from the flame, potential for danger. Adrenaline rushed through my body. I knew immediately this would be a lifelong affair.

That morning, conditions were calm and cold, perfect for an easier inflation of a hot-air balloon. The heat from the flame kept *Yellowbird* standing upright. I checked the important crown line was tied correctly at the basket, that all gas hoses were secured tightly, that the keys were in the chase vehicle and not in my jacket pocket. One final long burn and the basket lifted from the icy ground. We were free, becoming one with the wind, feeling as light as the air, released from gravity's grip and floating towards the heavens.

Sheep gathered at the fence, the only witnesses other than *Yellowbird's* crew, to my first balloon launch as pilot. As we drifted through the sky, there was no sense of motion, just a complete stillness, as if standing on an aerial platform with the landscape below, moving slowly and sleepily. I could see the complete story of nature below, the bends in the river as it told its own story of its relationship to the earth. The 360-degree view seemed never ending, just amazing. The New Zealand countryside was so green, so lush. While I was touched emotionally by my view below and beyond my basket, I had to draw my attention back to controlling my flight.

The balloon flew over a small farmhouse where the family rushed out in their pyjamas, looking up.

"Good morning," I yelled down to the upturned faces lit with glee.

"Where are you going?" yelled the little boy, running past their vegetable patch, chasing and waving to the disappearing balloon shape carved hard against the distant clouds.

One thing New Zealand is not short of is sheep and we were flying towards a large flock grazing in the paddock.

"Ruth, it is a rule of ballooning that we stay at least 500 feet above animals and that includes sheep," instructed Lawrie. "It is very important we fly high above dairy cows so as not to frighten them or they could lose their milk."

I took his advice and made a couple of extra burns to ensure the balloon was in equilibrium to continue flying level and not descend even the smallest distance. All this while watching the sheep spread over the field chewing the grass. Then one sheep reacted, possibly to the shadow of the balloon passing over the flock and began running in the opposite direction to the others. Immediately the remainder fell into line, following each other across the field, moving orderly, patiently, in time with each other. I wished I had my camera to capture this image.

Thirty minutes into our flight, the wind changed direction. *Yellowbird* headed towards hilly terrain. The balloon approached the crest, appearing to merge as one with the hills. Now what? I thought.

"Use really short bursts now to heat the air inside the balloon," said Laurie. "You will have better control closer to the ground doing that." he reiterated. I did what he said, shortening the burns to only two seconds at a time in comparison to the usual five second burns. I could definitely feel a better control of the balloon in flight.

Yellowbird reacted gently to the change of heat, rose silently over the treetops, missing the leaves by only a few centimetres. What a thrill to be able to view the trees so intimately, to feel so close to nature. On the other side of the hills, the land dropped away, leaving an empty space to feel the sensation of being untied from the earth once more. I was contour flying in an open wicker basket with a bag of hot air above my head, heavily intoxicated with my new emotions.

"We need to look for suitable landing choices now," said Laurie, "And landing a balloon is the most difficult part of your flying. The faster the wind speed, the larger the landing space must be, as the balloon could tip over and drag. Look for potential obstacles such as fences, trees, crops, animals and of course, power lines."

I could only nod silently in reply. My thoughts were a tangle of anxiety of possibly falling into the power lines, being burned to a crisp or even hitting the ground on landing so hard both pilot and instructor could be injured or killed. I glanced at Laurie, who appeared completely relaxed. I took a few deeper breaths, discarded my earlier fearful imagining. I recognised I must concentrate fully to feel the balloon's response to my control at the burner.

The balloon passed over Kerepehi. Gently, it moved into a descent to fifty feet above ground level. I made short burns to keep the basket flying level until we could reach the field of thistles in our forward path. Skimming across those thistles, the balloon finally came to rest on a gentle slope. Touchdown! I had just flown and landed a hot-air balloon all by myself. The enormity of what I had achieved was almost overwhelming. My emotions were dancing furiously. My first piloting experience had been without strain or disaster. Had taken me 27 kilometres in two hours, 15 minutes. The date: March 23, 1976. The seeds of long-distance ballooning were sown in my mind that very morning. I had wanted to fly on and on across the Tasman Sea to Australia.

For days I moved around my Mairangi home contemplating, scheming a way I could find funds to buy my own hot-air balloon. Such a luxury our budget could not afford. It became obvious to me I would need to find a company to sponsor my balloon.

A week after my first balloon flight as pilot, Kevin and I were invited to a friend's house for dinner. The group was a party of 10. Seated across the dining table from me was an elegantly dressed male in a navy suit, white shirt with red and navy striped tie. Don Macdougall was a Tupperware Vice President from Australia visiting New Zealand and was at the dinner as a special guest of honour. Conversation around the table was lively. Wine flowed freely. I found the atmosphere around the room quite congenial. At some time during the night, I began to tell the story of my balloon flight with Jim Greig, with my fascination for ballooning. My imagination was alive with excitement as I searched to find answers to questions being thrown across the table to me. I could feel my smile growing wider. I noticed Don's smile – megawatt, I would say. At no time did I see Don as a prospective sponsor. I was just happy to share my enthusiasm and dreams.

By the time we shook hands and said farewell that evening, he had offered to consider a balloon sponsorship. Both of us clearly saw the image of the Tupperware name floating across the skies on a red, white and navy balloon, the company logo colours.

"Promise me you will come to our company first, Ruth. Your passion to fly your balloon has been obvious. I can see you attending our Tupperware rallies, sharing your flying achievements with our sales teams. You would be an exciting spokesperson."

With those words ringing in my head as I walked towards our car with Kevin, I was quietly confident that a hot-air balloon would be part of my future.

With a slight turn of his head, Don smiled and disappeared down the path.

CHAPTER 12

Life for the Wilson family in New Zealand came to an end, June 1976. We returned to Australia with Kevin's promotion to Managing Director of the Australian subsidiary. Once more, I was looking at houses. Our next home, a white colonial in Wahroonga, was soon filled with all our worldly goods. Life settled into a daily pattern. Seeing my husband off to his job, waving goodbye to my sons as they walked to their school only one street from our home. I had set up a beautiful home, did my daily household chores, went shopping for groceries and asked myself, "Is this all there is?"

I was praying for positive news from Don Macdougall on a balloon sponsorship. At times, I wondered if I could do it all. Corporate wife, mother, balloon pilot, Tupperware spokesperson. My desire to escape to become involved with the unknown world of ballooning equalled my feelings of guilt at the audacity of my dreams of such future balloon flights.

To finish my instruction to gain a form of approval to fly, I had to return to New Zealand. For days, I held my internal dialogue with myself as to how and when I should approach my travel plans with Kevin. When we did talk, I was able to assure him I had arrangements in place to cover household duties and homes for our boys to stay after school until his return from his office. Frozen meals I had cooked for my period of absence sat in the freezer. While he was not overjoyed with my news, he never spoke outwardly against my desire to fly.

One of the brightest spots in my life was my growing closeness with my boys. They were of an age where I felt comfortable sharing my wisdom gained from personal struggle. My favourite book of that era was 'Illusions – The Adventures of a Reluctant Messiah', author Richard Bach. That and his earlier successful book, 'Jonathan Livingston Seagull' sat on the coffee table. I encouraged both my sons to read and over the years of their growing up, to read again. In a conversation with Grant years later, where

I was unsettled about a personal issue, he quoted sayings from 'Illusions' back at me to brighten my moment. It did.

I returned to Auckland to fly four more flights under instruction with Laurie Soffe. My first and second flight went relatively well once I got the feel of the connection between the heat from the flame and the balloon's reaction. I entered those flights from Paerata to Puni and Waiuku to Aka Aka into my logbook, signed off by my New Zealand instructor.

For my third flight, Laurie and crew picked me up at my Mairangi Bay accommodation at 4am for a 25-minute drive north to one of his regular launch spots at Orewa. My pre-flight preparation was approved, the balloon inflation went without incident, followed by a normal lift off. While inflight Laurie again went through the emergency procedures should there be a gas leak in the basket. I listened attentively. First, turn off the gas supply to the leak. Grab the fire blanket from the flight bag to have ready to extinguish any flame. Prepare to land as soon as possible.

So involved was I with absorbing this important information, I forgot to turn on the burner. The air inside the balloon cooled and was falling quickly, heading for a herd of Friesian cows. Laurie took the controls burning for a full 10 seconds to arrest the fall, to instigate climb.

"That was a good lesson for you Ruth, to learn what happens when you forget to aviate first and foremost. Your priority must always be to control flight of your aircraft."

He handed the controls back to me and we flew on for another 15 minutes. I still was feeling a little shaken by our near miss of cows, but I got us back on the ground, if with a few bumps till the balloon basket fell over, the envelope emptied of air.

My anxiety increased when Laurie made no further comment about whether I might have failed my test.

"We will finish with your solo flight on Sunday, Ruth. Let's see how that goes."

Sunday arrived with a north-easterly wind, gentle around 4kph. Laurie chose Paerata for my launch site, a site I was familiar with as I had flown there earlier. I kept repeating to myself as I prepared the balloon for flight. "You can do this Ruth."

Once in the air, standing on my own in the basket, hand on burner tap, I quickly realised I had to do this and do this on my own. The wind direction took the balloon once more towards the rural township of Puni, with scattered dairy farms and a few vegetable gardens I would need to miss. At the 55-minute mark, I could see clearly the Waikato River in the distance. I did not want to fly past that. An earlier landing would make it easier for the chase crew to access the balloon after landing. I commenced looking for a suitable paddock, while controlling a slow descent towards earth. Tension hugged my shoulders. My mouth felt dry. I so desperately needed a safe landing to shore up my confidence, but also to get Laurie's approval I so wanted.

I brought the basket down just above the ground with a few more burns to eventually settle on some dried cow pats. All gas taps were turned off when Laurie and crew arrived with the vehicle and trailer. I stood in the basket drowned in a mixture of emotions – relief the flight was completed, joy that I had embraced such an intoxicating passion for flight, anxiety that I might have to do another test while faced with limited time in New Zealand – till my thought moved to belief. Believe in yourself Ruth, I chanted silently over and over again.

At first, he said little as he strolled around the balloon, then approached the edge of the basket. I waited further with shortened breaths till he finally spoke.

"You are a natural in the air with a great sense of touch. I have been training another person for over a year and he still cannot fly the balloon level," my examiner said.

And thus, in late November 1976, after four balloon flights and only one solo, Laurie Soffe signed my Approval to Fly Balloons. I was a pilot.

Ten years after my New Zealand flights, Australia introduced more stringent rules and regulations for student pilots to gain their private pilot certificate. Apart from the solo flights and the 16 hours of training with an approved instructor, pilots had to take exams in Air Legislation, Meteorology, Navigation, Aerostatics, before gaining their certificate. But in my day, Meteorology was when I woke before dawn, walked outside to feel if there was any wind on my face, whether or not it was raining. If all appeared stable, I would make the decision to take my balloon to the launch site, proceed with inflation unless the weather had changed dramatically.

Navigation – my first rule of thumb was to look up at the clouds, at their speed and direction. Next was to grab a handful of dried grass to throw into the air to see what direction the ground wind was moving to point the balloon for a safer inflation downwind. It was always a rush to get up before the wind picked up at a faster pace. Between first light and sunrise, my balloon was ready to go.

I didn't even know what Aerostatics meant until the Australian Civil Aviation Safety Authority established the Commercial Balloon License in 1986. Then I knew what Aerostatics meant as well as the other subjects. I sat all their exams, passed and was one of the earlier approved Commercial Balloon pilots in my country. Approved to fly passengers for payment along with access to flying through controlled airspace with all aircraft.

I was also granted an Air Operator's Certificate (AOC) to manage my commercial ballooning company, the first sole female in Australia to carry an AOC for hot air ballooning.

CHAPTER 13

Don Macdougall turned out to be as good as his word. My Tupperware sponsorship paid for the balloon cost and freight. A fee would be paid to me as pilot of the balloon. As no Australian balloon manufacturer existed at this time, a British built balloon, 25 metres tall, 17 metres in diameter, patterned with red, white and blue horizontal panels featuring her sponsor, *Tupperware*, around her white girth, was bought.

Kevin and I discussed the financial commitment of my decision. He was clear none of our funds would be spent on my ballooning activities. I reassured him the cost of the balloon plus my travel and accommodation expenses were absorbed by my sponsor. In addition, they would pay me a fee to fly and any unseen expenses not covered by my sponsor would be covered from my fee.

My balloon's maiden inflation took place at Red Hill in Victoria a few months after I had gotten my Approval to Fly certificate. Two male Melbourne balloonists, long out of ballooning now, joined me, helping with the heavy work of lifting the balloon from the trailer. It was something one person could never do. They tied the thick tether ropes between the balloon's basket and vehicles as anchors. I heated the envelope and my new balloon gently rose upright to stand still on the ground. With a little more heat, she left the ground and floated to the end of the tether ropes. I repeated this exercise a few times until the wind grew too strong to continue making it an easy decision to complete the exercise. The balloon was packed away and loaded onto the balloon's trailer.

Over after-flight drinks, the group christened the balloon *Tarma*. We partied late, totally unaware a hammer was about to fall on my head.

There were only a few balloons throughout Australia in 1977. I was often called to tether fly *Tarma* to support charities that had booked the balloon through the Tupperware Head Office in Melbourne. It soon became usual for me to fly from Sydney to Melbourne to honour such bookings, collect the rental truck, then drive to the company's depot where my balloon was permanently stored to pick up *Tarma*. I had completed four of these flights when I was called into Tupperware's office. The hammer had found my head, devastating me.

The company's Head Office in America had discovered they owned a hot-air balloon.

They couldn't believe their Australian Office had approved something that might crash into a plane killing passengers. They ordered I be grounded immediately.

The fact the pilot was a woman was mentioned briefly, as was the cost of the insurance policy to cover the balloon's activities.

"What if I only fly the balloon at the end of tether ropes for a while to prove how safe ballooning can be?" I eagerly suggested, my heart pounding in my chest.

I waited with high anxiety for their response to my proposal. When it came, they granted me a six-month period for flight, but only on tether ropes. If there were no incidents, then the USA powers-that-be would review their decision.

Those next six months were torture.

I continually told the Melbourne office staff the balloon needed unhindered space because of its size for its inflation and tether flight. Half a football field would be perfect, I reiterated more than once. Whoever accepted the requests for the balloon had no emotional or personal involvement. Pure disinterest, I suspected. I had to suck it and see what was waiting as I flew south often, to fulfil commitments not made by myself, but by my sponsor.

I never had any experienced crew to assist. The small number of Melbourne balloon enthusiasts had their everyday job commitments. Whatever organisation or company that booked the balloon was required to assign three men to assist me with lifting the heavy gear from the truck, with two of my helpers responsible for holding the mouth of the balloon open so I could aim the flame through that mouth. The third male controlled the line at the crown or top of the balloon to assist with the rising of the envelope as it filled with heat. It also stopped the envelope from rolling left or right, or even out of control. These men would arrive individually dressed in their corporate suit with tie, black shoe-laced tied shoes. With little interest in the activity. With no knowledge or exposure to ballooning at all. Only five or six hot air balloons were owned throughout all of Australia, so the sport was generally not known.

For six months, I followed this pattern. Worked with men who had no attachment to the balloon. Men I had to instruct each time on the rudiments of their roles, who did what was required for an hour or so, then disappeared. My involvement with *Tarma* was a lonely relationship. I had to be strong to drive my enforced ballooning apprenticeship. The occasional tether flight would lift my spirits, such as supporting the Villa Maria Society for the Blind's appeal to raise funds to go towards the renovation of St. Paul's boarding school in Kew. March 2, 1977, the young blind boys from the school were fascinated as their hands felt all over the wicker basket and the burner while I described what they were touching.

While the balloon remained in a Melbourne warehouse, I could not share its magic with Kevin, Mark and Grant. I was sure once I did that Kevin especially, would be seduced by its uniqueness. Become more supportive of my new interest.

As I learned to juggle my various commitments, try to accept my sponsor's trial flights with grace, I also struggled with a heavy burden of guilt I felt. Stepping outside the expected boundaries and responsibilities of wife and mother at this time in Australian society was not an everyday behaviour. I was not feeling much fun at all.

In general, women had not yet embraced their right to follow their own star once married. The feminist revolution was slowly gathering momentum, but I wasn't part of any group. I felt like I was on my own. I had to work out a way of staying true to my air affair without being seduced by the financial security my husband provided.

A constant battle raged inside my head. Was I doing the right thing, bringing a balloon life into my Wilson family? What if I killed myself? Who would look after my boys? Why was Kevin so distant from our relationship? Somewhere from the back of my mind came my new personal mantra. "You must be true to yourself, Ruth". For days following such mental guilty thoughts, I would find an inner quiet by accepting that ballooning would always be a part of my journey. I never thought of myself as a pioneer, never really thought about the numerous firsts I was taking on. I just kept telling myself to stay strong, believe in yourself, Ruth E.

As my flying commitment increased, I realised I needed help in my home. It was time to discuss this with Kevin. I proposed we bring Youko, our Japanese housekeeper, to Australia to work and live-in. To my relief, Kevin agreed. With Youko managing mealtimes and taking care of other household duties in my absence, daily life could continue without the interruption of my not being at home. Mark and Grant were happy as they had spent their younger years with Youko in Japan. She was like family.

With a new sense of independence plus an income from my balloon sponsor, Tupperware, I set up Action Ballooning in 1977. It was the first commercial ballooning company in Australia owned and operated by a sole female pilot, mother and wife. I was 34 years old.

Six months after having *Tarma* grounded, the Tupperware suits acknowledged my perfect flying. I received approval for free flight away from any built-up areas in Australia. I hooked the balloon trailer to my car, loaded my flying gear plus Mark and Grant and drove to western New South Wales. Kevin chose not to join us because he was playing golf. A friend and my cousin agreed to meet there to crew for my first flight in *Tarma*, free of tether ropes.

Mist rose from the Belubula River as the sun spread its wintry fingers across the Canowindra landscape. At 0700hrs, the balloon's basket left the ground and climbed to 1050 feet, tracking 235 degrees. My younger son, Grant, aged seven years, his blond hair curling out from under his green safety helmet with his nine-year-old brother Mark beside him, stood in the basket's corner. This was a moment of close bonding. Love filled my heart as I watched my sons peering over the basket side, absorbed in the stillness of their first balloon flight. The pain of all those demanding tethered balloon flights I had performed faded away. Fun was kissing my lips.

Early in 1978, a change of management occurred at Tupperware while I was in hospital for surgery. The newly appointed manager was unsupportive of their company's hot-air balloon project. Without my knowing, one of my ballooning peers spoke with Tupperware, not in a supportive manner of my piloting skills. Consequently, Tupperware cancelled our involvement, sold their balloon to the usurper for a ridiculously low price. I was emotionally shattered at this loss, the unexpected betrayal by another balloonist. I also had to rebuild my physical energy after my surgery.

I felt a huge sense of loss. No balloon sat in our garage, nor did I have access to any to fly. My grief during this period was profound. Many days I sat with tears, alone. What helped me accept such a betrayal was my growing belief in karma, a belief I discovered while living in Japan. I would not wish anything negative on the man now flying my first balloon. I left that to karma. He eventually ran into financial problems, causing him to sell the balloon.

I have little recollection of daily life with Kevin over these troubled few months. I continued to attend school sporting activities each weekend with Kevin to support Mark and Grant.

Later that same year, I was sitting in our Wahroonga garden staring at the clouds dancing through the sky, creating various shapes and forms. I made a clear decision to try to find another balloon for myself. I knew I could not ask Kevin for financial support. That would not be fair, as we had reached that decision much earlier. I would have to ask the local bank manager for a loan. Though, financial institutions at that time were not receptive to granting loans to women without signed permission from their husbands, permission which I did not have.

As I parked my car in front of the newsagent across from the bank, I found unanticipated support. The latest issue of POL, a monthly magazine that had established a new standard of content, design and photography with a strong focus on raising awareness of the status of women, featured a photo on the front cover of myself with my balloon. Armed with a couple of copies of the magazine, I walked into the bank manager's office.

"How can I help?" he asked.

"I need a loan to buy a hot-air balloon," I replied, trying to sound as if this was an everyday request.

He wasn't really sure what a hot-air balloon was, as there were very few in Australia, and the sport had little recognition in the media as well. No passenger balloon ride business existed either. I put the magazine in front of him on his desk, assuring him I would be earning lots of money through flying my balloon. Passion fed my confidence.

He commented. "I'm afraid I see something of a problem."

Of course he did. Bank managers did not support women in business, let alone business conducted in an unknown field.

"Okay," I said with trepidation. "What?"

"Will you have sufficient funds to buy a trailer and pay for insurance?"

I was so surprised I took a minute to answer. "Um, not really."

"Well, then let's make sure you have enough to get you comfortably started."

Before I knew it, he signed the paperwork and passed it across his desk for my signature. My urge to reach across his desk to hug him had to be controlled.

In doing this, Mr. Henderson became one of my angels, camouflaged as a dull suit. He turned out to be an essential mentor along my life's journey. We had spent no more than thirty minutes together. He changed my life, but I never saw him again.

With sufficient funds, I phoned my ballooning friends at the British balloon manufacturers and ordered a Thunder Balloons' balloon that took six months to arrive in Australia because of long dock strikes in England.

The day my personal balloon G-VAMP arrived from the United Kingdom brought much jumping with excitement by both my boys and me. It never entered my mind my husband was nervous of losing control. That came later the first time he saw my new balloon. We took the full equipment to his company's large car park on a late Saturday afternoon. When I directed him to place a rope in position, he argued with me I was doing it wrong. Instead of joy, there was tension during the afternoon. I strongly resented his lack of willingness to support and respect my position as pilot.

I had taken a traditional role of mothering from the age of 10, moved into a marriage at 20, where I continued with nurturing and mothering. Now at 34, I was attempting to learn to listen to my own needs and desires. The sky became my playground once more. This was where I truly felt at home, no longer fragmented by the demands of daily living. Success in my chosen world of ballooning grew. My relationship with my husband presented no positive change. The young, emotionally fragile girl he had married was growing into a stronger, independent adult every day, with every flight, but neither of us wanted to address this change in the balance of power.

Women's magazines featured articles on my involvement with ballooning. I proudly sat them on our large coffee table. When Kevin arrived home from his office, I mentioned the magazine articles. He walked straight past the coffee table to our bedroom. I never saw him pick up any one of those magazines. His silent response hurt me. It also made me more determined to stay connected to my personal journey of flight, to be that questioning soul above it all. Perhaps if we could have talked about it, he could have told me my flying caused him pain or upset. I could have told me about my joy in the air. But we did not talk.

Wherever I could, I took my boys with me ballooning to share my passion. Each invited a friend along as well. They never showed any fear for my safety. I suspect I, along with my hot-air balloon, initially was a bit of a novelty to both them and their friends. And I reminded them often - 'thank you for choosing me to be your mother'. I wanted each son to grow up owning a part of the responsibility of our mother/son relationship.

CHAPTER 14

When the article appeared in the Woman's Day weekly magazine, journalist Martin Saxon had written: *"There's no mistaking balloonist Ruth Wilson is a free spirit - she floats around as free as a bird. Not just the sheer physical floating around in mid-air with clouds for company and the world at her feet. But deep down inside, where it really matters. Ruth, a vivacious bundle of energy, is also patient, open and cool and one of the best women in a man's game. Inevitably, there's a conflict sometimes. The day we met, Ruth was ballooning for charity in Melbourne. Everything was ready. Burner on. Balloon filling in slow motion. Then flame. In an instant, the 200 degree centigrade burner had gutted part of the lower skirt of the balloon. It hurt her that she disappointed the crowd. It hurt her more to see the balloon, almost reaching its most majestic - then lying burned and unable to fly. 'There's a part of me deep down inside that is very sad,' she said with a faraway look in her eye. Even there on the ground, I realised why Ruth Wilson is the free spirit she is.*

"To float through the air looking down on life is truly beautiful…one's spirit soars and the depth of one's emotions is wonderful… it's a rare experience…it brings joy, wonder, magic and a special lift into your life.

Ruth Wilson is as free as the air she breathes."

The suited corporate males assigned to help with the inflation at the above event reacted with fright when the burner flame was blasted in their direction. They jumped away, dropping the material around the mouth of the balloon they were holding open for the flame inflation. Material floated quickly into the flame, scorching a large burn hole. I immediately turned off the flame, the gas, pulled the ripcord to deflate my balloon. I fell to the ground on my knees with ash from the burnt hole floating around. Feelings of devastation soaked through my body. I felt as though the burn had happened somewhere on my soul. My gear was packed onto the balloon trailer. The corporate helpers headed for their cars, for their usual normal day's work in their offices. I drove to the empty motel room, my Melbourne accommodation, for the night. The following day, I located a local sailmaker who replaced the damaged material with new. *Tarma* was ready for flight once more, her cosmetic surgery unnoticeable.

Two weeks prior to this incident, I slept through a powerful dream of fire. A yellow forklift truck scraped its steel fangs under the wicker basket of my hot-air balloon and effortlessly lifted the 942 lbs onto the tray of the one-ton truck. At that moment, the forklift began spinning around. Crunching and belching, the yellow monster bore down, cornering me near a brick wall. 'Send it Ipec' signs were scattered around the room. An overhead fluorescent light was broken at one end, but still working. My knees shook, my vision blurred as I surrendered to the forces around me.

My fear turned to fight as an explosion of flames filled the room. Fire! The hot orange-red tongue licked my feet. I refused to be destroyed. The intensity of my decision supported me as I floated through the flames into a welcoming, cool, empty darkness. I had survived, was alive and healthy.

This Melbourne balloon flight was my first since that precognitive dream.

On the day of that flight, I collected my balloon from the warehouse where it was stored, briefly noting the 'Send it Ipec' sign on the wall plus the broken light. There was a faint mental retreat to my recent dream experience, but Martin Saxon was waiting to interview me for Woman's Day magazine, so I focused on the job at hand. I remained oblivious to what was about to confront me.

It took further precognitive dream experiences before I began to recognise that the dream state opens channels of communication between the waking and sleeping realities to allow the utilisation of unconscious or super conscious knowledge. As I continued to believe and accept the integrity of my being, I found it easier and fascinating to listen through my dream world. I began trusting messages and appreciating the greater glimpses of the magnificent realities surrounding me.

I taught myself during those early flying years to master my ballooning in many demanding situations through warnings from my dream state. In accepting this, I grew to believe that specific events occurred in my unseen world prior to manifesting in my everyday physical world. It could be said I was growing more passionately into a fatalist, a person who holds specific beliefs about life, destiny and the future. I was listening to my inner guidance, using my growing knowledge as a barometer for my decisions.

My love of living life to its fullest through my ballooning contributed to one magnificent dance towards appreciation of what I felt was my destiny.

CHAPTER 15

During those early years of my ballooning, I continued to fly with only a wicker basket, three fuel tanks and the balloon's envelope above attached to the burner frame. I carried only a compass plus topographic maps of the flying area with me in the basket. No radios for ground contact communication were used. The sport of ballooning was growing and membership in the sport's national body presented the opportunity for pilots to find help with crew. Eventually I was fortunate to find three or four regular crew to assist with inflation and to chase my balloon. During one of my earlier competition flights, I invited one of my four male crew to act as navigator.

"Where is the target in relation to the railway line?" I asked my trusty navigator.

"What railway line?" he answered.

"The one we are flying above," I stated quietly.

My decision was made there and then. I would do all my competitive flying in the basket alone. If I won, I won by my own skill. If I messed up, the responsibility would be all mine, not another's. Consequently, after my first World Championship where I did take a navigator, I chased targets in hot-air ballooning competitions alone in my wicker basket while the majority of competitors flew with a co-pilot/navigator.

The pioneering days of Australian ballooning are long past but not forgotten. Days when I used handfuls of dry grass thrown into the air to check wind direction as opposed to current behaviour using helium filled party balloons. Extensive weather information is now available on site with our Apple watches, mobile phones, helium weather balloons floating out of sight, offering wind speed and direction information for our pilots to be able to choose a safe and suitable flight direction. When flying in controlled airspace, pilots communicate with the relevant Control Tower, maps are clearly marked with sensitive zones, no fly areas and approved altitudes, with a list of emergency numbers attached on the back.

My challenge with my early flights was to tack the winds to land as close as possible to a road. That way, my chase crew could see the balloon for final retrieval. Many friendly farmers invited me for tea and toast while waiting for my crew to arrive.

The many 'firsts' the balloon accumulated included our appearance at the 1977 Hardie 500 Bathurst car race. Motor magazines and other media outlets carried the image of the start of the car race with the Tupperware balloon (*Tarma*) prominently displayed as part of the action. My sponsor was thrilled.

Being surrounded by armed guards on landing *Aerius*, was another first. Cologne, Germany celebrates its annual Rose Montag Festival every February. In 1978, four balloons launched from Kolner Verteiler to participate in the festivities. I was at the controls of *Aerius* with a clear vision of the city. A light fog licked at the horizon with temperatures at eight degrees Celsius. After 18 minutes, my balloon was positioned above the start of the snake-like tribe of costumed people, dancing and clapping to music. Mounted police lead the procession, their horses showing no reaction to the balloons above. Ten minutes later, the street procession twisted to the north, where no wind wanted to go that morning. Reluctantly, the partying crowd waved farewell to the pretty hot-air balloons above.

The drizzle of light rain dampened spirits in the grey frosty morning sky. With very little gas in the tanks, I needed to come back to earth. *Aerius* floated down, just missing a few large trees, to land in the grounds of the Perfume 4711 Company with its high fences and metal locked gates. Once the company guards were reassured, the smiling, innocent, Australian pilot was eternally grateful to be safe on the ground at Ossendorf, they invited me and my crew for coffee in their company canteen.

While in Germany, I was approached to fly the winner of a magazine promotion. Wolfgang Schaff had written of his desire to fly in a hot-air balloon to fulfil his dreams of escape and challenge in contrast to many other readers who wished for material objects. A quiet, retiring man in his late 20s, fair hair with shy green eyes, Wolfgang assisted with preparation of the balloon's equipment for flight. The burner flame spluttered weakly due to the freezing temperatures, but eventually *Aerius* wobbled slowly to an upright position. Cameras clicked to record Wolfgang's realisation of his wish. The balloon drifted upwards where the air felt pure and chillingly refreshing, but winds were light and variable. After two hours and close to lunchtime, the uncomplicated flight ended on snow next to a typical local pub, with smoke rising from the chimney.

The township of Canowindra, 332 kilometres west of Sydney, played host in 1979 to nine balloons and their crews – *Pegasus, Destiny, Moonraker, Jayskye, Wiz, Lovely, Puff Too, Australian Flag* and *Vamp*. I flew *Vamp* carrying Channel 7 television news cameraman, Bernie Keenan, while Carol Thatcher interviewed me together in the basket. The marker was dropped. *Vamp* landed soon after, followed closely by the Channel 7 chopper, with pilot Terry Lee at the controls. Empty fuel tanks were exchanged for full ones so Bernie could continue filming strapped to the outside of the chopper. His air-to-air shots of the balloons completed the TV News story. After searching the paddock unsuccessfully for over an hour to find my marker, the group ceased doubting the landowner's comment "probably eaten by one of the cattle." The carcass of a starved cow nearby in the dry creek bed bore grim testimony to the severity of the drought that year.

Then there was the flight hired by Fontana Films to shoot a segment on reptiles for John Laws World, a Channel 10 program. I inflated *Vamp* on Razorback Mountain. Once airborne at the end of short ropes with John Simpson, the cameraman beside me, John Edwards brown snake handler, released a bag of snakes under us. Snakes slid everywhere. The camera whirred beside me. I held my breath as my basket fell towards the ground. Visions of snakes in the bottom of my basket had me hit the burner tap for flame heat to climb away to safety. The story went to air.

Feeling so proud to be included in aviation's Schofields Air Show – the first balloonist invited to participate. Launched skyward at 1328hrs on a calm, stable Sunday as twenty parachutists floated towards an earth landing with Grahame Hill yelling, "Hello Ruth" as he winged past my balloon.

It is interesting to look back on media interviews where I spoke from the heart. My belief stated in the September 1979 issue of Cosmopolitan Magazine remains unchanged: *"I suppose I feel we have a destiny path in life and that if we're moving along it, then we're content achieving and experiencing things, and if we're off it, then we're looking and striving. For me, ballooning is a total experience and definitely a spiritual one."*

It was also an expensive one. The first time I saw an advertising dirigible, it was perched on a roof in Europe. I had never seen this form of advertising in Australia but saw potential for income. I bought one, shipped it to Sydney and set about finding customers for this new aerial marketing concept. Christmas 1977, my inflatable balloon sat on the roof of the large Hornsby shopping mall with a Merry Xmas sign for all to see, my first assignment. I had accessed the roof, along with two males, inflated the stationary balloon with a heater, secured it with ropes, stood back, pleased with myself. Two days later, it was gone. Some mischievous person or persons had cut the ropes, deflated and taken my ingenious idea from me.

My sense of knowing how to be a corporate deal breaker was shot down. I had no insurance, nor had I negotiated smartly with the shopping centre management for them to cover it with their insurance. I should have used different tie offs from the rope that was so easily cut. It never entered my mind that a person or persons would do such a thing.

'Bad luck' was all the Centre management could say to a distressed 34-year-old woman standing deflated. I had lost face, lost money. My new financial venture had failed.

CHAPTER 16

A couple of months later, I tucked away my thoughts of my dismal aerial advertising entrepreneurship, accepted an invitation to fly at the annual Zell-am-See ballooning event in Austria. Curious thoughts about my upcoming first flight in snow and close to mountains kept me awake on the long flight from Australia to Europe.

One of sixteen pilots to launch from the snow-covered Zell-am-See airfield in February 1978, I flew low at first, playing with the valley winds in my borrowed red, white and black balloon, *Aerius.* A few lazy cottony clouds drifted unknowingly through the brilliant blue sky. As pilots searched for various wind patterns, their balloons dipped and bowed as if in one celestial dance. The snow-covered Austrian Alps rose majestically nearby. The temperature was -2 degrees Celsius.

We had flown 26 kilometres in nearly three hours. I opened the last tank of gas. The alpine village of Taxenbach lay below. Miniature cars pushed through the slushy wet snow on a twisting road fronting the shop and buildings. On the northern side of the village were high-tension electric power lines. A mountain peak sloped back from the winter road and railroad tracks, rising to 11,250 feet, the towering watchdog of village life. I noted the balloon's altitude at 8640 feet. There was nowhere to land safely. The air grew stiller.

I checked the sky to see what the other balloons were doing. Could only pick out the *Rheingas* balloon southwest of my balloon and climbing. The pilots, Norbert and Wolfgang, were searching also for wind movement. Their balloon found a wind shear to disappear at speed over Gross Lockner at a height of 12,465 feet.

With the small amount of gas left, it was decision time. I opened the burner flame to heat the balloon, climbed to 9,250 feet, searching for even a touch of wind to draw the balloon across the village, away from the obstacles below, towards the side of the mountain. Powder snow reflecting rays of sunlight and blowing patterns down the leeward mountainside lay below my basket.

Smoke rising from a farmhouse on the side of the mountain became the target, my projected landing spot. I stopped holding my breath when I found the lightest of wind to move *Aerius* towards my target. I did feel nervous, though. Even a little shiver, but possibly from both the cold and nerves. Had never landed a balloon in snow. I was concentrating hard, burning for heat, for an approach into the deep snow. The radio broadcast from *Rheingas* broke into my thoughts.

"We have landed heavily in a pine forest. Balloon is damaged but we are both okay. We are at 7250 feet."

With a huge sigh of relief, my balloon now had moved away from obstacles below the basket. I brought it down onto the mountainside. The landowner ran through the snow, waving a bottle of Schnapps with six tiny glasses to greet his aerial visitors. "Hello, I'm from Australia. There's a balloon in trouble over the mountain" were the words this Austrian farmer heard from this Australian pilot.

His strides shortened, then slowed to a startled halt. He stared. A female pilot stood before him, an English-speaking female in her multi-coloured flying gear with Ruth printed across the front of her helmet. He stepped cautiously towards the basket. Short and stocky, his eyes hidden by bushy brows, the bucolic host talked quickly and incessantly in German, his ruddy cheeks moving up and down in time with his mouth.

"I'd like a schnapps please?" almost pleading in my drained state after such a demanding flight finish.

"Only men," he indicated, pointing at my German crew who had arrived in our chase vehicle. "You go to kitchen with wife," was my interpretation of his garbled German/English.

I refused to move. Reluctantly, he finally offered me a glass. One glass of schnapps, then I reluctantly agreed to leave the guys to pack up the equipment, to celebrate on their own.

While I warmed my body in the farmhouse near their log fire, the lady of the house fussed with homemade biscuits and coffee. Lisa, her 12-year-old daughter, stood shyly in the background, pretty in that blond Germanic fashion, slim and already as tall as her father.

"What do you want to do when you grow up?" I asked her.

"I must stay here to help around the farm," she answered in broken English.

My mind retreated to my 12-year-old self. To my constrained life. To my world, where I had not yet learned all things were possible.

"Maybe you could become a balloon pilot," I suggested. Lisa reached for my silver fountain pen engraved with 'Ruth E Wilson, Aeronaut' I handed her. I left the farmhouse praying my intrusion into her tiny life would inspire this young Austrian girl with her decisions for her future life direction.

Next day locals and balloonists pulled together for a successful rescue by sled of the *Rhinegas* balloon. All met later at a hotel warming up cold bodies with the popular local drink, tea with rum.

1942 My maternal grandparents William & Lillian Thorne with their family.
L to R: My mother Joyce Thorne, brothers Graham (seated) Bill (standing) Thelma

1946 My mother Joyce Thorne marries Edward (Ted) Lawson

1963 I married Kevin Wilson in Bowen

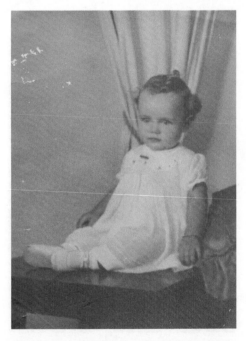

17 months old living with and loved by my grandparents in Rockhampton

4 years old in Collinsville. Ready for family celebration. At my favourite water tank.

Ron & Ruth Lawson with cousins Leslie & Colin Trathen at Queens Beach home

My Queens Beach Lawson family home

1959 My family - Back Ruth Ron Glenda Front: Mum Keith Dad

1960 I was crowned Queen of the Coral Coast Beauty Contest at Horseshoe Bay Bowen

1962 Ron joins the Army. Ruth (R) Glenda holding baby Jeffrey (L) Keith in front

With Kevin in Madison USA

My boys, my joys: Mark 3yrs Grant 12 months old

December 1971 Grant shovelling snow while Mark watches in our Madison USA home

August 1973 Mark celebrates his 6th birthday with his Mum, Grant and friends Japan

1977 at our Wahroonga home with my boys. Grant (L) Mark (R)

Mark & Grant with our pet dog Nicky in Wahroonga

My boys Grant and Mark with me in a tip over balloon landing. All wearing our helmets

1988 Celebrating Grant gaining his balloon pilot certificate

1989 World Ballooning Championship Saga Japan. With my son Mark as Pilot.

"Tarma"

Tupperware my first balloon

Vamp my second balloon

Just right my third balloon

Kodak my fourth balloon

Odyssey my fifth balloon

Misty Blue my sixth balloon

Aurora my seventh balloon

Regula Hug-Messner my gas ballooning mentor

On a hydrogen balloon flight in Germany

My early ballooning fire resistant jump suit with sponsors

CHAPTER 17

At the briefing for the first Australian Ballooning Championship held in Belconnen ACT, I was subjected to sexism, discrimination, prejudice, hostility and inappropriate discourse. The Flight Director, a male balloonist from Sydney, looked at me as I entered the room and stated loudly in front of all therein, "What are you doing here? There is no way a woman will ever fly in any event I organise. Anyway, I don't think you are experienced enough."

I had never met him before. Naively unprepared for this personal attack, I chewed on my top lip in an attempt not to cry in front of my male peers. I could feel my cheeks inflamed. Feeling fragile, I retired to my motel room, burst into tears, sobbing into the faded white pillowcase. I kept repeating, 'This man is projecting his own imperfections onto you. Do not surrender your power to him'. Soon I wiped my eyes, threw cold water on my face and returned to stand at the back of the briefing room. An armour of indifference sheltered me from further hurt from the bullying balloonist.

The following morning, October 14, 1978, a Judge Declared Goal, where the Flight Director chose the target for balloons to fly to, was set for the first task. Bill Watson won flying in his balloon, *Wiz*. Tony Norton, a Victorian balloonist, invited me to fly in his balloon and placed second in that task. The following morning, a small number of balloon pilots stood on the shores of Lake Ginninderra. The same Flight Director who had insulted me, informed the competitors he had not been able to get permission from the Civil Aviation Authority for the balloons to fly over the lake. It was decided amongst most of the group Bill would be given the title of Champion, as he had won the one task flown.

However, World rules state, to be recognised as a sporting event and for a champion to be declared, at least three tasks must be completed on not less than two separate flights. Bill Watson could not legally claim the title.

It had been a painful introduction for me to competition ballooning.

Indicative of the kind of treatment I experienced at various times in those early days of my flying due to challenging existing gender roles and patriarchal structures.

I thought of the long article which appeared in the national ballooning magazine of a reckless pilot launching in dangerous winds, who should have stayed on the ground. I was the only pilot who chose to fly on that occasion, while nine male pilots remained grounded. It had to be me as the referenced pilot. I felt very hurt at the nastiness of the story. The winds were no stronger than 10kph; my flight was long, with a safe landing. No damage to the balloon, pilot or passenger. I sat at my kitchen table and wrote a long letter of reply. As I finished, I reminded myself it takes two people to start a battle. That I would ignore the attack, not give oxygen to the article. My reply went into my waste bin instead of the Australia Post mailbox.

Alan Moult, a photojournalist, who was covering the 1978 Canberra Nationals wrote in GEO, Australasia's Geographical magazine, in a 1980 article on ballooning and balloonists, *"their determination to fly was typical of the lengths to which people bitten by the ballooning bug will go – despite officialdom, lack of funds or narrow escapes. It reminds me of a touching scene at a Canberra balloon meet a few years ago. Ruth Wilson – at the time Australia's only woman pilot – had been refused permission to compete in the 1978 Australian Ballooning Championships because she was 'not experienced enough'.*

As a tearful Ruth was being comforted by those who knew of her flight experience in the tough school of tethered flights at country shows, I saw a glint come into her eye. It was an inner signal. The next time I saw her was at the 1979 championships at Greenethorpe, New South Wales.

Her performance during the two-day event was superb. It was woman and machine against the elements. They soared, they swooped, they hovered. They were daring and sometimes cheeky, and they knew it. There were tears in her eyes again on Sunday night when she was crowned Australian ballooning champion. In June this year, she'll be taking on the world's best at Battle Creek, Michigan.

I pity them."

CHAPTER 18

Eleven months after my initial painful contact with competition ballooning, I claimed the title of Australia's first Hot Air Ballooning Champion. Two years earlier I had participated at the World Championship in York, United Kingdom. As an Official Observer working with the competitive pilots, I learned the official rules of balloon competition. This grounding in international competition contributed to my breaking no rules in my years of competitive balloon flying.

But for now, I hooked up my trailer with my new balloon, *Vamp*, so named as she carried the UK aircraft registration of G-VAMP and drove to Greenethorpe in western New South Wales to compete in the 1979 National Hot Air Ballooning Championship. My logbook recorded 50 flights to date, with a total of 28 hours as Pilot-In-Command.

I was determined to be included in the Australian competition flying this time.

Saturday 0759 hours, my balloon left the ground for the first task, an Elbow Bend. The pilots had to fly to a point then seek winds that would take their balloons back along the same track, or as close to that as possible. Bill Watson's angle was smaller than mine taking first place, while I scored as runner-up. My flight time was two hours and covered a distance of 37 kilometres. During drinks at the local pub, I overheard a small group of male pilots commenting on the morning's flight. "She only finished second because she followed Bill". I was tempted to move over to the group, to challenge them, but it was more important I conserve my energy for the next day's competition flight. I finished my drink and exited the pub, trying to wash away the hurt I was feeling. I certainly had flown my own race.

Saturday 1635 *Vamp* launched from the Kindra property to compete in the Fly In task, seeking winds to fly to the target at the Greenethorpe Gliding Club. I dropped my marker on the target to take first place. Bill Watson placed second.

The atmosphere at Sunday morning's briefing was tense. Because of the scores, this was a contest now between two pilots, Bill Watson and me.

A Hare & Hounds task to be flown solo (pilot only in every basket) was set. The weather was perfect for ballooning. People scurried around the launch site in preparation for flight. The Hare balloon launched first with all the others (Hounds) instructed to wait a further 10 minutes before chasing the Hare. As soon as that waiting period expired, *Vamp* was first into the sky. There would be no chance of any comment that I followed another pilot. Confidence hugged my shoulders.

My eyes were fixed on that Hare balloon, climbing, dancing on the clouds together, falling from clouds at the same time, both creatures of the sky. The Hare balloon touched down. The crew laid out the target. I shortened the burns to control my balloon's descent towards the target, glancing quickly behind to check where the other balloons were. I was way in front of them. Bill Watson was at the back of the pack, drifting off course to the west. My mind became cold, concentrated with thoughts only of securing the 1000 points to win. I dropped my marker close to the target, then flew on to a safe landing. I had won the task; Noel Canning second; Bill Watson third. Roger Meadmore, Phil Kavanagh and Tony Norton finished somewhere on the list. Cannot recall the names of any others.

Three tasks had been completed on three separate flights. Australia had its first official ballooning national championship, plus a champion of the sport. Being declared that first champion was a sweet victory over the male chauvinism thrown at me. Celebration followed, with lots of hugs from my family and crew, plus my visiting Canadian girlfriend, Wende Anstruther.

Sunday afternoon, a special task was flown for the large crowd of spectators. It was not a designated official Championship flight. This was a first for all pilots participating. Parachute Le Mans was a race where a skydiver joined a balloonist in the basket to 4000 feet. The balloon was then to descend to at least 3500 feet before the guest skydiver jumped out of the basket. The chase crew was required to collect the skydiver first, then to retrieve the pilot and balloon. First team back to the launch site would win.

Bill Rosenberg was assigned as the skydiver for our attempt.

"They call me the Hawk," were the first words he said to me.

The afternoon winds were increasing. My balloon was rolling from side to side. I tried to shoot flames into the envelope for the inflation. The basket was also dragging along the ground. David Bowers called a few men in the crowd to come to help hold the basket in place. There were now ten people straining to hold the basket as I fought the conditions to get *Vamp* upright. The leaves on the downwind treetops were dancing frenetically.

"Quickly, jump in," I yelled at the Hawk as the wind started to lift the balloon upwards. In his red and white jump gear with his camera strapped to his helmet, he stood beside me, his eyes black and piercing. His anticipation of the thrill of falling free was obvious. His eyes had a crazed look to them.

"Give it heaps, babe!" was the second time he spoke to me.

"She's too hot already. Don't call me Babe or tell me how to fly my balloon," I yelled back at him. One could cut the tension between us in the basket with a knife.

The balloon's crown temperature registered 110 degrees Celsius. *Vamp* climbed at 700 feet per minute to overtake a couple of higher balloons to reach the required 4000 feet. I pulled the rip line open. The top opened. Heat escaped immediately and *Vamp* began a quick descent. "We're at 3600," I yelled at my skydiver passenger.

"I'm staying till 3000 to give you extra weight for a quicker fall," he yelled back over the burner noise. He climbed out to sit on the basket edge. "Give me a countdown," he threw at me.

My whole body was quivering. All my senses were stretched. I had heard the expression 'adrenalin junkies' - at that moment, both definitely qualified. "33, 32, 31, 3000 feet," I screamed. The Hawk turned and winked.

"Geronimo!" he yelled, jumped and was gone. I leaned over the side to watch his body weaving through the air. He pulled his ripcord. He was going straight in to land in the field below.

My initial plan was to land past the wheat fields. I changed my mind. I would follow Hawk straight down. I prepared for a final hard landing. Maps and the first aid kit were tucked tightly into place. Pilot light off, rip line in my hand ready for deflation. *Vamp* hit the ground heavily, basket tipped over, going nowhere. I wriggled my body. No injuries. Out of the basket I scrambled, started packing up equipment. My crew arrived a few minutes later. My *Vamp* team was first back to the launch site. Our recorded time: 26 minutes.

I hugged my two sons, Mark and Grant, while friends and spectators cheered as the *Vamp* team broke open the champagne. Judy Lynne, working as the PR person for the event on behalf of the sponsor Lovely

Lady Pancakes, congratulated me. It was obvious to me Judy had become seduced by the world of ballooning. And I was right. In a short time, she was flying the sponsor's new balloon.

Noted Sydney journalist Lenore Nicklin, covered the Championship for the Sydney Morning Herald and wrote:

"Piloting a six-story high tan and orange beauty called VAMP Ruth Wilson was a clear winner - she came first in two events and second in the third. 'I flew my heart out,' she said, wiping away tears and drinking victory champagne. Ruth feels that ballooning is her destiny. "When I am flying, I feel I have total responsibility for my own safety, and I accept that. But the thing I enjoy most is the magic, the joy and wonder that a balloon brings to people in everyday life," she said. "The highs are so high. It took me three months to get over flying over the Austrian Alps. People who fly balloons feel life is not so restrictive - that all sorts of things are possible."

CHAPTER 19

As 1980 unfolded, I was caught between three worlds.

Corporate wife and mother, aviator with a strong passion to fly, but just as fascinating to me was the blossoming exploration of self and spirit.

Not long after the family had resettled in Sydney, Australia, I had found my way through a web of personal contact to meet new people who touched my life momentarily at the library of the Psychical Centre in Carrington Street, Sydney. There I met people of all ages and backgrounds. People who accepted the idea of reincarnation, contact with the spirit world, the power of healing and other metaphysical realities as a normal part of their daily existence.

My grandma's 'sixth sense' began to make sense to me. I began to see spirit form, to appreciate my knowingness more strongly and regularly. I was definitely full of joy when dancing on the clouds, totally in tune with the balloon's movement at one with the wind. I still had to learn how to open up to allow myself to receive universal love, how to displace the destructive thinking that clung to the cliffs of my mind specifically with regard to my marital relationship.

Because of such thinking, I was moving further away from my relationship with my husband. We were a couple whose individual needs were not being met with our lives moving in different directions. Our common ground was our sons. On the surface, we remained polite to each other, carried on for the family's benefit while an underlying tension spread throughout the relationship.

One night, after numerous unhappy thoughts about my current home situation, I fell asleep. In the early hours, my spirit rose out of my sleeping body, walked across the floor, exited through the bedroom walls. I was flying across the top of the Sydney Harbour Bridge through the night sky. When I landed, a tall being dressed in long white garments stood in front of me.

"Where am I?" I asked.

"You are on Arcturus," was his reply.

The mental dialogue between the two of us continued.

"You need never feel insecure, Ruth. Try to remember your power."

With those words, a bunch of pure gold roses appeared in my left hand. I stared at the roses. In response, those roses instantaneously disappeared in a puff. Gold roses no longer existed.

"Whenever you need support, you can call upon the Brotherhood of the Roses," my ethereal advisor told me. "Accept the practice of journeying in your dreams. Guidance from the 'other side' will be available for you."

CHAPTER 20

Why all sorts of things were possible fascinated me as I continued to develop a proclivity for the metaphysical. My exploration of 'the other side' of life reflected my growing discovery of self. A variety of books found in my local library fed my soul, amongst those the writings of Pythagoras.

In 529 BC, his Pythagorean University in the Greek colony of Crontona located in southern Italy, admitted women and men regardless of race, colour, political persuasion, religion or financial independence. Through unique studies and research at that time, Pythagoras grew to be recognised as the founder of modern mathematics, musical theory, philosophy and the science of health.

His adaptation of the simple numerical system to a symbolic representation of human life and expression gave the world the study of numerology.

"Evolution is the law of Life. Number is the law of the Universe. Unity is the law of God." Simple words I had read and recalled easily over time.

My life's ruling number is nine, calculated from the digits in my date of birth.

Ruling nines are said to be responsible, extremely honest, idealistic, ambitious, humanitarian, with a serious attitude to life and unsuccessful with saving money. I studied this interpretation and could not question the validity of the words looking back at me. This was a description of my orbit without doubt.

A Handbook of Astrology for Australia & New Zealand written by Jane Bennett and Craig McIntosh sits amongst the numerous books lining the large bookcases in my study. The charts of 41 well-known Australians and New Zealanders are featured. An entry on page 193 follows Gough Whitlam (Australian Prime Minister 1972-75).

Ruth Wilson

Ruth is probably one of our most intriguing entries. A publicist during the week but, more notably, a highly successful balloonist. Ruth won the first national championships in 1979 and was runner-up in the second event in 1981. Ruth first found ballooning in 1975 when in New Zealand on a magazine assignment. Within a few months, she was flying her own balloon under sponsorship. Ballooning has taken Ruth around the world as she has competed throughout Europe and America. We can expect to see Ruth's autobiography in the next couple of years.

The opportunity to further develop my intuitive gift using tarot cards and numerology was unexpected. My friend's art gallery in Hornsby, a northern suburb of Sydney, was struggling financially.

"Would you take bookings for readings at my gallery?" Judy asked. "I need to get more people into the gallery." I happily agreed.

On the day the journalist from the local newspaper appeared for a reading and interview, he entered the room with a definite lack of enthusiasm, a sceptic. He scribbled notes, personal information from the reading, his interest blossoming, departing with a thank you and smile. His published article was full of enthusiastic support for my readings. The locals flocked to the art gallery. The hive of activity drew gallery sales. I returned to my home each evening, often drained of energy but full of a sense of achievement through helping others.

There was JP. He had returned home from work to find his partner had left, taking all the furniture and paintings from their shared home. JP was quite distraught. Kept threatening to end his life. The usual one-hour session turned into two. I worked calmly with him, encouraging him not to give his power away to his ex-lover. His partner, Ken, had shown no signs of discontent with their relationship. JP was as much in shock as in pain. He left the reading armed with new core beliefs to carry him past his struggle. He called a week later to offer thanks.

There was AK who arrived, quite sceptical but curious. The cards showed clearly an oncoming death of a close family member. AK acknowledged she had not seen her parents for a few years due to a quiet estrangement. She commented she would fly to visit them soon. Four days later, my phone rang. "My mother died last night," I heard the pain in AK's voice. "If you knew my mother was going to die four days before she did, that meant her time was up. Knowing this has made it much easier for me to let her go," explained a reflective AK.

Working with people seeking clarification of their life direction, questioning the stability of relationships, of proposed job changes and travel plans could be quite draining of my energy. Additionally, the responsibilities of family life plus my balloon flights began to take a toll on my emotions. After six months, I put my cards away.

CHAPTER 21

I woke early feeling peaceful. The first light of the day filtered through the curtains. My husband slept soundly, wrapped up in his own personal demons. Then I recalled my dream earlier in the night.

My dream where I was standing naked in front of the bathroom mirror examining my breasts. When I squeezed my right nipple, a greenish colour fluid appeared. Alarmed, I squeezed the left side with the same result. What a strange dream, I thought.

Two weeks later, I stepped out of the shower, grabbed the towel, commenced drying myself. I looked into the mirror and began checking my breast. I squeezed my right nipple. A greenish colour fluid appeared. Recalling my earlier dream with such clarity, I began examining both breasts with much more concern. It was then that I found the lump in my left breast.

"We should put you in hospital to check surgically and do a biopsy," said the surgeon.

I rested silently with the curtain half pulled around my bed for some privacy. The outside world bustled forward through traffic jams, girlfriends lunched, people going about their daily work while I worried whether or not I had breast cancer.

The woman sharing my hospital room was older. She had not stopped chattering with her visitors since I slipped into my bed to await my fate. To distance myself from their conversation, I reached for the two books sitting on the bedside table. A J Cronin's the Citadel and Hotel by Arthur Hailey, author of the popular Airport book. The back cover of The Citadel stated, 'this is the story of a young, rough, idealistic doctor and his apprenticeship in life." I selected the other book that carried the stamp, The Free Public Library of the Borough of Madison, New Jersey, on the inside cover. I got as far as page two when they came for me.

Rolled into the operating room for what I believed was a check on the lump, I was told as the anaesthetic wore off, a third of my left breast had been removed. The lump was precancerous.

"We removed the tissues just to be safe," said the doctor as I lay there under the white sheets.

"You had no right to take that action. You should have waited until you explained what was happening in my body, discussed the options for treatment with me. Not just take away one third of my breast. I am really angry with you." Silent words not said aloud.

As the pain slowly subsided over a few days, I determined I would be strong enough to meet my commitment to fly my balloon at the Annual Darwin Beer Can Regatta.

The surgeon told me I was crazy. Not in so many words, but that was his opinion.

With one month to prove him wrong, I leaned on my growing belief in the power of the mind to create my personal reality. I formed a clear, precise picture of my balloon on Vestys Beach, contributing colour to the craziness of sixty home-built boats made from beer cans afloat on the harbour. Through my programmed visualisation and affirmations, I drew healing energy from the universal force into my breast, the wound and throughout my body generally, weakened by surgery. I would close my eyes, breathe in deeply and slowly to send soothing, healing, nourishing oxygen through my body, my brain waves slowing to tune to my higher self.

At the beginning of my relaxation, waves of blue then purple light would emerge through my closed eyelids. A feeling of peace surged through my body. After a concentrated period of peacefulness, a beautiful white shining light would appear, expanding in size to embrace my whole body. There were moments when a sharp shooting pain would sear through the breast incision. I interpreted the sensation to be one of the wound drawing larger quantities of healing energy visualising the scar tissue healed; the muscles growing stronger and resilient.

There were nights that passed without much sleep. Nights dulled by incandescent thoughts about my breasts now varying in size, whether or not the medical staff had won their battle over any suspected cancer cells possibly lingering, searching for the next area in my body to attack.

It would have been easier to allow myself quiet times. To allow the natural healing process to take time, but my desire to get back into my balloon basket was powerful. I was also determined not to feel a victim, to control my thought processes that wanted to grieve about the loss of part of my breast.

It became a daily exercise to dissect my moods, to recognise negative feeling was just that and I could control such thoughts. Creating images of myself standing in my wicker basket floating above the Australian bush would lift my mood. Gratitude would come calling, settling in for long periods of time.

Local Darwin media fussed over the female pioneer adventurer with her balloon, *Vamp*, the first ever to be inflated and tethered in Darwin. I sent a clipping from the local paper of my balloon in Darwin with his patient at the controls, to my surgeon.

Once more, my ballooning had offered a refuge from my personal pain.

CHAPTER 22

As the winner of the inaugural official 1979 Australian Hot Air Ballooning Championship, I left without fanfare to compete at my first World Championship in Battle Creek, USA. I would fly *Gumball*, loaned by Americans, Leo and Jill Eisenberg. It would not be an easy journey for me. A few months earlier, I met Simon Fisher, an Australian balloon pilot based in Adelaide. He offered to be my co-pilot. It could be fun flying with Simon, I told myself. I bent my rule on flying solo in competition. Often it was fun, but also our strong personalities would clash in the basket.

All competitors were only eight minutes into the first flight when extreme weather arrived earlier than expected. Eighty balloons suspended like teardrops against a blackened sky began drifting every which way. But mostly not to the target displayed at the Kellogg's International Regional Airport, closed to air traffic to accommodate this event. Over 200,000 spectators stood expectantly, waiting for the balloons to float lazily overhead.

"Is that rain, Simon?" I asked, looking up into the crown of *Gumball*. It was Sunday, June 21st, 1981 1850hrs.

I felt decidedly uncomfortable in the air. The harmony I usually felt with my balloon and the air was not there. As *Gumball* levelled out at 1200 feet slightly off track towards the airport, the rain fell heavily, soaking the nylon material of the envelope. Water rippled down into the basket. The other balloons remained airborne, with the storm worsening.

Simon checked our map to calculate the balloon's required approach to the target. His eyebrows creased and folded as his tension mounted. "We will miss the target at this altitude. I think you should climb higher to find a different tack, Ruth".

I looked up past the outside edge of the balloon at the black, angry sky. Shudders ran through my body. It would be sheer terror to climb higher into a sky that could dispose so easily of unwanted intruders.

"I disagree with you, Simon."

"You are here to win the World Championship. If you expect to succeed, you have to be daring and aggressive," he threw back at me.

I hit the burner to initiate climb knowing intuitively the decision was wrong. As the wind carried the balloon further away from the target, anger raged through my body because of my capitulation. I recognised my action was not because I thought Simon was a better pilot. I reacted due to exposure to years of conditioning that the male was the more dominant force and should be obeyed.

As *Gumball* approached the perimeter of the airport, the roar of engines cut through the wet sky as a C-5 Galaxy Military transport plane moved down the runway and took off, ignoring four balloons edging the airport perimeter. Turbulence and wind shear from the plane's climb hit the aerostats, causing them to momentarily look like squashed ping-pong balls. *Gumball* maintained her shape and level of flight but was caught with a strong change of wind direction. We were flying even further away from the crowd and target. There was no harmony with the winds that morning.

Gumball finally landed safely in 'The Home of the Fighting Rams' ballpark. Our ground crew rushed to help pack the heavy, soggy balloon. My yellow wet jumpsuit clung to my body, outlining well-shaped breasts, tiny waist and rounded hips. Thunder rumbled across the sky, lightning spread its forked fingers in repeated flashes as hail hit the ground. Other teams were not so quick and minor repairs had to be carried out during the night on hail damaged balloons to be airworthy for the event the next day.

The only other female competitor, Toshiko Ichiyoshi from Japan, badly damaged her ankle during her landing in this first task. She withdrew from the Championship and returned to Japan. She never competed in Worlds again.

Battle Creek resident Earl Chapin was outspokenly "anti-balloons" in the media leading up to the Championship. He strongly believed his hogs might die from heart attacks caused by fright from the burner noise associated with balloons above his property.

All pilots were warned by the Competition Director Tom Sheppard to mark their maps 1000 feet minimum altitude. Do not land on Mr. Chapin's property, was repeated at the flight briefing. Two balloons flew low over the Chapin property. One landed thereon, causing Earl Chapin's blood pressure to boil. The local sheriff, Jon Olsen, was called. Word got around. Don't mess with Mr. Chapin. But I would meet him. My nerves were raw at this thought. The wind blew my marker inside his property's fence. I would have to meet Mr. Chapin to retrieve my marker so my flight could be scored. When I did, my Australian accent softened his response.

"Is everything okay, Earl?" asked the local sheriff, who arrived to check out potential problems.

"Yep," he blurted back as both pilot and hog farmer headed to his fence to collect my marker.

Teams awoke on the last day of competition to no predicted tornado but to light winds. After six tasks, Canadian pilot Del Michaud was in first place. I had climbed to 17th in the standings. As the only female competitor, I was thrilled with my results. At the final competition briefing, I noticed a poster with the words, "Life's Greatest Thrill is Tomorrow!" Tomorrow had arrived. This would have been "tomorrow's thrill" if I had reached both targets. The day turned out a thrill for American Bruce Comstock, whose focused flying shone to finish closer to targets than Del to win overall. Del Michaud finished 9th in the Championships.

The next morning, 104 competitive and fiesta flyers combined for a final salute to the people and city of Battle Creek for ten days of unparalleled warm hospitality. These people had endured bumper to bumper traffic, long food lines, crowded toilet facilities. All that was forgotten as they responded to the majestic magnificence of the colourful balloons bursting from the field, throwing cone shaped shadows over the gathered masses. An open letter sent to all balloonists stating "if you run into trouble, land at 19th and Andrath. You can even land on our greenhouse roof if you want" was representative of the fantastic reception from the folks of Battle Creek, Michigan, USA.

I had finished in 32nd place in my first World Championship in a male-dominated field of 82 pilots. More importantly, after a week of decision making with my flying in tough conditions, I had reached a point in my personal growth. I finally accepted it was okay to trust and act on my own knowing. In that tiny space in the wicker basket, I had embraced with amazing clarity the awareness that both men and women are spirits in an earthly body with knowledge born and gathered over many lifetimes of multidimensional experiences. That knowing is an inner quality which both men and women possess, which has nothing to do with gender.

That I would bury my conditioned response of feminine surrender and try to learn to appreciate personal interchange with males on a more equal basis.

At the awards banquet, eighty-two pilots from twenty-two countries dreamt of victory – next time.

CHAPTER 23

Sound asleep in my Wahroonga home, Kevin travelling overseas on business, I woke with a start. Hovering on the righthand side of my bed closer to the ceiling was the spirit image of a Native American sitting cross-legged. His arms were folded out in front of him. I particularly took note of the three feathers on the left-hand side of his head. I sat up and smiled at him.

"What are you doing here?" was all I could say out loud.

My night-time visitor's look was one of love. Strength emanated from his strong jawed, handsome face. His black hair fell to his shoulders. An overwhelming feeling of love radiated from my visitor. He maintained a steady, penetrating look into my eyes. While there was no physical voice tone, I heard the following words: "Have courage and follow your inner guidance. Recognise your 'knowingness'. There are basically only two core emotions - love and fear. All other emotions spring from either love or fear. Remove fear from your life then your core base for all your decisions and actions will emanate from love. That very thought will open up realms of possibilities and much happiness."

His image gently faded away. Was his visit a result of my sharing flight on the Native American reservation a couple of weeks earlier? I had piloted the *Qantas* balloon at the 1981 Albuquerque Balloon Fiesta. After landing on an Indian Reservation during my last flight, I was greeted by a local family. The mother leaned across the basket's edge to ask me to fly her blind 19-year-old son. I felt delighted to be able to do this, to bring a new experience to both mother and son. With a small amount of gas left, we launched and floated to the end of the reservation – not far at all – but far in my passenger's imagination, I am sure – far in my joy at being able to share.

I eventually fell asleep, but not before pondering on how thin that veil was between myself and the 'other world'.

My curiosity about my Native American visitor would encourage me to seek out the history and culture of the various North American tribes to search for this extraordinary being. I found images of the Mohawk Indians wearing three white feathers but had not found the face I was looking for. The symbolic meaning of feathers in their culture dealt with ascension and spiritual evolution to a higher plane. Feathers also represented the power of the thunder gods, along with the power of air and wind, both of which were a huge presence in my life. On a trip to Boulder, Colorado, a few years after this nocturnal visit, I saw the painting of the Indian Chief Walking Bear dressed in shades of sky blue, black and white with a twenty-two feather back shield in an art gallery. The painting now hangs in my living room, along with an original Navajo peace pipe plus two framed pictures with Native American wisdom below:

"Walk tall as the trees,
Live strong as the mountains,
Be gentle as the spring winds,
Keep the warmth of the summer sun in your heart,
And the Great Spirit will always be with you".
Brule Sioux War Chief, Nomkapha, who lived from 1832 – 1915.

"The only way to pass any test,
Is to take the test.
It is inevitable".
Chief Regan Black Swan.

Within weeks of this spiritual encounter, I was defending my National Champion title. Chasing the winds, dancing on clouds, falling through clouds, floating above clouds in Northam, 45 minutes northwest of Perth in Western Australia. Throughout that week of competition, I soared, conquering clouds. Acclaimed cinematographer, Jan Kenny, was despatched from Sydney television to cover my title defence. A dedicated crew supported me in the quest to retain the title of Australian Champion. George Chapman and Debbie Lynn got me off the ground, were there when I landed. They kept me going when my energy began to fade.

Under international rules, after the minimum required three tasks over two separate flights have been achieved, the Event Director must advise the competitors when the final competitive task would be flown. At the Thursday morning's briefing, I requested that important information from the Flight Director. I wanted to know when the final competitive flight would be called. The officials refused to clarify. No satisfactory answer was offered.

Friday morning dawned, bringing rain. No flying. After six days of competition flights, I was still holding the Championship's title. If Friday had been the designated final championship flight, I would have retained the title of National Champion.

Saturday, the officials called the morning's flight a competition task: Judge Declared Goal with the target 15 kilometres from launch. I tried unsuccessfully to bury my belief the Saturday task was called in an attempt to take the title away from me. My mental turmoil during the competitive flight did not help me find my harmony, to find the winning winds.

Bob Dickson's marker hit the target to win the Championship. My drop was only a touch outside of his. My score dropped me into the runner-up position by 67 points.

I had not conquered any clouds this morning, both emotional and physical.

The Australian Women's Weekly stated on September 9, 1981: "Ruth Wilson is a romantic who loves the freedom and peace of her sport. But she is also at the top - a winner in a field largely dominated by men. A win or place will entitle her to compete in the next world championships in Paris. Some of her comments during the interview covered: "My son asked me if I will leave him my hot-air balloon when I die. I said I would, he thought about it, then said 'you won't. You will be like a Viking and go down with the ship'".

CHAPTER 24

In late 1982, my marriage finally ended. As I grew more desperate to live in an equitable partnership, I headed towards a resolution that was not made easily. After months of marriage guidance counselling, Kevin and I were told 'this marriage can't be saved'. Our separation, previously edging its way towards me, had increased to a gallop. And Kevin was standing there ready to let go the reins. Neither of us was involved in an affair with another person. Consequently, our divorce was non-confrontational.

My belief that death was never the end of any relationship carried over to my divorce as well. I worked diligently to stay connected to Kevin, not as his wife, but as the mother of our two sons. "Be loving and positive" was my mantra to help me find the necessary strength to support our sons through this painful time.

It was only when standing alone on my balcony looking at Sydney Harbour sparkling at night I allowed tears to flow, to sob uncontrollably. The ache that I had not been able to achieve a fulfilling, happy home life, different from my formative years, weighed heavily on me. My personal pain of mother guilt for causing my sons, whom I loved and adored such pain, kept me awake often long into the night. I knew I had to learn to forgive myself, but how to do that I had little idea. And then my dream state showed me how through the following emotional nightmare.

I was treading water at one end of a long swimming pool. Kevin was moving around in the water at the other end of the pool. I glanced to my right to find Kevin exiting the pool. At the same time, all water drained from the pool, leaving me standing on the tiled pool floor, legs apart. I moved to the pool exit door. It was locked. I began to scream. Help! Help! Not a person heard me. After some time, I managed to unlock the door. Found myself hitch hiking a ride from a roadside. A car full of people picked me up but would only take me with them to the hotel where they had booked. Once there, I realised it was a hotel Kevin stayed at on business trips. I called management to ascertain if he might be a current guest. They refused to disturb the guest in Room 9. I yelled abuse at them, cried till one of my roadside rescuers pointed out Room 9 in the message. My kind rescuer went to Room 9 on my behalf. Kevin was there but would not come. I ached for his arms around me, for reassurance all was safe, that our love was safe. My heart ached.

I woke from this dream in my bed, tears streaming down my face, my neck so stiff I could not turn it to the right. My whole body hurt. I stumbled out of my bed towards the shower. Stood under hot then cold water to wash away the pain, to release the emotional tension from my muscles, followed closely by drinking two cups of coffee. Later that day, I spoke with a counsellor about my dream. She offered her explanation that water translated as emotions in dreams and my dream story told its own message. I gradually gave myself permission to cease carrying the full responsibility for my marriage breakdown. To finally realise Kevin also carried some responsibility for our broken connection.

As a couple, Kevin and I maintained a non-complicated divorced connection. While relationship love had died between us, we maintained a warm relationship as parents to our two sons, eventually as grandparents to our two grandchildren. On Kevin's 86th birthday, all his family including myself, knowing his days were numbered celebrated with him. Twelve days later, he sadly passed.

Any marriage or relationship ending can be difficult to embrace, but my life during the 1980s consisted of passion felt through flying, achievement through work, growing awareness of spirit on one side; a broken family, scattered friends and an empty personal relationship on the opposite side. For the couple of years following the end of my marriage, I worked as a consultant in the entertainment world as the publicist on the movie One Night Stand, involved with the Coolangatta Gold movie as well. It was my work with the Michael Edgley International Harold Park Paceway promotion that coloured my months after my divorce.

Years later, mother guilt attempts to dance around my ears, but I eventually smack it away knowing my two sons live loving adult lives. What more could a mother want?

After my divorce, I set about building future castles in the air.

CHAPTER 25

My castle in the air for 1983 was to travel to France in August to represent my country again in world ballooning competition. And I had to find funds for that castle.

The French organisers had levied a large entry fee the United States balloon teams opposed, eventually boycotting the event.

It was now two hundred years since man first severed ties with the earth in 1783 in a balloon in France. I intended to be part of the 1983 special celebration, so I accepted and paid the entry fee.

The Castle of La Pervenchere, 20 kilometres north of Nantes, was the official launch site for the Championships. I rented a chateau for my team of eight, a mixture of Australian and German personalities. My elder son, Mark, accompanied me to France as support with this aerial challenge and there were many. Grant with his father headed to Canada for a father/son holiday.

On the first competitive flight, a Japanese pilot flew directly into my inflated balloon standing ready, waiting for clearance to launch. I stood helpless in my basket, watching his balloon basket's edge rip a long tear in my rented balloon carrying a *Qantas* sponsor's sign, now useless for flight. Both balloon and pilot were forced to remain on the ground. No score. No competition points. Unbelievable. I felt devastated. Mentally and emotionally. My dreams of finishing in at least the top 10 totally shot down on that first day. There could be no recovery from a loss of a possible 1000 points. What a disappointing way to start the week. And it never improved.

Mid-week 80 balloons were lined up on a launch field waiting to be unfurled and inflated. The competition director had instructed all to standby while a raging storm passed. He then shocked each and every pilot by stating, "There is no official competition but if one pilot chooses to fly, he will be scored." The British pilots complained loudly. Australian pilot, Peter Vizzard, advised me if I flew not to go to 1400 feet. His weather balloon had been clocked 30 knots at that altitude. I was unaware what Gren Putland, the third Australian competition pilot, was contemplating.

It was the French pilot who took on the challenge first. His balloon lifted off, its sides caved, hit by the surrounding wind shears. A Dutch pilot, Mathijs de Bruin, was next. His balloon almost flattened from top to bottom. I had never seen balloons behave in this manner. I reached for my helmet, taking time to secure the neck strap till I could feel my breathing settle. The pilot next to me started his inflator fan. Tension danced all over my face. My darling concerned son walked over, put his arm around me and said, "You don't have to prove anything, Mum. We all love you."

But I felt I did have to prove something to myself. I made the decision to fly. I studied the map closely, noting the large bend in the river, a church, other points of interest along the track to the target area 15 kilometres northeast of the launch site. My plan, once airborne, was to search the ground for these points of interest to work out if I needed to adjust the balloon's height left or right to find the correct wind to track to the target. It was as simple as that. No electronics were part of the ballooning scene. Even radios to talk with ground crew were banned.

"I'm going," I stated, tightening the strap on my helmet.

The flame from the burner spewed heat into the balloon. I lifted off alone at a great speed. The balloon finally stopped climbing to level out at 1400 feet. I was standing in the belly of the blackest cloud in the sky. I could not see anything. Confidence had deserted me. Terror had found a new acquaintance shimmering up and down my legs. A balloon pilot, not game to spill any air from the top of her aircraft in case the whole balloon deflated mid-air, stood in the centre of the basket holding onto the sides firmly. Who was this person?

"Please God. Let me get down safely. I will never fly in these conditions again," I whispered to the wind.

The cold air around the balloon caused it to begin to fall. Clear of the cloud, the balloon was situated right over the bend in the river, obviously on target to the goal. My spirits soared. Confidence blew Terror out of the basket. "I was being rewarded for being so brave," became my thought mantra, focusing now on the balloon's flight path.

Only a small number of pilots flew, flying much lower at tree top level north of my track. At no time did I think I should descend to join the pack, to be safe with a comfortable score.

The French villages all look alike from the air. The fast winds had whipped the balloons away so quickly. With no radio contact allowed during competition, the ground chase crews were having difficulty finding their balloons. I was quite close to what I thought was the goal as light rain began to patter down on the top of my balloon. I brought the balloon down to treetop level and prepared for a fast descent into a field. The basket hit hard, tipped over and dragged for five metres, then stopped. As I stood up, a bull sauntered from under a tree in the corner of the field. My main concern was to keep it from trampling on or eating the material in the balloon. "Shoo!" I kept yelling at the beast. He would come closer, lower his head, stare at me, obviously trying to decide what to do with this intrusion into his territory. He retreated back to his earlier resting spot while I gathered the envelope into a tight ball of material, then sat on the basket to wait for my crew. Meanwhile, they were driving up and down country roads asking the locals, "Did you see the *Qantas* balloon?"

Nearly three hours had passed when they finally ran into the field in the dark. Martina and Karen burst into tears, having been convinced something dire must have happened to me. After a late dinner and drinks, the team started to find a funny side to the whole exercise.

My balloon had moved two kilometres south while caught in the turmoil of cloud at 1400 feet. The river bend I flew over turned out to be the bend further south on the map. I did not win that task, but won the respect of many of my male peers.

From France, Mark and I travelled to London to stay with Carol Thatcher at the Thatcher family home. We were invited to No. 10 Downing Street for drinks to meet Carol's father, Dennis. I enjoyed lively conversation with him, answering his questions on the various aspects of balloon flying. Prime Minister Thatcher was at Chequers, but I had the great pleasure of dining privately with her and Carol three years later on a visit to London. I found Carol's mother gentle, an intriguing, enquiring woman.

Since my first overseas ballooning trip in 1977 to York in England, as an Australian, I had travelled further than all others to participate in the sport. And I spent my own funds, any and all savings to honour my sport and my country.

Ballooning had given me a sense of my own creative and spiritual identity. It did not answer my questions about my genetic identity. The ache to learn about my biological father would not go away. Not long after my return from Europe, I flew to Bowen in North Queensland to finally talk with my adopted father about my life and his.

CHAPTER 26

The Queens Beach pub was full, mainly of men leaning on the bar with glasses of cold beer in front of them. Outside and across the park, the ocean sparkled, a vivid blue with white caps dancing erratically. Father and daughter were sitting on adjacent stools, both downing a beer.

"Is this really young Ruthie?" asked Alfie, my father's friend. "Is she still flying those things in the sky?"

"Yes," I heard the pride in my father's voice.

My father had been widowed and living alone for 15 years. I was three years old when he married my mother, three months later adopting me. I knew no difference until I was 31 years old. I finally wanted to talk with him about my biological father.

"Glenda told me you were not my real father," I said as he sipped his beer. He turned to look into my eyes, resigned, almost relieved.

My insides were churning, but I was on a course of discovery.

"Can you tell me anything about my birth father?" a question asked, overflowing with expectation.

"I never asked your mother about your father. I did not want her to think it was important to me, so I cannot help you," he said. "Maybe your Uncle Bill, your mother's brother, might know."

I was stunned at his answer. My expectation shot down by a couple of sentences. A confirmation to me that said a lot about the relationship between the two people who undertook a journey of family together, who spent 24 years living as husband and wife. I would not judge. I had been as guilty of inadequate communication in my own marriage.

After a few more beers, father and daughter drove home and prepared dinner together. Later that evening, we talked more about his life, his early droving days. Finally, I gathered enough courage to broach the subject of my pain at the beltings with the iron cord he handed out particularly to my brother, Ron.

"I thought I was doing the right thing by disciplining him. Besides, my father used to belt me with his whip," he said as tears rolled down his face.

My hard-working, quiet father had pain written all over his face, pulsating from his body as well. We talked long into the night, probably the only time any person had listened to his story. Only thirteen years old when his own father died. As the oldest child, he went to work to support all his younger brothers and sisters. I felt overwhelmed with sadness. I struggled to find something in his story that reflected joy, laughter, frivolity and fun. There was nothing. I thanked him for being my father. Hugged him long and hard. Slept little that night, overcome with emotions I could not control. I sensed he was heading towards the end of his life. I was not wrong.

Once back in Sydney, I tracked down my Uncle Bill in Warwick by phone.

"Do you know who my birth father was?" I asked him. Emotional tension choked my chest. A sense of excitement around finally knowing about my father beamed out of me.

"Yes, I was 16 at the time. Your father was an American serviceman who loved your mother very much. They wanted to get married, but because of religious differences, our parents would not allow Joyce to marry. In those days, people had to be 21 to marry without the parents' consent. Your father went off to fight in New Guinea. About six weeks later, as I was leaving to go to school, a telegram arrived from one of your father's friends with the news the Japanese had killed your father."

My uncle could not remember my birth father's name, hard as he tried.

After thanking him, I put the phone down. My sense of loss incredibly painful. I stared into emptiness, soon flooded by my tears. Later, I thought about my recurring dream experienced over many years. I was a soldier hiding behind a thick bush. A row of Japanese soldiers advanced, thrusting their long guns into the shrubbery, searching for their enemy. I could see the Japanese soldier's face clearly as he began to thrust the bayonet through the bush towards me. At that point in the dream, I always woke up, my heart racing, often in a sweat.

Could that have been my father killed by the Japanese?

I had discovered a huge love of Japan and its people in the years I lived and worked there. Now I was trying to accept the death of my biological father in New Guinea at the hands of a Japanese soldier.

In more rational moments, my mind created images of two people in love during wartime, one of them an American pilot, the other my mother.

"That must be where I have gotten my love of the air from," I told myself often. "I have American blood running through my veins. That must be why I am so drawn to that country. To the Native Americans." There were days when I felt empty and angry. I had no name, no personal details about my biological father, no information on my American relatives. He would have had parents, relatives in the States who would never know of my existence. I was a secret daughter.

I contacted the Queensland Births & Registry by phone, hoping to find my father's name on my original birth certificate. I was told when a child was born to an unmarried couple at that time, the father had to agree for his name to be added to the birth certificate. I believed my father was deceased prior to my birth, killed by Japanese soldiers. I gave up trying to find his name with the Government Department.

In the meantime, my cousin sent an old sepia photo from the 1940s. He had found it amongst a bundle of photos belonging to my deceased Aunty Thelma. The man was dressed in an American uniform. The name "Louis Campbell" written on the back of the photo. Could this be my American father?

I wrote to hundreds of Campbells in the United States asking if they had a relative who had been in the Services stationed in Rockhampton in the 1940s. Many kind letters were written in return. Not one fitted the missing bit from my personal jigsaw puzzle. I would console myself with, "It really does not matter who your parents are, Ruth E. You are a reflection of your inner self, the spirit that pulses in your being." I would forge ahead with my life till the next time the urge to discover my true past proved overwhelming.

Then my darling younger son came to me with a request. From a young age, Grant showed interest in being an actor. Now at thirteen, he had made an appointment with an actors' agent in central Sydney city. Would I drive him to the meeting and sign his contract? I have to admit I was not impressed with where I found us, even sceptical, but I would always support him. I handed over the funds for his required publicity photos and registration. The day after this signing, his new agent called with a casting job for a television series, 'Harp in the South'. Grant got the role, one of the main characters in the series. My scepticism unfounded. And he has remained working in the entertainment industry ever since. I felt immensely happy for him, extremely proud also.

CHAPTER 27

My landline phone rang.

The nightlights of Sydney Harbour blinked through my Neutral Bay home windows. The scent from the jasmine bushes underneath the living room window drifted towards me. Rivulets of water ran down the sides of my tall glass full of vodka, tonic and ice.

"Ross Spicer," he said after I picked up the phone. "I am a friend of someone who crews for you occasionally. She has invited me to go ballooning with her over Easter. Told me we would be flying with your balloon. I thought I would call to introduce myself, see if I could help in any way."

"I was considering cancelling the weekend," I replied. "I need a chase vehicle as mine is sick."

"Use my 4WD," he replied. With those few words, Ross stepped into my life in a huge way. My feelings of 'it's all too hard doing this on my own' faded away.

On April 7, 1984 he experienced his first flight in my balloon *Vamp* over the wheat fields of Canowindra. Brown hair strongly flecked with grey, manly build, Piscean sensitive nature and eyes that mirrored his passion for life, Ross was always there as my Crew Chief. His personality was larger than life. We became flying partners and the closest of friends.

When my darling brother Ron shot himself, it was Ross I phoned who listened to the pain in my voice as I recounted my story.

The telephone call came in the early hours of the morning.

"Are you Ruth Evelyn Wilson?"

"Yes, I am" I replied.

It was the Nambour Police.

"Do you have a brother, Ronald Owen Lawson?"

My heart started pounding, dreading the worst. "Is he okay?"

"He is in the Nambour hospital. He shot himself. He is calling for you."

I walked into the hospital, not knowing what to expect. I was not prepared for the sight of my brother, who had put a gun to his right temple and shot through his forehead. Heavily sedated, he lay in bed in a caged area adjacent to the nurses' station due to his pained belief everyone was determined to kill him. Ron's whole face was black and swollen. Where was my blond, blue-eyed, handsome brother? My love for him brought tears streaming down my face. My pain for him had me murmuring repeatedly, "Oh Ron, oh Ron, what have you done?" I sat to listen to the doctor repeat the story Ron had continued to repeat to all who approached him. I felt destroyed, inadequate to heal his distraught pain.

Ron and I were 30 and 31 years old when we found out we were adopted. When Ron discovered his father was an American serviceman, he became more emotionally fragmented. Why had our mother not married his birth father? My brother had been christened Gene Owen at birth. His name changed to Ronald Owen on adoption as Gene was too American sounding. The story that his birth father wrote letters to our mother during the war, had written with a proposal of marriage on his return to the States, confused Ron. Till he was informed our mother had never received any of the letters written by her American lover. Certainly not the last one Ron's father had sent. Our mother's parents had kept his letters from her because Joyce had met George Edward Lawson, who had proposed and agreed to adopt both of her children, Ruth and Gene. Life was moving forward. Best to leave it as is, was the decision of our grandparents.

After years of emotional and mental turmoil, Ron left Sydney to drive 25 hours non-stop with guns in the boot of his car to kill our adoptive father. His dysfunctional childhood and Vietnam service finally had taken its toll. After driving without many breaks, he arrived at our Queens Beach home about breakfast time, stopped long enough to eat something, had a conversation with our father where only the two of them know what was said. Ron was not a killer. He climbed back in his car, started driving south for Sydney. By the time he reached the outskirts of Nambour twelve hours later, he had become paranoid. Lack of sleep, trauma and stress played with his mind.

He imagined the police cars he saw were coming to get him, so he turned off the road up a dirt track. Once out of his car, he dug a mound to shelter behind, got his guns from his car. He was in battle mode once more. Back in the jungles of Vietnam. Then he saw them; Viet Cong creeping through the night jungle towards him. The fear of being caught and tortured was too much for him. Better to take his own life. Placing the gun's nozzle to his right temple, he pulled the trigger.

I did not know he even owned guns.

Ron's continuing paranoia drove him to distrust the doctors and nurses. Through all his confusion, the only person he felt safe with was his sister, calling for me repeatedly in his drugged state. "They want to kill me," he told me as I held his hand. I would put my body between his and everyone else to appease his anxiety. I could do little more.

The doctors wanted to strap him onto a stretcher to fly him back to Sydney, to the Repatriation Hospital. I argued strongly against the strapping bit. I knew I could protect and reassure him during the plane flight. The airline staff was wonderful. Once all passengers were on board the plane, Ron and I were shown to the two front seats, with Ron next to the window. I hugged and smothered him with my body at flight launch and landing. We were escorted off the plane first, into the ambulance, then driven to Concord Repatriation hospital.

Once the medications had subdued his bouts of paranoia, he was allowed to move around the hospital to sit in the garden to smoke. He started to talk, slowly and gradually at first. When I finally heard his troubling story, I took him into my arms and we both sobbed tears of pain.

"I had been out on patrol for many days, lost count as day and night roll into each other," he stated softly. "My patrol had just returned to base camp when everyone was called out. The commanding officer stood in front of all the men, told us that an enemy patrol was suspected of being in the area. A patrol would need to go seek them out. Step forward any guy who feels he can't or doesn't want to go back out," invited the Officer.

Exhausted from the continual fear of being killed in the black of night by a Viet Cong grabbing him and lack of sleep, my brother and three others who had also returned from patrol stepped forward.

"Well men," said the Officer, "Now you know who the cowards are, the men you will not be able to trust beside you."

With those words, my brother lost all sense of manhood, maleness, sense of self. A deep bloody incision to his soul and mind caused him to bleed, mentally and emotionally. And the bleeding never really stopped.

While recovering from his self-inflicted gunshot wound and hospital experience, he would sob in my arms, "I am not a coward! I am not a coward!" My passionate reassurances fell on deaf ears. I sat in the hospital grounds listening quietly to Ron and other psychologically scarred Vietnam Vets. All were faced with a long journey in front of them back to some form of life normalcy. Whether they would get there was questionable.

The doctors put Ron on permanent medication. The Army gave him a disability pension to live on, but he seemed unable to find reward or meaning to his life.

The Nambour police had confiscated Ron's guns. A friend of his eventually sold his Seiko 22 Hornet and the Weatherby 224 Magnum plus ammunition for $1200 on August 8, 1984. He sent the receipt to the police. Of course, Ron lost his gun licence. Over a number of months, he slowly returned to everyday life and moved back to his home with his family in Morayfield in Queensland. But his torment stayed with him. And his pain stayed with me. I returned to my Neutral Bay home, returned to my every-day responsibilities.

I found an outlet for my pain by connecting with Reverend Ted Noffs at the Wayside Chapel in Potts Point, Sydney, who needed a Public Relations consultant to spread the word to promote his concept of Life Education. His preference to educate children about the damage drug use does to their bodies included creating Healthy Harold, the friendly giraffe. For a number of months, I carried a Harold the Giraffe banner on my balloon and promoted this work.

The following year, my son Mark gained his ballooning pilot certificate on his 18th birthday, the earliest age one could. An exciting achievement for him. An even greater thrill for me to observe and share my son's love of and skill flying a balloon.

CHAPTER 28

When I faced my death in the air, I was totally unprepared. My ongoing belief over the previous years that I could accept any possibility when I flew was shattered, albeit momentarily.

High wind conditions kept most of the competitive pilots grounded. I was one of only a few who launched. From my basket, at an altitude of 1100 feet and a distance of 630 metres, I could see the target clearly. High tension power lines stood as sentinels to the target area, a formidable obstacle to the challenge of reaching the goal, to score points, to win. My plan was to sneak over the top of the lines, once clear, pull the ripcord to spill hot air from the top of the balloon. A fast descent into the target area would follow. I soared.

The wind had increased to 18 knots. All my senses were stretched to cope with the increased challenge. Suddenly, the balloon was falling out of control. A vice-like grip of nature had taken control. Balloon and pilot were falling fast. Burner taps were full on. Flame was pouring into the belly of the balloon. Not only were we falling, but there would be no sneaking over power lines. The balloon would become entangled in them at gas tank level. Fire and electrocution would dominate the sky.

The lines loomed closer and closer. I could count the twisted threads carrying their lethal force of electricity. Faced with an absolute conviction I was going to die, my thoughts rushed to my belief only my physical being would perish, my spirit would live on. With such acceptance, I felt the panic leave my body. An incredible calm settled through me. I sent loving thoughts to my sons, praying they would continue to understand and accept my passion for flying, not condemn it. With only centimetres to go to contact, I emerged from my calm, prayed with intense feeling to the depth of my soul, yelled to the heavens. I had to fight to stay alive.

"Please don't let me die! I am not ready to die!"

In that moment, the balloon altered its descent, swept upwards towards a low-flying dark cloud. Away from the lines, away from contact.

Overwhelming waves of relief flooded my body. I fought off light-headedness. A vague recollection of concerned faces staring upward from the ground flashed through my thoughts. I had to get the balloon and myself back safely on the ground. Seven minutes later, the basket hit the ground positively, tipped over and dragged 45 metres across the paddock. I slowly crawled out from inside the wicker basket to lie on earth. Stunned, surprised I was still alive. So thankful. My crew ran from our chase vehicle.

"Are you okay?" I heard them yell.

"I'm fine," I replied. I tried to stand. My jelly-like legs folded, but I had survived my serious brush with death.

It took months for my nightmares around being burned alive to stop. My memory of that flight has faded but visits me occasionally. Gratitude also I was not taken.

CHAPTER 29

He was sitting in the seat next to my assigned number. We smiled at each other at the same moment. I turned away to buckle up my seat belt. "Nice energy." That's what went through my thoughts.

Eventually my companion stranger asked, "Are you flying home?"

"No, I am visiting from Australia. I have been at the 1985 World Championship in Battle Creek, Michigan. Now going to Ottawa to balloon, then to Calgary to visit friends, to fly commercially for about three months," I replied with a smile. "Have ballooning commitments in Europe next year."

"Calgary is my home. I have a cabin in Banff I use for a retreat. It really is a beautiful area of the world. I'm in Ottawa for business meetings this week."

The tone of his voice was delicious. Conversation flowed easily and by the time the plane had touched down, I had accepted his offer to join him for lunch while in Ottawa.

The official ballooning launch site was at Le Breton Flats. Garry Lockyer, the Event Director had arranged for me to fly his partner Cheryl's US built balloon, *Calypso*. At the first flight I lifted off accompanied by Kathy Thompson, a staff journalist for Ottawa's daily paper, the *Citizen*. The following day's edition carried a beautiful front-page photograph of *Calypso* floating low over the suburbs of Ottawa with Kathy's article:

"Between me and oblivion far below, there was only a waist-high basket which bobbed every time I moved. No nets, no railings. 'My God,' I thought briefly, 'What have I got myself into?' We descended slowly, majestically and I was able to take a look around at the clear morning sky, streaked with pink and gold. Beneath us was Ottawa in miniature, with tiny cars and trees as delicate as parsley."

"You have a message, Miss Wilson," said one of the reception staff at the hotel as I walked through the lobby.

"Lunch Thursday, 12.50 at your hotel? Call me. Geoff." I called but was not able to meet due to my media commitments that day. A meeting was confirmed for the next day.

Geoff took my arm as we walked into the restaurant, relaxing easily in each other's company, enjoyed our food and wine, shared stories of our lives. I spoke comfortably about my earlier divorce. Geoff had been married and divorced twice. His business demanded lots of travel between offices in Canada, USA and South America. Both of our lives were full of travel. He appeared to find my ballooning stories fascinating. I wondered momentarily if I had found a communion of souls. We agreed to reunite in Calgary.

Richard Bach, author of 'Jonathan Livingston Seagull', 'Illusions' and other books, wrote in his 1985 book, 'The Bridge Across Forever', "Did you ever feel that you were missing someone you had never met?" I had identified strongly with his words for a number of years. Like Richard Bach in his biplane searching for his soul mate, I travelled the world to fly for adventure, challenge, competition and financial reward. With every flight and landing, I met new people, but never the person I was missing. Could Geoff be that person?

I liked the way he ran his fingers through his hair, his dress sense was elegant but casual, his height, but it was his natural sensuality that stirred me. His eyes danced between softness and hunger. His animal spirit was strong. I felt powerfully drawn to it. My years of celibacy finally dropped away like icicles melting in the sizzling midday sun.

I spent most of my spare time in Calgary with Geoff. When the weather generally was stable, I went flying. Time for departure from a country I had grown to feel could be my permanent home loomed.

"I would love to take you to the cabin in Banff to share your last four days before you have to leave," he said down the phone.

"When could you pick me up?"

"Give me two hours and I will be there," he replied. I felt the smile in his voice.

The last light of the day spread across the sky as we drove off Banff Avenue into Geoff's garage. His cleaning lady had turned on the lights, left a bottle of champagne in the ice bucket. Bits and pieces of food sat on the table. Deer were standing in his backyard, easily visible from the kitchen window. Time was running out for us. After a night of intense passion, I reluctantly prepared to venture back into the everyday world. Before we left, I hid a small, intimate gift in Geoff's overnight bag for him to find after my departure. I told myself that whatever this was between us, it had wings.

"I will be back," I whispered into his neck as he held me tightly. The bustle of people at Calgary airport was just a blur as I walked onto the plane to take me away to chase targets in further ballooning competitions. Buckled up in my seat, a mischievous smile continued to play across my lips as I relived our incredibly intimate times together. Ballooning was my primary source of income. A commitment to fly at Chateau-d-Oex, an alpine village just a short distance from St Moritz in Switzerland, had to be met. Later in the year, I would compete in the Europa Cup in Pforzheim, Germany.

Fate had definitely handed me a pack of cards. At this point, I only hoped they would be shuffled correctly.

CHAPTER 30

"Watch out for mountain turbulence and avalanches," The Flight Director's words settled into my brain.

In Chateau-d-Oex Switzerland, we were a three-woman team. Regula Hug-Messner, Marta Trindler, both Swiss balloon pilots helped me lug the balloon on a sled across the deep snow to our dedicated launch site. As the registered pilot-in-command, I cautiously took to the sky. Other pilots eventually followed to fill the overcast heavens with multi-coloured balloons dangling like earrings against the sky. The Eiger is the highest alpine peak in the Swiss Alps, but Mont Blanc at 15,771 feet was easily identifiable in the distance.

Winds change quickly around mountainous terrain. After 35 minutes in the air, the balloon changed direction to drift up the side of the mountain. A craggy peak loomed. My decision to land was made quickly. Ground contact happened faster than anticipated. The balloon was deep in white virgin snow about 80 metres from the nearest road where the chase vehicle waited. The three of us commenced packing up our balloon. The swoosh of a balloon's burner sounded close. Another balloon landed beside us.

That was how I met South African pilots, Rick Makin and Herbert Gearing. They had brought the first balloon to South Africa in the early 70s. It did not matter they knew not how to fly. They assembled the balloon together, then took to the sky, like the pioneers who, back in 1783, stepped into a balloon to prove man could fly. Now our new South African friends were using their masculine strength to help carry out the equipment of both balloons, piece by piece, to the road. It was an easy decision to celebrate our near misses of Swiss mountain topography. Two Swiss, two South Africans and the lone Australian headed for an Italian restaurant to drink German beer.

My next European adventure brought shock and relief in even measure. Shocked to see one of the German crew clinging to the edge of the basket, his face white with fear, his legs dangling below the basket as the balloon I was piloting climbed higher and higher.

The organisers of the Europa Cup held in Pforzheim near the Black Forest in Germany had offered me a balloon to fly with crew support plus free accommodation. In return, they had used my photograph with the Australian female pilot angle to gain media publicity for the event. I was reunited with *Lenor*, the balloon I flew in France in 1983. Flying accurately during the week, I was placed in 8th position prior to the final flight scheduled for September 28. I had no premonition that flight could prove potentially fatal.

As *Lenor* stood upright ready for flight, I poured extra heat into the envelope to be sure the balloon would be sufficiently hot enough to climb high to clear downwind power lines. Turning to the ground crew, I called 'let go', then turned to face the front of the basket. The balloon left the ground and sailed upward. Higher and higher, the balloon floated. I turned back to wave thanks. That's when I found my unplanned passenger. Adrenalin surged through my body, my legs trembling. He will die if he falls! He can't fall!

Relief as my passenger and I sprang into action immediately lifting and heaving the stricken man over the edge into the basket with much force. He fell onto the balloon basket's floor instead, landed on his face and broke his glasses. He lay there for the remainder of the flight.

Once I knew my unwanted guest was alive and breathing, I went searching for my friend, Confidence, to gain further control. Flew for another twenty minutes before landing the balloon. The uninvited crewmember was subsequently diagnosed an epileptic. This had been his first fit. He explained later he had a mental blackout, could not remember the balloon leaving the ground but regained consciousness high in the air while clinging to the basket. He never returned to ballooning.

There were lighter moments during the Europa Cup.

A large bouquet of long stem yellow roses with a note that read "Welcome to Pforzheim" signed "The Marathon Runner of Pforzheim" with a phone number was in my room when I first arrived. One of my German crew called the phone number.

"Could he fly with me on Sunday?" was the request. My reply was negative, but I invited him to join the crew to chase the balloon.

Early on Sunday morning, the hotel front desk phoned my room. Mr. Annt was at reception holding the largest cake with the greeting "Welcome Ruth!"

Over his shoulder, he carried a cloth bag. All his marathon medals won, including his Olympic gold medal from in his early days of marathon running sat therein. He was nearly 70 years old and had sent the yellow roses.

Mr. Annt joined my chase team, while thousands of others were forced to stand behind the control barriers. He was charming. A delightful person and so proud of all his accomplishments and medals.

After my return to Sydney, Ross Spicer and I were successful in obtaining a *Toyota* balloon sponsorship. Together, we walked into the office of the Toyota Marketing Manager who greeted us. His first words. "I am telling you now I am not interested in a balloon." We left there an hour later with a sponsorship agreement. I was flying *Kellogg's Just Right*. Ross took responsibility for flying the *Toyota Hilux* balloon.

Often, we would play together in the sky, masters of our individual balloons. We always had fun. Ross would bash the keys on a piano to fill the room with great music, could jive and dance beautifully, filling a room with his energy. He could have been a romantic threat to my Canadian partner, but my loyalty remained with Geoff. Ross remained a huge presence in my life until he died in a ballooning accident.

CHAPTER 31

I qualified for my next World Championship. My decision to go or not ate at me daily.

The expense would eat at my savings for a real estate purchase, one of my life goals. The need to put myself to the test; to challenge myself; to feel that affair with myself when I am outside my comfort zone refused to be silent. Powerful emotions rose like a huge wave through my body, drowned my thoughts about not going against spending my savings. I waited till the last moment to forward my entry form.

My logbook shows from August 31 until September 4, 1987 I was in Schielleiten, Austria, flying practice flights. The World Championship commenced two days later, September 6. My son Mark, 17 years old, was with me as crew. Grant and his father were holidaying in Fiji.

"Have you brought that balloon trailer all the way from Australia?" one of the American competitors asked incredulously.

"Yes, I airfreighted all my gear, including my enclosed trailer," I answered with a quiet smile. Hiding my saboteur thought that I had spent a ridiculous amount of money to do just that.

"She's really serious, isn't she?" I heard him mutter to the accompanying guys as they walked towards their own gear.

My other crew members had travelled from South Africa, the United Kingdom and Australia. Rick Makin, David Finney, Simon Fisher, Martina Schmidt and Sharon Kenny, a global team of five friends who gave of their time, their emotions and their dedication along with my son Mark to help me in my quest to do well in my chosen sport.

It was a challenging championship. The flying area was close to Graz. The surrounding terrain quite hilly and undulating. Often our flight paths took us down into valleys over small villages, upward over nearby hills. Many wind changes caused pilots to rethink their selected flight plans in mid-air to try to reach their targets. Most people have life moments that stay with them. I had one of those at this event. Years later, my memories of that moment have me in my basket, acting like an eagle diving for its prey to eat.

On an afternoon flight, each pilot had declared his own target before lift-off. The wind was coming from the south east. Selected targets would be towards the north west. At launch, the wind had changed 180 degrees. Moving now in the opposite direction from the north west. With the changed wind conditions, over ninety balloons would fly further away from their pre-flight selected targets. I chose to stay on the ground, to be patient, to assess a viable alternative flight plan. With only two minutes left before the launch period ended, I observed the high clouds scudding across the sky, moving straight towards my selected target. My decision to shoot high to find that fast wind in front of the clouds was instant. With the burner on continually, the balloon climbed through 3000, 4000, 5000, 6000 feet. At 6950 feet, my balloon reached the wind shear. We were moving with the clouds in the direction of my target.

I knew what I had to do. Had to judge the exact moment to pull the ripcord. To spill heat, to descend at an accurate speed and angle to hit my target. It was daring and risky. I went for it. Swooped. Like an eagle with its eye on its target. And we fell. Falling through wispy clouds. The balloon's sides gently flapping, soft, accelerating faster towards the ground. I held my nerve, resisted the natural impulse to burn to fill the balloon's envelope with heat. I let the balloon sides flap. My heart was flapping also. *VH-JUS* and I were as one as we skimmed over the target.

To swoop in a balloon from almost 7000 feet down to five feet in a distance of less than two kilometres remains one of my most memorable flights. I also won that task. During the next morning's briefing, a few of my male competitors congratulated me. I smiled gently in reply.

Each flight is its own story. The winds for the evening flight on the last day in Schielleiten were ridiculously fast. After two aborted landing approaches, my balloon hit the ground, dragged across the grass, finally deflated close by a farmhouse. The balloon and basket lay on its side. I crawled out of the basket to lie flat on my back in the grass adjacent to my basket, catching my breath, elated with my flying, hugely relieved I was not hurt. Appearing above me stood the farmer, a toothless 92-year-old. He was wearing his farm gear, plus a leather apron and a jaunty, well-worn cap. He shuffled sideways from foot to foot. So excited. Pointing to the sky. Questioning. More excited when my team arrived. Our host wanted to hug and pinch Sharon and Martina, both young and attractive. His daughter, in her 70s, served us home-made wine in the field. I thought it better not to stay too long. The excitement might prove too much for our elderly host's heart.

Flying solo in all tasks I finished 15th from 71 competitors from 23 countries. My final score above that of the USA Champion, the Canadian Champion and the current Australian Champion. The final Awards Banquet was held at a grand old castle set in a magnificent garden. A string quartet played classical music. Over 1000 balloonists in black tie evening dress enjoyed the elegant atmosphere that was purely European: a fine finale to a fabulous feast of fun.

A reunion with Geoff in Calgary followed. Comfortable in each other's company during those first few days, I became aware our personal relationship was slowly changing. Phone calls when he was away with his business trips east were returned much slower than during our earlier days. I began withdrawing emotionally, shutting down to protect my feelings of vulnerability. The clouds I was dancing on were growing dark and stormy. After three weeks, I looked for a final commitment from this man I had been faithful to for just on two years – the longest emotional relationship since my divorce. The tension between us was as prickly as the thorns on a bougainvillea branch. His response brought no surprise. Disappointment and hurt, yes. My emotional pain was submerged under my inner knowing. My shuffled cards had fallen apart.

Two days later, I returned to Sydney, not with a relationship, but armed with a financial plan.

I flew to Brisbane in Queensland to invest in real estate. I had not the funds for a house but looked at apartments. When I arrived at the Ellis Street, Kangaroo Point apartment block, black clouds hovered above threatening rain and hail, humidity was high, as was my anticipation. I spilled out of the lift, walked into the apartment with the realtor. I knew I had found my little piece of real estate. I did not know then that fourteen years later I would spill into that same apartment drenched from tears at the loss of a loved one. The contract to buy was signed on day three, a tenant installed by day seven. My real estate life plan was coming together, but not my romantic personal plan.

After completion of my real estate deal, I returned to Sydney. Australia's Bicentenary was looming. Enthusiasm for the year's celebrations was beginning to build. Threads of thought or emotional attachment to Geoff were being shredded from me. I had work to do. Lots of work. Geoff became a disappearing memory. I became totally immersed in the organisation of the Trans-Australia Bicentennial Balloon Challenge, scheduled for March 31 to April 15, 1988.

Letters, faxes and phone calls from many parts of the world were a constant stream. International teams were busy finalising their travel, accommodation across the continent from Perth to Sydney, transportation of all ballooning equipment, vehicle hire in Australia and the many details such an adventure requires. My stress levels overflowed when Customs requested a guarantee in writing of $264,800 to ensure every pilot left the country taking their 52 balloons imported for the Challenge with them. I didn't have such funds available personally. Lost a few nights' sleep until I decided to approach a senior executive at the Commonwealth Bank. Once the bank accepted that my company would go guarantor for the above amount, I slept, albeit restlessly. I had mortgaged my Brisbane real estate investment.

A Letter of Guarantee was forwarded to the Customs Department just days before the Challenge commenced. The international balloons released to their owners.

CHAPTER 32

In 1988, Australia had a 200th birthday party – an acknowledgement of white settlement in 1788.

And the Trans-Australia Bicentennial Ballooning Challenge captured the good and bad of partygoers everywhere. Over 700 participants from seventeen countries celebrated the nation's birthday, the anniversary of white settlement in 1788, across the continent from Perth to Sydney over 16 days.

Twenty-three pilots from the United States, 22 Australian pilots, seven from the United Kingdom, four from West Germany and Japan, three Canadian, two French and one each from Finland, Denmark, Austria, Netherlands, Hungary, New Zealand, Yugoslavia, Poland, Sweden, Switzerland and their crews were some of the party guests.

To kick off the party, over 900 invited guests mingled at the Black-Tie Cocktail Party at the Burswood Casino Perth on March 30. That night, I paced my bedroom floor. The wind outside my hotel room refusing to drop. At first light, the winds remained too strong for safe ballooning. After a sleepless night, trying to hide my disappointment, I faced the national breakfast media. In the interest of safety, the scheduled flight had to be cancelled. An American pilot had written me a letter during the night. I spoke clearly as I read his words to a national audience.

"Dear Ruth,

As I laze in my bed this morning at 4am listening to the wind howl, I was disappointed. But more than that, I felt bad for you. What were you going to tell them? You know, 'them' - those whose lives have not been touched by ballooning - those who might not understand.

Tell them that ballooning teaches us many things. It teaches us how to be patient. It teaches us that in life, some of our most wonderful experiences involve circumstances over which we have very little control. It teaches us that we have to be ready, but that sometimes we must wait.

Tell them that we have travelled here from as far away on this planet as you can get, and we are ready. Probably no one is as disappointed as the pilots, but we are patient and our spirits are not dampened.

Tell them to stick with us - to be patient with us - and when the weather is right, we will not disappoint them. They will be thrilled, and they will never forget it. But today, we must wait.

Tell them to remember one of our favourite Aussie expressions:

No worries mate - she'll be right!

We're still smiling....Howard Solomon."

As the host of this amazing party I joined the entourage of 78 vehicles and trailers, plus the official TNT Pantech, the Elgas LPG tanker, the mobile medical emergency team, the balloon repair station, the media van, Bus Australia full of journalists, eight international documentary crews as we left Perth for Merredin. Challenge Officials Geoff and Vicky Tetlow, Tim Molloy, Phil Hanson, Danny Galbraith, Wally Williams, Cec Andrews, Wiz Gambier, David Finney and Rick Makin while supporters in another 85 vehicles joined us to head east for the first stopover location. Adrian and Ann Clements had already departed as forward scouts.

A colourful lot of adventurers in various modes of dress set the theme for the celebration across the nation. American Stetsons, Louis Vuitton khaki and blue jackets, Dutch clogs and black pantaloons, Virgin Airlines outfits, the red, white and blue Challenge jacket, convict dress, neat trim orange *Just Right* overalls dotted the countryside. The jungle greens of the Australian Army team, 55 strong, led by pilot Darryl Stuart, had entered their own balloon. They also provided crew and vehicles for balloonists from Poland and Hungary,

My elder son Mark flying my *Just Right* balloon wrote on his CV for the official event program:

Age eight, fell over his first balloon rope. Age 11, assisted on crown at first National championship as part of the winning team (first taste of victory).

Age 14, fan expert at National Championship (risky). Age 14, mouth crew World Championship Nantes, France (an awesome experience).

Age 18, completed 10-year apprenticeship by finally reaching the pinnacle of the balloonists' hierarchy, that of the PILOT. Age 19, Crew Chief at Nationals in Barossa Valley. Age 20, crewed at the World Championship in Austria, 1987.........

His crew consisted of Chris and Kaye McLeod, David St. Clair, Penny York and Prue Ireland. His brother Grant, also a balloon pilot, partied along as well as a crewmember for the assigned media balloon during the Challenge.

The weather pattern from Perth had flowed through to Merredin. In the interest of safety, once more the black flag was raised. No flight.

My comments addressed to the assembled media contingent were strong and clear.

"Hot air ballooning is one of the most weather dependent sports. In a situation where nature is supreme, learning to come to terms with such a disappointment is part of the challenge. Australians will see all aspects of this dynamic sport. This includes being grounded."

During the final stages of the Challenge, the party reached Dubbo. I made quiet time to check previous media coverage. Some of the event's highs and lows featured.

Day 3: April 3. Kalgoorlie - Locals sat around at the Cruikshank Oval in the centre of town on picnic blankets drinking from their goblets waiting for the aerial giants. Canadian Alistair Russell won 15 ounces of gold donated by the Shire. A few balloonists protested the flight because of thermal activity. The medical team, Dr. Peter French and Mary Ann Offer, reported only minor bumps and bruises from some of the bad landings.

Australia's only Two-Up school is based in Kalgoorlie. Two-Up is a gambling game played with two coins. A spinner tosses two coins in the air. He must throw two heads to win the game. Balloonists wasted no time in learning the refinements of the game. No word on how team Dakota Roughriders fared with their gambling.

The following morning, the cavalcade set off early to drive across the Nullarbor Plains, some 2000 kilometres east to Kimba in South Australia. Nothing in between except the occasional petrol station plus two time zones to cross. Past dry saltpans and along the longest stretch of straight road in the world were the towns: Cocklebiddy, Madera, Eucla, names on the map. In reality, nothing more than a motel and or service station.

Rolf Slattern from the Dakota Roughriders balloon team wrote:

"Who starred in 'They Shoot Horses Don't They? Who was the 'losingest' hockey coach in UND history? What's the capital of Tasmania? Who is Leonard Sly? Can Captain Jim sing the Sioux Fight Song?

It's 6:00am. April 3, 1988, the Dakota Roughrider Aeronautical Expedition and 77 other hot-air balloon teams from 18 countries are pulling out of

Kalgoorlie, Western Australia and heading east once again. Seventeen hours, a dozen 'petrol' stations, far too many bangers (sausages) and several hundred trivia questions later, we are still an hour out of Ceduna, South Australia and driving hard. The conversation has gone nowhere.

'There was a young girl from Ceduna', begins Rich Burns, who has not attended UND and consequently has an excuse for such outbursts. He observes that Ceduna rhymes with tuna, which leads to endless possibilities, each more unfortunate than its predecessor, but all hilariously funny after nearly eighteen straight hours of driving on the wrong side of the road. We are tired, tired of the songs, tired of the limericks, tired of road killed kangaroos, tired of grabbing fast food from places that would lose a cook-off against Wilkerson Cafeteria and tired of a highway that stretches straight and level into endless nothingness, but we are in the Trans-Australia Bicentennial Ballooning Challenge and nothing was ever better."

A Land Cruiser lost a wheel, other vehicles endured punctured tyres, a broken axle and gearbox difficulties. This was THE Challenge.

Ballooning fever hit the small town of Kimba on the Eyre Peninsula. The population of only 900 people almost doubled. Kimba opened its heart to the Challenge. Sheep shearing, vintage car display, parachuting, model airplanes, beer-barrel rolling competitions, lizard races and an old-time dance showed our overseas guests how Australia partied. Teams were billeted in local homes. Many pilots took their hosts aloft for their first balloon flight. Sweden's Ingemar Lilja landed in his host's garden. Became a local hero.

The flying was spectacular. Increased winds dragged late landing balloons across outback red dirt. An English pilot was heard to comment. "This landing field is as big as four English farms." At the half-way point of the Challenge, David Levin USA, was leading the point score, Jean-Robert Cornuel, France, in second place with Josef Starkbaum from Austria, third.

Day 8: Barossa Valley – My son Mark won the morning's task to hold overall lead in the Challenge. With flying conditions perfect in the rolling hills of the wine-growing district in South Australia, over five thousand people watched the balloons drift above wheat fields and vineyards. The media clamoured all over Mark, at only twenty years old, the youngest participating pilot. He quietly shared his moment of glory with his team. A proud Mum toasted him with champagne, also.

Day 10: Mildura – Excited to have hot air balloons visit their town as a first. The Challenge participants were welcomed with enthusiasm but also with rain and wind. A few pilots inflated their balloons for the crowd. The expedition continued onto Broken Hill, a mining town in outback New South Wales, a drive of 300 kilometres north through kangaroo and emu country.

Day 12: Broken Hill brought drama. As the teams gathered in front of the Pantech, the mobile briefing spot, our meteorologist read out his weather and wind speeds for the morning's flight. "Eight to ten knots," he said.

"You mean inside the Pantech, Wally. What's the winds on the outside?" called Ross Spicer and everyone broke into laughter, including good-natured Wally.

The immediate terrain around Broken Hill was bush country. Scattered trees covered the red dusty soil, preventing easy balloon landings. Many pilots flew long distances, searching for space to land their balloons. American pilot Howard Solomon was particularly sensitive about landing his new balloon in the outback-red dirt. He was last seen disappearing over the horizon towards the northwest. A local was quoted: "This is Australia. There's nothing that way except the desert and Alice Springs, 1500 kilometres away."

Solomon's chase crew couldn't find him. Tim Molloy, a fixed wing pilot and Challenge Official, charted a light plane to search for the missing pilot and balloon. Word came through on the outback-wireless channel. Howard was on Walbridge Station and was fine. While the search was on, the media and documentary-makers at the Command Centre pushed their microphones in front of my face.

"Wasn't it irresponsible to send pilots up in those windy conditions?" they questioned.

"This Challenge is about the ability of a person to make decisions and accept responsibility for their own safety. It is an individual's choice to fly here and how they party during this celebration," was my determined reply.

My words were lost on the media, hungry for negative images. As I walked to my motel room later, I collapsed due to lack of sleep and induced stress. The event doctor injected me with a drug. I slept. Four hours later, the media got their sensational balloon crash story.

The afternoon official flight was cancelled because of high winds. Pilots were given the opportunity to fly to pick a silver ingot donated by the town, off the top of an extended cherry picker. The value of the ingot: AUD$8000.

It was made very clear this was not officially part of the Challenge. Anyone who chose to fly would be flying a personal balloon flight under that individual's own insurance policy. A large crowd of spectators as well as balloon officials were gathered around the cherry picker, holding the ingot high above the ground. Other teams who had chosen not to fly in the interest of safety stood around the ingot target as well.

The official launch period closed at 1730hrs. It was 1725hrs when I checked my watch. My inner voice was telling me drama was on its way. To stop all flying. I lifted my UHF radio to call the launch official.

"Danny, I'm closing the launch period now. Advise any pilots in your area not to fly," I stated clearly.

"You're too late. *Wyoming* has just left the ground," was his reply.

When I saw the balloon in the distance, I accepted trouble was on its way. The yellow and brown balloon continued flying low over the town to get the drift to the ingot. The anticipation of their success was pulsating from the crowd around the field. Cameras were snapping. People were cheering loudly. From the ground, I could see the rate of descent of the balloon was too fast. I shook my head, took a deep breath, then reached for my car keys. A lot of heat had been spilled from the top of the balloon to descend to reach the ingot. Now the burner was full on trying to stop the downward fall. The balloon missed the ingot.

Gasps and shouts came from the crowd as the basket collided with the corner of the rooftop of a nearby house. The air conditioner fell from its casing. The balloon toppled sideways from the impact. The burner still on, it shot fire towards the envelope above. Flame licked a large hole in the side of the balloon. The intense heat caused the balloon to rise again, just missing power lines along the side of the road. The crew regained control. Landed the balloon close to a nearby gully. I drove up. Exited my car to hurry to the basket. The medical team followed. The crew climbed out of the basket. Jerry Elkins had bruised ribs, the other two guys badly shaken but with no injuries. I handled the situation with calm, directing the thronged media and locals, still under the effects of the calming medication administered earlier that day.

"She has ice in her veins," commented a local departing the scene.

"If only they knew," I whispered to no one in particular.

The damage to the house amounted to $2000. Jerry's insurance policy covered that.

The sympathetic townsfolk of Broken Hill presented Jerry and his crew with $1000 for 'having a go'. Jerry borrowed some fabric from another pilot. The repair station had his balloon ready for the next competition 826 kilometres east at Dubbo on the Macquarie River. Jerry finished in 7th place overall to take home some prize money.

Day 14: Dubbo - Only one more flight until the final hurrah at Bankstown Airport.

Weary pilots, crew and officials gathered in Dubbo for the final competitive briefing. Flying conditions were excellent. The townsfolk of Dubbo saw a dynamic display of tactical skills as pilots challenged each other. Around lunchtime, the computer spat out the results. American, David Levin first by 13 points to the Australian Army team's pilot, Darryl Stuart. Masahiko Fujita from Japan placed third. It was indeed a demanding challenge.

At the convict party hosted by Dubbo that night, I finally relaxed and danced till the early hours. Graeme Scaife of West Sussex and his crew, Brian Smith and Kevin Cooper, were filmed wearing tee shirts that stated, *"I had a Met Briefing from Wally and survived"*. Finally, I could laugh out loud.

A mass ascension at Bankstown Airport in western Sydney offered a visual treat for the seven thousand spectators, a photo opportunity for the media and a bid farewell to the Australian birthday celebration.

Participants had travelled over 6000 kilometres in 16 days. All pilots' skills had been extended, balloons had been damaged and repaired, a French pilot had broken a leg, a Danish crew person broke her ankle, relationships started anew. Others ended. By far, the overwhelming feeling was one of good times best summed up by the winner, American pilot David Levin.

"It was great. We got to see a lot of Australia, to meet a lot of people and spend time with them. And fly balloons that I love to do. I don't believe there was anything dangerous about the flying conditions. Any injuries sustained or damage done to balloons was purely pilot error. I watched some of the landings. The pilots concerned did not handle them properly in the conditions."

The twelve officials had done their job to the best of their abilities. At varying times, the enormity of the responsibility overwhelmed me. Just recalling the event chokes me with emotions. Moving a contingent of characters across a continent, throw in competition ballooning, numerous mad parties with weather a constant worry. No mobile phones, no GPS, no sophisticated weather information, populations of ten towns reliant on the event as their Bicentennial celebrations – is it a wonder at times I couldn't breathe properly, or that I fainted with exhaustion?

The mammoth logistical exercise that took me five years to bring to fruition would be seen on television by millions of people around the world. Foreign and Australian film crews travelling with the Challenge captured an event that was truly a Celebration of a Nation. 'The Up Over Down Under' documentary can be found on YouTube.

At the final Black-Tie Awards Dinner on Sydney Harbour I thanked my team, who had helped raise the awareness of ballooning both nationally and internationally. Australian balloon sales had increased. Sponsors were also thanked. In my day job, I owned and managed a Public Relations company. Henkel Corporation, based in Chicago, was one of my clients. I negotiated their financial support for David Levin's participation carrying their Natural Source Vitamin E banner during the Challenge. A successful connection for all parties. New faces were attracted to the sport. New boundaries to the sport had been set through endurance ballooning.

The Trans Australia Bicentennial Balloon Challenge was a first of its kind. It had created ballooning history, leaving the participants with their individual stories of dare and devil to share over many years to come. As Challenge Director, I believed I had the most compelling story of all.

As part of the organisation of the event, I ran a media campaign calling for Australians to participate. To crew for those pilots who needed assistance. Penny York was one person who wrote of her enthusiasm to be part of the celebration. Over 6000 similar letters were received. When Penny arrived at my office to discuss her participation, I had no available team for her. As Penny walked into the room, I heard my inner voice state loudly and clearly -

"She's Mark's woman in life."

I was initially shocked with such a profound message. I had heard my inner voice clearly many times previously and reacted immediately.

"I don't have a team for you Penny, but you are in the Challenge. You can be my assistant if we can't find a team for you to crew. I then encouraged my son Mark to invite Penny to join his team as crew. He did. Penny's mother, Kane, had encouraged her to enter; I made it a reality. Their fate was settled. Eventually they married.

And along the Challenge track somewhere between Broken Hill and Dubbo, I became aware of an American balloonist, his energy, his laughter and the way he held others' attention when he spoke. I found him quite attractive, even his air of aloofness. But my attention was required on those final legs of the Challenge. I knew where my responsibility lay. It wasn't with chasing a personal, even romantic, connection. The party at Dubbo we danced, we talked easily. Such a pleasure for me to relax, to allow the over-riding responsibility of such an enormous event fade away. I looked forward to more times together. And we made time. After the final Awards celebration, we knew we had only four days till he flew back to the USA. I was once again building a romantic long-distance relationship. We made plans for a reunion once I returned to Calgary in August.

It was July 29, 1988, when I received the letter of cancellation of the guarantee from the Commonwealth Bank. My belief that the 52 international pilots would do the right thing by returning to their various countries with all their ballooning equipment had been vindicated. I had worn this financial stress over a quarter of a million dollars for four months.

American journalist Mary Dahl Woodhouse on the Challenge wrote, *"The Balloon Challenge was a one-of-a-kind adventure. Midway through the trip, participants were already planning how a similar event could be handled in their own country. But it took Ruth Wilson with her commitment, imagination and love of the sport to do the first one. None other will ever be like it."*

CHAPTER 33

Immediately after the Balloon Challenge, my elder son, Mark, drove to Canowindra with my *Just Right* balloon to compete in his first National Ballooning championship. All week he sat in first place, his skill at the burner obvious to all who watched him. On his final task, he missed his goal to finish in second place. He had qualified to represent Australia at the next World Ballooning Championship to be held in Japan the following year, the youngest competitor at that time ever to do so. My heart sang for him.

My younger son, Grant, was becoming more in demand with his television commercial work and flying my balloon socially on various weekends in the country with his friends. I marvelled at his calm when at the balloon's controls. He also was a natural in the air.

After the years of working on the Balloon Challenge, I felt mentally and emotionally exhausted. I began planning my permanent departure from Australia, believing there was not much more I could do or wanted to do with ballooning in my home country.

Sipping a beer on my home veranda while watching the sunset days after the Challenge had ended, I was woken from my reverie by the ringing of my phone. I rose to answer. "Ruth, it's Jean-Michel from the Challenge". The French voice was melodic. I struggled to recall his face from the hundreds of people I had met recently across the country.

"I was with the French film crew shooting 'The Flight of the Kangaroo' during the Challenge. We are now in Alice Springs with more scenes to film. The pilot of one of our balloons has to fly back to France for a family emergency. We need a replacement pilot urgently. Would you help us, please?" he asked.

"I am flying to Canada August 1st. Have a lot of unfinished Challenge work to complete, reports to the Government and sponsors. Can you find someone else?" was my answer.

"We have called around. Nobody seems to be available or willing to join us." He sounded dejected and tired.

"How long do you need me?" My resolve was slipping. I could feel my emotional urge for adventure taking over my logical mind.

"We have finished filming on Cork Station in south-western Queensland. Just need to shoot around the Red Centre at Ayers Rock, a flight over the Barrier Reef with a final landing shot at Avoca Beach, just north of Sydney. Two weeks maximum," Jean-Michel assured me.

I considered his request. There was no offer of payment for my involvement, but that did not discourage me. I heard the need with his request. I told myself I could help with their film work and finalise my Challenge reports. Grant was involved with his television work and Mark was flying balloons commercially in Calgary so I could go.

The French expedition had two balloons, one for filming, the other balloon as part of the documentary. I would be joining French pilot, Dany Cleyet-Marrel, I hesitated at first. Convinced myself, it was only for two weeks. I finally agreed. Flew to Alice Springs to join the team as their second pilot. I also felt better saying 'yes'. Just a rescuer at heart.

The team of five was at Alice Springs airport to meet me. French director Christian Zuccerelli and Jean-Marc Péchart, cinematographer, greeted me with warm appreciation. In addition to my pilot skills, I took over managing the expedition's logistics. As an Australian, I had a better understanding of approvals required and speaking English was far superior when dealing with Australian authorities.

The expedition drove south to Ayers Rock (now called Uluru). We stopped for accommodation at Curtin Springs Station, 200 kilometres east of the Rock. I exited my car, walked to the working sheds. Aussie stockmen sat around drinking tea from enamel cups. Biscuits sitting still in their wrapping paper lay scattered around the table. I thought of my drover/stockman dad. I felt at home. I stepped confidently into the work shed.

"Who's in control here?" I asked with a broad smile.

"I am." The voice came from a corner at the back of the room.

"Hi, Ruth Wilson. I'm with a French film crew and we need beds for the night. Is there any way you can help us please?"

"Ashley Severin," he said while walking towards me. "Curtain Springs is a family-owned property."

I extended my right hand to shake his. I felt his surprise. But he responded.

"Let's see what we can find." I followed him out the screen door into the red dirt.

Three generations of the Severin family owned and managed the cattle station. Peter Severin, with Ashley and his son Ben, had plans to grow the property and business into a tourism destination. The flat-topped Mt Conner that forms part of the triangle that includes The Olgas, Uluru and Mt. Connor, rose out of the desert on the Severin property.

Our team was made welcome. Beds were found. Drinks were downed. By bedtime, permission was offered to fly over the saltpans on station property. Even over Mt Connor itself. What an unexpected win. The French director and cinematographer were aglow with visions to capture for their film. I slipped away to my bed, excited about new and different landscapes to gaze upon.

Sleep evaded me. But when the alarm rang, I was out of bed with my enthusiasm trumping any tiredness. As dawn broke, Christian Zuccerelli was strapping himself plus camera into a harness ready to hang from the top of my balloon. I proceeded with my inflation, as did Dany with his balloon. By the time the sun was making itself known, my balloon was airborne, Christian capturing unique images hanging outside my envelope.

I stood in my wicker basket, controlling the balloon. We drifted towards and within meters of Mt. Connor, a flat-topped sandstone and rock mountain standing 300 meters above ground, similar in length to Uluru. The winds adjacent to the rock face changed direction. In minutes, the balloon was floating the length of the mountain. Changing colours throughout the rock formation were spectacular. Red kangaroos and a small mob of rock wallabies skipped away from the noise of the balloon's burner. Thumbs up to Christian to ascertain if he had filmed our native animals. His thumbs up back made my heart sing; Dany's film crew were shooting our flight.

Our marvellous day ended with more drinks from pure Aussie outback hospitality. Plans for the following day solidified before bedtime. The saltpans streaked with yellow, purple and pink due to the recent rains would be our destination. Ten-year-old Ben was keen to fly with me. I couldn't say no.

Our flight began gently, proceeded easily over the saltpans, all part of an ancient inland salt-lake over 1 million acres in size. The isolation of the country was mind blowing. I was so lost in my emotions at the beauty of it all, I missed the slight changes the wind made on the pans. Dany flew high, signalling they had all the footage they needed. I waved as his balloon faded into the distance, ready for their landing.

It was only a moment in time. But a moment when the thermal hit. My balloon behaved erratically, spinning in circles, changing shape. We had to get on the ground and quickly. I was conscious of my responsibility for dear Ben. I ripped out the top of the balloon. We hit the ground positively amongst the spinifex, edging the salt pan. The road was three kilometres away. We had a situation, but both of us were physically safe. The balloon also. I knew our crew would be trying to access the area to find us. Time ticked by. Ben was calm. I appeared calm. My insides told a different story. What joy and huge relief I felt when I heard Ashley's Australian drawl on my UHF radio.

"Are you near the north/south fence or the east/west one, Ruth?" I knew immediately our wait for rescue was over.

There was a moment of sadness when I drove out of the station and waved good-bye to our hosts. The team had experienced real Aussie outback hospitality. Fantastic ballooning experience as well. I felt a real connection to the Severin family. I promised I would return. Two years later, I did with another French filming/ballooning expedition.

After the Mt. Connor filming, the expedition headed north to Alice Springs. I contacted a local pilot to arrange a flight together over the forbidding McDonnell Ranges. After three-hours airborne, all balloons landed within 200 metres of each other. In the open spaces of the Red Centre of Australia stood people from France, Ireland, United Kingdom, Canada, South Africa and Australia, spirits high, laughing and talking, a sight to acknowledge. Meanwhile, a frilled lizard slept nearby in the sun.

The 14-day filming expedition I had signed up for had expanded to day 26. At 1540hrs I stood on the beach at Port Douglas in North Queensland questioning my decision to agree to join the filming expedition. I could not abandon the team now as I explained to Peter, my potential romantic partner, on a long phone call to his home in the States.

The exercise with this section of filming was to fly a hot-air balloon from Low Island perched in the Coral Sea, part of the Pacific Ocean, to the mainland. To film the spectacular coral reef from the balloon with an additional film crew shooting its flight from a helicopter.

The crystal blue, calm early morning sea was rapidly growing angry. The wind velocity increased from 5 to 18kts. Low Isles was a green and white speck on the horizon. A crowd of locals gathered around. The two zodiacs were readied for the ocean; one carrying the hot-air balloon basket and equipment, Christian, Dany, Jean-Marc and the zodiac captain Jean-Michel. All the film equipment and personal baggage wrapped securely in plastic bags were in the second boat with the remaining team members. I clung tightly to the rope handle on top of the second zodiac. After a wet journey across the Coral Sea, the equipment was unloaded onto the sandy beach. I wandered off to meet Graham Grant, the lighthouse keeper and his wife, Bev, who had tendered the light for three years, to seek their support.

As the sun set over the mainland, all adventurers settled down for a night under the stars. The waves lapped rhythmically close by onto the shore. But there was wind, about 14 knots of wind. For a gentle lift off the next morning, we were looking for a maximum of eight knots. I spent a restless night trying to sleep. At first light, the trees on Low Isles in the Pacific Ocean were shaking their leaves. Instinctively, I knew a decision to fly this morning would prove foolish.

A phone call from the lighthouse to Cairns Met provided details of the upper wind conditions, 20 knots from 175 degrees at 3000 feet, they advised. The project needed a 130 to 160-degree vector to ensure the balloon would reach the mainland. Also, the sea had remained rough throughout the night, making an ocean retrieve of the balloon by the zodiacs if needed, very difficult. The flight was cancelled. Tomorrow would bring another opportunity.

That evening, eight adventurers sat on the white sand under a full moon eating, drinking and laughing, sharing a personal closeness, that special camaraderie which exists during most team expeditions. Eventually, all found their own spot to throw down sleeping bags. I chose the northern tip of the island with the water lapping only metres away from my resting spot. But the wind licked my face, so I snuggled down further into my sleeping bag. The moon shone light as far as the horizon. The ocean rippled constantly, seemingly oblivious to those who planned to fly across her. The wind had not dropped. Would we have to cancel again? I recalled the three dolphins swimming with the zodiacs to the island. I clung to my belief I would fly.

Saturday 0600hrs. There was wind, lots of wind. I felt a huge pressure to fly. The film crew stood around waiting for my decision. The helicopter company on the mainland waited for the call also. I knew the inflation would be challenging in the wind whipping around the nearby palm trees. Could I do this? Do this professionally with cameras on me? I was searching for Confidence, but she was teasing me, refusing to be found. I bit my bottom lip. Turned to the group and nodded. Let's go. A launch rope was tied to a nearby tree, the balloon inflated, finally upright. Dany climbed into the basket quickly, followed by Claude with her camera gear. Our balloon insisted on rocking from side to side. A strong burst of wind uprooted the anchor tree, the basket dragging towards the water lapping onto the island. The burner threw flames upwards into the envelope, water covered the basket floor. Claude dropped her camera gear onto the floor. In a matter of minutes there was clear sky between the balloon and the ocean below. 0805hrs the balloon had reached 3000 feet drifting north. Claude had retrieved her camera and commenced filming. On board the circling helicopter were Christian and Jean-Marc filming and photographing this historical first flight from Low Island to mainland Australia. The two black zodiacs gave chase, moving through the ocean, leaving a white choppy wake that stretched back to the island's edge.

Misty clouds wafted over the top of the balloon, threatening to fall down to engulf us. I stopped burning to let the balloon cool. We were falling, falling from clouds. Burner on again to level out. My relief we had gotten airborne was replaced with overwhelming awe. From my aerial platform, I could see for miles. The view was spectacularly unforgettable. The coastal sweep from Port Douglas to Cape Tribulation with its lush tropical rain forests ran parallel to the coast, hugging the Great Dividing Range. It resembled a dark green dragon basking in the sunshine. Confidence had found me and was hugging my shoulders.

Our flight direction took us towards the mouth of the Daintree River, an obvious landmark spilling into the Pacific Ocean, 45 kilometres north of Port Douglas. We were definitely gathering a variety of footage for the 'Flight of the Kangaroo' film. I went searching for a westerly wind direction to carry us away from water. I found it at 3600 feet. Once over land, I brought the balloon down to treetop level. *Benammour* flew level over the Greater Daintree National Park, the oldest living tropical rainforest on earth. I felt a huge privilege to float across this wonderland, to look down into the belly of the forest knowing over 400 species of birds, 13 of which are found nowhere else, nested. A huge percentage of our country's bats and butterflies settled here also, a world listed heritage site.

Past the mangroves, towards the sugarcane, we flew. After the intensity of the rain forests, we were looking at one large pale green waterbed. The cane was ready to be cut. The farmer was winding through the fields on his tractor, chasing our balloon. A grassed field close to his house was waiting for the balloon and its passengers to claim it. It was imperative I find the ground winds to land there. If I missed the landing, we were over dense forest once more. Low on fuel. Sensing, feeling for the smallest of wind change, I found it. To my great relief, I flew the basket to ground.

Landowners Mary and Dudley Jack and children hurried towards their aerial visitors. Our chase helicopter touched down in the same field. Christian and Jean-Marc emerged glowing with professional excitement and yelling, "Fantastic footage, magnifique!" The reunion of the group sparkled with celebratory champagne, tales of each person's observation of the flight, with laughter and hugs. The team had covered over 10,000 kilometres in six weeks, where the essence of the Australian landscape had been captured from a balloon.

'The Flight of the Kangaroo' documentary was viewed throughout Europe.

CHAPTER 34

I gathered my enthusiasm for change even though the French filming expedition had left me drained. My departure flight for Calgary was rushing towards me. Arranged for my furniture and effects to go into storage in Sydney, attended a farewell party Wendy and Phil Kavanagh organised. I stood outside my Neutral Bay home with two suitcases. Felt no misgivings at all about my new direction, a move to fly balloon commercially in Canada. To explore a potentially promising relationship with an American man.

The difficult part of my new adventure was leaving my son Grant behind who, with his best friends James, Crewsy, Mark A, Grant T, wrote on a card 'without you the pack's just not gonna be the same! You'll be missed! Goodbye'.

The easiest part of my new adventure would be a reunion with my son Mark, who was to celebrate his 21st birthday, two days after my arrival in Calgary.

My recent romantic interest, Peter, lived in Colorado, where flights from Denver to Calgary made our reunion easy. Our friendship, our connection, blossomed. We shared a love of aviation and dancing at the Cotton Club at least for one night during his visits. Summer moved into fall. We planned that I would spend the Christmas and New Year holidays with him in Colorado. Memories of our sharing during his absence continued to build. And fly-fishing was amongst such memories.

On one of his Calgary visits, we went fly-fishing. We wound our way through the hills in my black pick-up truck to the Bow River. He pulled the rods and reels from the truck. Initially, Peter demonstrated how to fly-cast Bow River style. After some practice, I felt confident to try alone. My instructor moved further down the river to his casting spot. We remained in those spots for over 20 minutes, both casting, with me trying to remain patient.

Then Peter caught a brown trout, to great whoops of joy. Not to be outdone, I caught a tree on the riverbank, hooked solid, fell backwards into the river with the stream filling my waders, drenching my hair and clothes.

"You will have to change into those spare clothes of mine in the bag in the back of the truck. We are too far away to get you home to change," an obvious remark.

Standing there in jungle green tracksuit pants and check hunter's shirt, I put my arms around his neck and kissed him. Fly-fishing still reminds me of cold, wet feet.

Within a short time after my arrival in Calgary, I was flying passengers with Del Michaud's company. The other designated commercial pilot was my son, Mark. Both of us would often be flying our separate balloons over Calgary at the same time. On one of those mornings, Mark's balloon was caught above a skyscraper building in downtown Calgary. The wind had dropped to zero. An absolute stillness mapped the air. Mark persevered, burning all the gas in three of his balloon tanks, using up most of the available gas in his last tank. He was searching for just a tiny fraction of wind movement. When he found it, the balloon moved off the building. With short bursts of flame, Mark flew the balloon down the side to land on the railway tracks between the buildings. My heart was full of respect and admiration for his skill and calm under such challenging circumstances.

"I think I have aged 10 years this morning, Mum," he said when I caught up with him. I appreciated his feelings. Caught out with wind dropping unexpectedly to zero, my balloon perched over the top of beehives, over thick forests, powerlines, over water in various countries, had aged me too. In all situations, I'd been blessed to find the smallest wind movement to escape potential danger, even lethal. Mark eventually returned to Australia, finished university and moved to work in the corporate world.

Summer flights in Calgary were conducted late into the night with 21.30hrs landings quite acceptable. Summer flights in Australia were not so popular as our weather patterns rarely allowed for stable, safe evening flights. To beat the summer heat of the day with threatening thermals, most Australian pilots made early starts, meeting their passengers around 5am, airborne by 6am at first light, on the ground by 7am.

The Canadian autumn offered fabulous photographic opportunities of yellow and gold leaves intertwined with green for those who chose to fly. And autumn was my favourite time of the year for any ballooning activity. The heat of summer had disappeared. The cold of winter was yet to embrace us all, but the period in between was a pilot's blessing. Mostly the air remained stable, winds not too demanding, always a blaze of flamboyant autumn colours below.

Calgary winter arrived. With it came snow. Too cold for passenger flying. I would take the smaller balloon out to fly in -10 degrees to promote the local sponsor. It was not unusual for the wind to increase, to fly to the farmlands east of the city, to drag through the snow on landing. End up with a basket full of snow on top of me. One flight dragged 12 metres. The crew needed a shovel to empty the snow out of the basket resting on its side, so I could then climb out, alight with my biggest smile at the craziness of such a scene.

Such a flight would not happen in Australia, a country without heavy snowfalls at sea level, only on our few mountain peaks, the tallest at 7310 feet or 2228 metres. The colder weather of winter presents the hot-air balloon with more friendly conditions. In essence with flight, the temperature inside the balloon's envelope must be hotter than the outside temperature to climb. With the winter cold temperatures, less flame was required, less wear and tear on the ripstop material of the envelope. Spring and autumn invariably brought good flying conditions in most countries.

The views over the Bow River from my apartment north east of Centre Street NW were stunning. I had found this two-bedroom, one-bathroom apartment and felt at home as soon as I first walked inside. Lots of white. Walls of that colour, curtains and blinds also white. The lounge and two single seaters were white leather. Both the living room and main bedroom floors were covered with a red Turkish pattern large rug. A pale green rug covered the guest bedroom floor. I added a few personal touches I had shipped from Australia. Mainly photos of my sons, my family shots and other ballooning paraphernalia. Always a vase of flowers.

In the depth of winter, the river would ice over. My drive down the hill to the city was challenging, with my truck skidding on black ice many times. I looked forward with huge enthusiasm to Peter's visits. Loved sharing my personal space with him.

I welcomed 1989 wrapped in the arms of my American lover.

CHAPTER 35

My eyelids opened. I reached to turn off the alarm. My first thoughts of the new day followed. It's all about the wind. Will the wind allow me to fly the exclusive flight booked by the Chief Executive of an oil company for his son's 30th birthday gift? As I showered quickly to warm my body, my thoughts stayed in the air, endeavouring to intuit my ballooning day ahead.

At 0500hrs I called the Calgary airport met officer for a February weather report.

"It's a beautiful morning for a flight, Ruth, 2 - 4 knots all the way up," I was told.

The meeting point for the flight was at Riley Park, downtown Calgary. The time 0630 hrs.

"Good morning, Tom. Ruth Wilson. I'll be your pilot this morning," I said as father and son approached the balloon basket.

Concern spread all over Tom's face. This was something I had to contend with often when passengers were faced with a young female pilot. As I prepared the balloon for flight, I started my regular spiel designed to put such folk at ease.

"I do love flying around Calgary, but my favourite place to fly is where I won the Australian Championship," casually said. How many times had I said the same statement to assure mostly male passengers I knew what I was doing? It worked every time, eventually drawing a more visibly relaxed passenger towards the basket. Tom was not one of those. His son showed no concern at all.

Other balloons arrived at the park, began preparing for flight. I loaded maps and radios into the basket. Just prior to lift off, I noticed the leaves on the tops of the trees in the park were swaying a little too fast for the predicted 2 to 4 knots. Today I would reach for my mobile phone, check weather information that allows for decisions whether or not to fly. In Riley Park in 1989, there was no mobile phone. I began to feel uneasy, questioning my decision to fly, discarding my inner voice's warning. It was touch and go whether to fly or not. With the other balloon company inflating their two balloons close to my launch spot, I chose GO. With both passengers now on board, I hit the burners. Our balloon lifted off from the park, reached tree top level, distorted through a strong wind shear, knocking some of the heat out of the envelope. We had lost power to climb, but we were too high and over trees, so unable to land. I had one option. I kept the burners shooting flame into the envelope. We would continue our climb, our flight.

The commercial centre of Calgary stood on the balloon's path. Our track was heading directly towards the highest building in the city. After calculating the angle of approach and speed, it seemed inevitable the balloon would hit the side of the tallest building, about two floors from the top. There was no instruction in the balloon's manual about pilot action when colliding with a building. My stomach churned, my nerves were stretched to the point I could feel my legs begin to shake, just a shimmer. I was facing potential danger, an accident. I had visions of the balloon hitting the building, collapsing, sliding down the 22 stories to hit the street below amongst heavy morning traffic.

I could hear Calgary Control Tower calling me, but I could not answer. I was frozen with my intense assessment of our position. I was trying to wet my lips so I could brief my two male passengers on the possible upcoming collision when a wind swirl saved us. It blew around the top floors of the building, grabbed the balloon, moving it horizontally and parallel to the building, away from the building's edge.

Tom's knuckles were white at launch, but he had relaxed as the balloon moved closer to the building. He then started waving. The balloon was only about five metres from his boardroom. His staff were standing at the window waving to him. I had unknowingly flown him towards, then past his company's boardroom. This titan of the corporate world was duly impressed and said so loudly.

While Tom was enjoying his aerial moment, my balloon was flying towards Calgary International Airport. To renewed relief on my part, I reached for my VHF radio to call Air Traffic Control.

"Calgary Control. Requesting clearance to 7000 feet please," I did not recognise my own voice, usually so strong and confident, but quieter, full of relief.

"Is that you, Ruth? We have been waiting for your call," the male voice answered. "Any problems?"

"All positive," I answered. And everything was positive with the flight. We had not hit any building. My passengers were never aware of any potential danger. As the pilot, I had remained outwardly calm and in control.

"Clear to 7000 feet and have a good flight."

A couple of days later, I flew a teenager only days before his death and stared down a police officer.

I picked up the phone to hear the voice say, "The doctors have told us that our 15-year-old son has only two weeks to live. His final wishes are to go on a balloon ride and to meet Wayne Gretsky, a famous Canadian ice hockey player. Can you take us for a balloon ride?"

On the morning of the scheduled flight, I met both passengers at the usual launch site in Riley Park. It had snowed heavily the evening before. The city looked as if it was covered with white icing sugar. Most people and their dogs were all inside because of the snow, as the balloon floated towards the northwest.

The father stood beside his son, both looking over the edge, pointing at landmarks below. They appeared relaxed, enjoying the view from above. A long entourage of cars full of family and friends followed the balloon's progress. I remained silent, not intruding on their close connection. After the balloon landed and all the people had filed out of their cars, champagne bottles were opened. The mood was jubilant. When the Sheriff's car drove up, the atmosphere changed. In Alberta in 1989, it was illegal to drink alcohol in the open. An anxious feeling descended on the group.

"Leave it to me. I will speak with them," I said and walked towards the patrol car.

"Good morning Officer, I'm Ruth Wilson and the pilot this morning."

"We know you balloonists usually drink champagne after flying and we're just checking," said the man in uniform.

I looked straight into his eyes and said without hesitation.

"I have been flying balloons all over the world for the past 14 years and this has been a very emotional flight for me this morning. I have just flown both a dad and his 15-year-old son who has been given only two weeks to live. This has been his final wish. We have had a wonderful flight and I believe it deserves to be celebrated and yes, we are drinking champagne toasts."

He removed his sunglasses, looked me straight in the eye, and said, "Ma'm, I have a 15-year-old son. You go right ahead and celebrate. Enjoy your morning." He reversed the police car, turned around and drove off.

I returned to the group with a tear or two in my eyes. My passenger passed over 10 days later.

The month of January had passed. Peter and I had not been able to spend time together after my New Year visit. I felt the distance between us. Began to mentally fight with myself. I thought often about death; about the father and son I had shared a basket with not so long ago. Reacted emotionally to my memories of the compassion shown by the local lawman, allowing us to bend the law in favour of family love. Dark clouds settled over my days after that flight. I was feeling stranded, emotionally lost. I was missing Mark, now back in Australia. I was missing Grant also in Australia. As time moved towards mid-February, I began to doubt the probability of a long-term commitment with Peter.

I even considered retiring from flying.

"I am giving ballooning away. It's so hard doing this on my own," I said to my friend Michael Kelaher. I heard the chuckle in his voice even before he spoke down the phone.

"I was about to climb into a balloon basket recently when I turned to the pilot and asked. Do you know Ruth Wilson who flies balloons? He turned, looked at me, nodded his head and replied:

"Serious feathers, that one."

CHAPTER 36

"**I'll be back in about six weeks,**" I assured my Canadian friends, waving good-bye, disappearing through Calgary Airport Immigration. It was February 17, 1989, my birthday. Fate would have other plans for me.

At a stopover in Auckland, I did a tarot card reading showing my friend Ute, now divorced, would marry a man she would spend time with while she was in another country. As I flew on towards Australia, little did I realise the man Ute would marry would be Kevin, my former husband.

My younger son, Grant was following his star. His work with stage, television and filming had been steady over the ensuing years. He was also an excellent balloon pilot. We celebrated his February birthday together in Sydney.

Early March, I drove to Canberra to fly at the Balloon Festival, an annual event to celebrate the founding of Australia's capital city. It was where my life was about to change direction without my even knowing. It was where I met Shawn Mackinga, an American pilot. He was new to the ballooning scene and I had yet to meet him. Two days passed before that happened.

Day three brought rain, forcing flying to be cancelled. The event organisers arranged for a bus trip to a winery for lunch. He entered the bus, walked straight to the empty seat beside me and smiled. "I'm Shawn," were his first words as he reached for my hand. "Ruth Wilson," I said, returning the smile.

"I know who you are and I've heard a lot about you," he replied. The die was cast. Our futures would be powerfully intertwined.

After the festival with two weeks before my scheduled return trip to my Canadian life, I drove to Mudgee to spend a couple of days with my dear friend and balloonist, Ross Spicer. My plan was to then drive north to stay with Jeni Edgley at her property near Nerang to film a promotional video using my balloon. Shawn joined me on the journey north to meet up with his Gold Coast friends. Neither of us could suspect what was waiting ahead of us.

As we drove down the hill into Alstonville, a quaint township in Northern New South Wales, smoke was pouring from the balloon trailer. The brakes on the trailer needed repair, so we relaxed at The Federal Hotel with a few drinks while the local mechanic worked his magic. Darkness was settling in as we headed out of town too late to reach both our final destinations. Instead, I made the decision to turn off the highway to Byron Bay for overnight accommodation, with the intention of continuing our travel the next day. That did not happen.

I blame the wind seducing me with perfect flying conditions met on waking. If the wind had been strong, no decision would have been reached to inflate *Just Right* at the Epicentre of Byron Bay, very close to the beach. In a parallel lifetime, both Shawn and I would have eaten breakfast, then driven north to follow a different life story. But my passionate need to play with the wind dominated my thought processes that morning. I inflated and launched into a mesmerising blue coastal sky.

The scenery below and reaching west as far as I could see, was spectacularly beautiful and peaceful. The ground below the basket rolled on, sleek and curvaceous, like a woman's hips and breasts. The magic I felt took my breath away. I floated alone in my basket at one with the wind. The energy slumbering through the hills and valleys of the hinterland awakened slowly at first, then built up to an amazing climax as it grabbed my heart and mind. Shawn was waiting with chase vehicle and balloon trailer at my landing field. My decision to stay and fly once more over the Byron landscape was made while packing away the balloon. That afternoon, I flew a second flight, landing my balloon at the Byron Bay Beach Resort, met the owner, who invited me to go marlin fishing the next day.

The full moon shone through the open window of the motel room while Bach's Air was playing softly in the background. The telephone rang. It was Peter.

I spoke softly into the phone with a touch of reasoning. "I have wanted to experience the power of marlin fishing for years." Silence. Peter was waiting for more.

"What's been happening in your world?" I asked, adding a smile to my voice. "So, I am quite excited at the possibility of going out to sea and using the fishing rod."

Little did I know I was about to come face to face with a seven-metre wave and have to fight for my life, not for a fading relationship.

CHAPTER 37

I stepped onto *Innovator,* the 32-foot fishing boat owned by my newly acquired friend David, for my first deep sea fishing experience. Anticipation zipped through my veins. I was 46 years old.

"How are you on the ocean?" David asked.

I paused.

It was a good question. I was athletic, confident, adventurous and outdoorsy, with streaked blond hair and tanned skin to prove it. But water was not really my element. An unusual quality for an Australian and a sporty one at that. The truth is, I'm not much of a swimmer. At 10 years of age, I once jumped off the high diving board of the town pool to show the boys I was fearless. Unfortunately, not knowing how to swim, I promptly sank to the bottom. I was saved by a tourist who'd been sunning himself nearby. Since then, I've had a certain trepidation about water.

"I don't know, David. I've never been on the ocean, but if a strong mind helps, I'll be okay," I replied with nonchalance. This at least, was true. I might not be good with water, but I was good with challenges.

Besides, it was a beautiful day. At 7am the air above the Ballina Marina was already 20 degrees. The sun was shining. And we were off to look for marlin! What we'd do if we ever found one was a challenge to be explored. Wearing a red cotton shirt, khaki-coloured shorts, Italian leather sandals and gold jewellery, I climbed the ladder to the bridge and sat next to Peter, the skipper, at the controls. I was carrying my Italian leather shoulder bag with me for security. I preferred not to leave my travel documents, jewellery, make-up, and my long-kept diary (in which I collected addresses) in my hotel room. So, I'd packed them into my shoulder bag and brought them aboard. In retrospect, perhaps this wasn't such a smart idea, but then in retrospect, whatever is?

I settled into my perch on the bridge, trying to acclimate to the bounce and sway of the boat. David, with my new ballooning friend Shawn, remained standing on the deck below me.

As the boat motored towards the Ballina bar on the east coast of Australia close to Byron Bay, I chose to remain central to all the activity, adjacent to the skipper. The sky was clear and I was getting the feel of the boat's movement. Then I noticed the waves were getting rougher as we approached the bar. Doubts began creeping into my mind. Would I get seasick? Wouldn't that be a touch humiliating after my confident statement earlier?

As we reached the bar, the skipper throttled back the engine. The boat started to bob, turning slightly towards the left. I sensed the skipper's indecision. I wondered if the conditions were normal or not. I had no experience of boats, fishing or oceans. The water around us was rough and unsettled. Was the skipper contemplating cancelling our fishing adventure? I leaned forward to see better through the Perspex window. Ahead, a large wave gathered, building to huge proportions. I remember thinking 'I didn't know water could climb perpendicularly.' I waited for the mountain to flatten as water should. But the wave continued climbing, higher, higher, until it towered over us, dwarfing *Innovator*.

In the split second before the thing hit, I said aloud, "This has fate written all over it, Ruth E Wilson." Then the raging water smashed through the windscreen. It ripped the chair I was sitting on out of its anchor. *Innovator's* bridge vanished. Seconds later, I found myself in the ocean. Huge mountains of foaming, swirling, angry water bashed me about. I gasped, trying to get air, and inhaled a mouthful of brine. I felt myself sinking. I could not breathe. My mind was screaming, "No air! No air! I am going to die." I was lost in the raging swirl as my lungs filled with water. Bubbles streamed from my mouth as my arms and legs flailed helplessly. I dropped still deeper. I had no idea which way was up, which way led to the surface and the precious oxygen I needed, or where the boat might be. I was drowning. I had to do something drastic to save myself.

My mind flashed back to that fateful day in the swimming pool and that terrible moment of panic as I hit the water - this was much more frightening and threatening and for a second I thought the challenge of survival too great. Then I heard a voice - my inner voice - it seemed calm but insistent. "Kick your legs. Keep kicking, Ruth, note where your shirt is". I could see the picture of myself very clearly in my mind. My shirt collar was floating above my eyebrows. My panic eased. I focused. The water's surface was above my head. That's where the air was. That was the direction in which I needed to swim. The sea around me spewed and churned. I kicked as hard as I could, thinking of nothing but the movement of my legs and the power needed to get me to the air I needed.

I broke the surface and inhaled my first sweet breath. Around me bobbed the debris of fishing lines and hooks. I raised my head in time to see *Innovator* gurgling as it sunk beneath the waves. I could see no sign of David or Peter or Shawn. I flapped my arms desperately, trying to control my panic. I was not wearing a life jacket. My lungs felt starved. I couldn't get enough oxygen. Blood seeped out of a large head wound above my left ear and settled around my left shoulder before dripping into the sea. My back felt weirdly numb, as though it should hurt, but didn't.

Suddenly Shawn broke the surface close by and yelled, "Stay away from the propeller". I couldn't fill my lungs or feel my spine, let alone see where the propeller was. Shawn swam towards me and grabbed hold of my left hand with one of his. In relief, I coughed up seawater. For a tiny moment, I believed myself saved. Then I noticed the land receding. The sea wasn't done with us. We were caught in a strong rip; both being dragged further out to sea.

Now the real fear began.

The rip towed my fragile, exhausted body through the swells like a sodden rag doll. Panic swept through me again. Were David and the skipper dead? Could the sea really snuff out life that quickly and easily? I clutched Shawn's hand. The water swirling around us was bone-aching cold, the ocean rough with deep swells. The wreckage grew smaller and smaller as the rip continued to drag us away from the shore. The next wave ripped Shawn's hand from my grasp and flung our bodies apart. I struggled to keep my head above the water. I couldn't reach Shawn. He was so close, yet so far away. He was not wearing a life jacket either. But he swam towards me again and we found each other's hand.

"Keep kicking your legs, I need to know you are still conscious," Shawn shouted as we struggled to remain at the surface. I kicked. I breathed. I would not pull him down.

I felt so impotent. We were just two tiny heads in a huge ocean. How could anybody find us? Blood leaked from my head wound and dripped into the water. My legs dangled over the dark abyss of the ocean below. Weakly, I kicked to keep from sinking. Jaws-like images floated up from the depths. I pictured a shark stalking me from below, rising and closing its teeth on my flailing legs. The look on Shawn's face said he may have been worried about a shark attack, too. Fear gnawed at my entire being and consumed my energy supply. I struggled to control my thoughts so I could retain sufficient physical energy to stay conscious.

We rode the crest of another angry wave and dropped into a deep trough of steel-grey water. Like a mantra, I kept repeating, "I am responsible for everything that happens in my life." Once I accepted that at some level, I had agreed to be a part of this story, to be here in the ocean. A huge surge of energy flowed into my body. I refused to lose hope.

But then, once again, we were swept to the crest of a mountainous wave. The feelings of extreme vulnerability and fear returned and all my previous positive energy drained from me; weak, limp, terrified, my head filled with negative thoughts.

All my pockets were swollen with water. The weight of my wet clothes began to pull me under.

I have a horror of the below. The concept of it. The claustrophobia of it. There are times when I feel I don't even belong on the ground. Air is my element. For years I'd been having an affair with the wind, the clouds. I'm a balloonist, a champion balloonist — and I belong to the sky.

In my long affair with flying, I had been bewitched by the art and grace of losing myself to the air. It's been my passion, my adventure, my way of escaping from everyday living.

How many people had told me I was mad for taking up that sport, such a *dangerous* activity they said? And they were right. As an elite ballooning pilot, I've had my fair share of disasters, thrills, close shaves, over the years. In the air, I understood and trusted the powerful natural forces around me - understood their patterns and quirks and designs. But this was different. I was being sucked *below*. My first time on the ocean and there I was fighting for my life.

Oh, the miserable ludicrous irony of it all.

"Get your shorts off," Shawn yelled while he tore at the buttons on my red shirt.

Stripped down to only red bikini briefs, I felt less hindered, less weighted, but far more vulnerable. I was swallowing too much water. Waves of vagueness began to engulf me. Through the fog of mind, my inner voice spoke. "You cannot die Ruth. You have been living on the edge of your heart's desire and have not yet loved fully."

"Hang on a bit longer, Ruth E. We'll be alright. I can't support you if you pass out. I am exhausted. Keep moving your legs," Shawn shouted at me.

"How will anybody ever find us in this huge ocean?" I whispered. This thought had refused to leave me. Our situation seemed so hopeless. I tried to hang on, to keep the fog from engulfing me.

"I can hear a motor now. It's a boat." Shawn's faint words fought through the greyness of my mind. "Damn, it's going away from us." I didn't have the energy to feel disappointed.

And then I saw fins. Sharks! Fins slicing through the water towards us. My mind started examining what my reaction would be when I felt the clamp of razor-sharp teeth around my body. Would I scream or accept my fate calmly? There was not a thing I could do to save myself. I felt no panic. My act of surrender to my fate, to my belief my spirit would live on, created a gentle essence vibrating through my being, an incredible calmness. I saw the shapes begin to jump up into the air, playing with each other, encircling us. Not sharks, but dolphins.

"We will be saved," yelled Shawn. "The dolphins are with us."

I was slipping in and out of consciousness as a boat appeared beside us. Male shapes and voices were leaning towards us. They lifted me from the sea. I screamed out because of the intense pain down my back. A male voice filtered through my haze. "Oh my God, look at her back. It's black." And hearing Shawn's voice in the distance. "Have you got something to cover her?"

As I was hurried into Ballina hospital on a stretcher, I was fighting shock, hypothermia, head and back injuries. Figures loomed over me asking, "Are you allergic to anything?" I think I said no. The painkiller, pethidine, was administered, followed by the intensity of one voice stating, "We're going to lose her. I can't find her pulse." I slipped into unconsciousness. I floated around in other worlds. On one occasion, I was swimming under the water to meet up with three dolphins. Communication flowed between the middle dolphin and me.

"We want you to build this balloon," stated my dolphin friend. An electric blue balloon with six golden dolphins depicted on the sides appeared in front of me.

"That will cost me $41,000," was my shocked response.

I heard the dolphin reply clearly, "You have been helped often. A film will be made of your life. This balloon is important and part of that."

The owner of the boat, David and the skipper, Peter, were rescued by men on a fishing trawler that arrived at the accident scene. Fortunately, both men were not injured.

On my hospital discharge, I went to stay at the Byron Bay Beach Resort to recover my energy and strength. Shawn was also hosted at the resort. My profound underwater dolphin experience stayed with me. I had lost my personal possessions in the boat accident. My large leather bag had sunk with the wreckage, along with my expensive camera and camera bag. Also, my new sunglasses I had bought in Canada as my birthday present to myself. I grieved irrationally for my sunglasses. Wished they would wash up safely on the shore nearby.

I had decisions to make. Important decisions. On whether to return to Canada or not.

Was Peter important in my life? Should I build the dolphin balloon, shown to me in a dream while in hospital? Where would I set up my new home if I stayed? Why had I been in this life-threatening accident? But the most important message I repeated to myself was I was not a victim. Not a victim of this boating accident. Not a victim, I had been blessed to survive. I was a survivor.

CHAPTER 38

My decisions were made. Calgary did not feel part of my immediate life. I would follow my dolphin dream experience and build the balloon depicting golden dolphins on its sides. I found a home in Coopers Shoot, seven kilometres out of Byron Bay. My Calgary friends shipped my possessions to Byron Bay.

Kavanagh Balloons built my vivid royal blue balloon with six golden dolphins depicted as shown to me under the ocean, registration VH-VLX. I named her *Misty Blue* after my favourite song by American R&B singer, Dorothy Moore. The final cost of *Misty Blue* was $41,000 plus some cents.

Who can explain how I captured that dollar figure as the balloon's cost during my unconscious conversation with my dolphin acquaintance?

Due to that clarity of experience, I believed strongly I was meant to stay in the Byron Bay area. Also, I was meant to write for future record of such an enlightened experience. *Misty Blue's* inaugural flight over the Byron hinterland happened on Mark's birthday August 3, 1989.

Word soon spread that golden dolphins were floating around the Byron area. I received a phone call from Estelle Myers, producer of a TV documentary on what she called the "human-dolphin connection" that had won commendation from the United Nations.

She explained to me dolphins have built-in sonar and communications technology that allows them to detect underwater objects, to talk to each other on several channels at a time over distances of many kilometres. Some can move through the water faster than a nuclear submarine. She added, dolphins were the only wild creatures that sought out friendly contact with humans. Most intriguing, dolphins seem able to communicate, mind-to-mind, with humans.

I understood exactly what she was saying as I definitely had experienced such communication post my boating accident. I shared my experience with Estelle, where I had communicated so clearly with the middle of three dolphins. But what impressed me was knowing while unconscious that such a balloon presented to me during the dreamlike experience would cost the amount it did.

I could imagine Estelle nodding knowingly as she continued with her story. Some dolphin trainers had told how they would lie awake at night, planning new tricks and next morning when they arrived at work the dolphins were doing those tricks without having been taught.

While phone calls with Peter were frequent, the tenderness in our conversation grew less and less. He could not understand my need to stay in Australia. I could not forget the overwhelming experience in the ocean as I had fought for my survival. My sons' faces remained with me and I often focused on my mother/daughter past relationship. But not once was my relationship with Peter a priority amongst my mental and physical turmoil. I will always remember my inner voice – 'you have not yet loved fully'. It was easy to appreciate my doubts about my feelings around our connection while waiting for his phone call.

There were sleepless nights when I tossed, grabbed the other pillow to hug, felt the emptiness in my bed, crying for the difficulty I felt towards my maintaining a deep committed relationship. I examined my personal emotional struggle repeatedly. I yearned for intense intimacy with another, but I could offer no sensible, clear reasoning for my behaviour other than I had not yet met the person I truly completely wanted. As the days slowly slipped by, finally so did my feelings towards Peter, who was not prepared to visit Australia because of his work and life commitments. We parted during a sad, disappointing phone call. This relationship had lasted 15 months.

I settled into a village lifestyle in Byron Bay in my home on Coopers Shoot. "Would you like to stay and help me establish a balloon ride business, Shawn?" I asked as we sat on the veranda surveying the rolling hills towards Bangalow.

"If I can work to get my commercial balloon licence, I will," he replied.

He had saved my life in the ocean. We had shared an incredible experience fighting to survive the elements. Through all that, I knew I could trust him. He had shown strength by taking the lead, protected me. I acknowledged I had a lot to repay him. Our connection was obviously very strong. I often wondered if and how we knew each other in previous lifetimes. I easily accepted our bond this lifetime was karmic only. I set about helping him along his ballooning career path. Shawn met his future German wife through my Byron Bay ballooning business.

Bay Balloons was set up and launched with a Montgolfier party on Byron Bay beach on August 3, 1989 with excellent media coverage. The phone rang for balloon flights, but also with numerous requests for complementary balloon flights to support fund raising for one charity group or another. I always complied with an open heart.

In the ocean, I had recognised my passion to push boundaries had driven me to forge my own life path. That fear would blot out optimism. That I had dived to the depth of my own vulnerability and used up much adrenalin fighting to stay alive. I now felt I was a different person from the woman who earlier had yearned to wrestle with a marlin, who yearned for challenge in competition ballooning, dreamt of flying over snow covered alps. I definitely felt softer and more fragile deep inside, aided also by the pain of my relationship break-up. But generally, I was really just happy to be alive, to have cheated a fourth possible death.

As I settled into the Byron lifestyle, I became more entrenched in the community spirit of the area. When well-known Byron Bay identities, hotel proprietors Tom and Cathryn Mooney, flew with me, then spread the word on the safety and joy of ballooning, bookings for balloon flights grew. And our personal friendship grew. Shawn gained his commercial licence and took over flying most of the commercial passengers in *Misty Blue*. I often joined him in the sky, content to be flying solo in my small personal hot-air balloon, *Just Right*. But life was not going to get any easier.

The thrill of inflating my balloon

Ross Spicer on inflation fan while I inflate my balloon

Australian Champion with trophy and sponsor Roger Meadmore

With Simon Fisher at 1981 World Championship USA celebration

Family Wilson support Mark at 1989 World Championship in Japan

Just achieved a world's First with Ron Llwellyn. Parachuted at night from my balloon

On this marlin fishing boat Innovator when wrecked on the Ballina Bar 1989

Flight of Moet Chandon special shape balloon from Low Isles for French doco

Inflating Moet balloon for short flight on Fraser Island Qld

My gloved hands on the burner of Aurora preparing to land

Packing up a balloon. Margaret Collins & Alison Batty help.

Flying in Dubai launching from the Burj Al Arab Hotel

UK & French Championship Brissac-Quincé Participating as an Official Juror

My first fixed wing solo flight from Bankstown Airport

My happy place Alpine Ballooning in Austria

Beauty seen from above during my Austrian flight

Winter flying in Austria

I am an official at the World Championship balloons in USA

I am with Tanys McCarron testing our small basket Our home for the GB Race

Detlef Göcke Balloonmeister prepares our basket for the Gas Balloon Race

John McCarron & Mark Wilson

Shawn Mackinga checks QNH with me

Heading to the start podium in Bern for 2018 Gordon Bennett Gas Balloon Race

Conquering clouds with Tanys McCarron above the Swiss Alps

Cold & checking my oxygen levels with Tanys McCarron above the Swiss Alps

Final landing after 18 hours non-stop & approx 410km Roveredo in Piano Italy

CHAPTER 39

I collapsed on the floor, screaming, hurting, in a state of shock. How could something I loved so much take someone I loved so dearly? Nothing eased my pain as I grieved constantly for someone who I now appreciated I had loved much more than I had been prepared to admit. Lethargy became my constant companion. It was a normal day with nothing to prepare me for the shock and pain on its way to my world. A simple telephone call was all it took.

"There's been a fatal ballooning accident in Mudgee. Ross is dead."

Ross owned a graphic arts business in Sydney and Jindalee, a property in Mudgee, west of Sydney where he ran a commercial ballooning ride business mainly on weekends. Memories of his phone call only ten days before his death continued to haunt me.

"Why don't you marry me and come and live in Mudgee and fly balloons with me?" he said down the phone. "We're a great team."

I had laughed, dismissing his proposal. "Call back when you have not been drinking."

"You have such a strong sense of self, Ruth E, that you will never surrender to any man," he said as he ended our phone call, his last words to me. Now I questioned if I had said yes, would life had been on a different path for him, for me.

Memories of the days I had spent with him in Mudgee six months earlier, flying, laughing and enjoying each other's company, would surface as I tried to fall asleep.

Memories of his support during my brother's attempt on his life in 1984 filled gaps as I tried to face daily responsibilities.

Memories of his ballooning accident on October 11, 1989 would be my first thoughts when I awoke each day. His balloon had settled onto two 11,000 volt power lines he had not seen strung across a field, the power poles hidden in trees. The wires and part of the envelope were tangled, but the basket slowly sank to the ground. Ross instructed his passengers to all leap together from the basket as he had been trained. As he hit the ground, he looked back to see one of his passengers still standing in the basket. He thought only of her safety. Ran back to try to help her from the basket. As he made contact, electricity grounded itself through his body. The charge was so powerful his boots and gloves flew off his feet and hands. His clothing became alight.

He died immediately, trying to save his passenger.

Two others escaped the basket. One of them was the husband of the lady passenger who had leaned on the gas tank, drawing electricity through her hip that Ross had tried to save. Her husband managed to drag her from the basket by her pullover to give her mouth-to-mouth resuscitation, but she died from heart failure on the way to the hospital.

Memories of our journey together in our balloons and in life would pop into my mind at unexpected times. The physical ache throughout my body would cause me to need to lie down, sobbing into my pillow. I lost interest in my balloon business and drifted through the days in a silent world of my own.

I tried to lean on my beliefs that death is only the shedding of the physical body, that Ross was close by but existing at a different vibrational frequency. I had been able to accept that belief when I thought of my parents and grandparents or others who had passed over. With Ross, I failed to grasp my wisdom I had so readily shared with many over previous years.

Four days after Ross' fatal accident, news came through I had lost another friend through ballooning. David Bowers died when his balloon contacted power lines in the Hunter Valley, a popular wine growing area north of Sydney. I had met David on my first balloon lesson in Auckland, New Zealand. He had just arrived from Yorkshire, England and made himself known to my ballooning instructor, Laurie Soffe. David came along and crewed during my training period in that country.

Later, when he moved to Sydney, he was my crew chief for a couple of years till he bought his own balloon. A Yorkshire man with a great sense of humour, brown curly hair and brown eyes, he had an eye for the ladies till he decided to marry Mary, a beautiful woman he had met on the boat on his way to New Zealand, renewing their connection once he was back in Sydney. I was amongst a small group of friends to attend his wedding and became godmother to his daughter, Clare.

David had phoned me to talk about Ross's accident Thursday evening. Sunday, he died.

"I am really tired, Ruth. Once I fly my weekend passengers, I plan to take a good break for a couple of months."

"Only you know your body, David. Please follow your instincts and be careful and don't fly if you are exhausted," was my advice to my friend.

We ended our phone conversation promising to get together for lunch the following week.

On that fateful Sunday morning as he brought his balloon down to land, one of the passengers noticed power lines further down the field and yelled, "Power lines, jump." The extensive media coverage a few days earlier on Ross' power line death had scared this particular passenger, who jumped from about six feet urging all the others to do the same. It was reported none of the other passengers were alarmed, but a scramble to vacate the balloon then occurred.

Only David and a lady passenger were left in the basket when the others all jumped. With the lighter load, the balloon took off quickly into the air again, flying towards the power lines. As the balloon brushed past those wires, one David was holding took the electric current.

He was killed instantly.

While all this was happening, the husband of the lady in the basket was yelling from the ground at her to jump. She did from a height but did not survive. The balloon flew on and eventually safely settled back to earth a few kilometres away.

Where I once believed ballooning was a mystical experience, I now felt disillusioned, emotionally battered, even bruised by my great love. The horror of losing Ross and David snatched away my usually positive attitude. A rising sense of detachment from all around me became my world.

For months after Ross and David's deaths, I flew only enough flights to keep my commercial licence current. Shawn held my business together till the day he sat down beside me on the veranda and shocked me.

"It's time to move out of your grief and take an interest in the business again," he said.

I sucked on the straw in my apple juice as I tried to find an answer. I had little awareness I had descended into a deep dark void, had removed myself so far from the daily rumblings of life. I certainly was not dancing on any clouds. I was more often than not falling from clouds. Dark clouds that invaded my thoughts when I looked into the future. I could see only the emptiness. Often unbearable. Mornings I woke to the sounds of birds singing in the treetops, my pillow damp with a mixture of tears and make-up not removed before retiring for the night.

Gradually, I leaned on one of my life's core beliefs.

You can't have a feeling without a thought. Practice mindful thinking to control your thoughts. Find positive thoughts, then positive emotions would follow.

I eventually felt my smile rising up deep inside my being, finding its rightful place on my lips. The darkness that had surrounded me faded. I emerged into daily life reminding myself death ends a life, not a relationship.

And feelings of hope insisted on intruding in my daily activities. My son Mark, just turned 20 years old, was representing Australia at the 1989 Worlds in Saga, Japan November 18 – 27. As the youngest pilot to take on this responsibility at a Worlds, I had hope he would gain from such an experience. His brother Grant and father Kevin would join Mark's team and I would be his co-pilot.

I try to minimise my life regrets, but my behaviour in the balloon basket with Mark competing in the 1989 Worlds is one regret I fail to diminish. During the three solo flights, where Mark was by himself in the basket, his flying skill shone. He won two tasks, scoring second in the other. He was a much better pilot without his enthusiastic, over-sharing mother beside him in the balloon basket.

CHAPTER 40

"**I want to do a world first,** Ruth E. Parachute at night from a hot-air balloon. Would you do it with me? I want to jump from your dolphin balloon."

When I needed Ron Llewellyn most, he parachuted straight into my life. Dragged me out of the pain I continued to feel through my loss of both Ross and David in my life.

On a sparkling Saturday afternoon with light breezes brushing the bushes along the veranda of my rural home, Ron surprised me with his request. A request that was to help me find my adventurous inner pulse again.

Two Mercedes metal grey sports cars roared past the front hedge that badly needed trimming as I murmured my reply to the night jump, "Love to." My nerves began dancing at the thought of such an audacious challenge. More wine was consumed as Shawn joined us. More frivolity danced around our conversation. Underneath it all, I felt a commitment to doing something extraordinary, something that could help me find my adventurous essence once more.

"I have a private fixed wing pilot licence, radio operator's licence, St. Johns first aid certificate, class 3 driver's licence, hold a chief parachute instructor, Master scuba diving instructor, ultralight aircraft instructor licence, plus a licence to navigate a registered vessel and I am a reasonable stills photographer. You will be in good hands," said Ron reassuringly.

I felt no opposing thoughts to my immediate decision to do this world record with him.

We had met at the Tyagarah Airfield just north of Byron Bay a few months earlier. I exited my car and walked towards him to introduce myself.

"I read about you and your ballooning exploits in the local paper," he said as he moved away from his Cessna to shake hands with me.

In 1981, Ron had established The Australian Air-Sports Centre at Tyagarah Airfield. An ex-Army officer with 10-years' service, Ron had been the leader of the Army parachute Display Team, The Red Berets, also a member of 'The Green Machine'. With his impressive skills, he joined the US Army's prestigious Green Berets and spent time with the Canadian Army parachute team. During a training stint with the British 'Paras', he jumped from 25,000 feet at night, but from a plane and carrying 45 kg of equipment. He landed in a Druid burial mound.

"I teach parachuting because I love it. I know exactly how my students feel that first time and throughout their training. I share their emotions," he shared with me.

"I was hoping we could launch my balloons from your airfield, especially with the afternoon winds blowing from the ocean," I proposed.

"That would be fabulous to have another aviation activity here at Tyagarah," and with those words, a lifetime friendship was formed.

Ron and his staff attended the official media launch of Bay Balloons and drinks at the popular Brunswick Heads hotel on a weeknight became a regular get together for us. Shawn and his growing list of friends often joined the party.

Planning for the exercise began. My days bubbled with anticipated excitement around my new challenge. With the balloon aloft for around two hours in the night sky, every possible direction of drift to avoid being trapped by mountains or forced to ditch into the ocean had to be calculated. The main area of our concern in the planning was the landing of the balloon after the jump. Ron had made many night jumps from planes at high altitudes. He assured all involved the actual jump posed little problem. The balloon could not land at night. Danger from power lines, village life and other obstacles precluded this. We needed sufficient light for a safe finish to the exercise.

Both of us flew in Ron's Cessna 182 over the hinterland of Byron Bay looking for a suitable launch site, found it, marked it on our paper maps. The next day we drove to Bexhill, knocked on doors to alert the residents we would be active sometime in the coming weeks. The balloon's burner noise may wake them. Everyone was very kind and wished us good luck.

I had flown a friend's balloon previously while visiting Montana in the United States, lifting off at night and landing after sunrise. I also had my night endorsement on my Australian Certificate. I began filling in the required Australian paperwork to gain approval from the Civil Aviation Safety Authority for our night flight. Australia is famous for its ability to produce 'red tape' faster than you can cut through it. The time from official notification of the attempt to the actual jump was 3-1/2 months.

As always with aviation, the weather was the major factor to consider. For six days I would wake at 0200hrs, stand outside, releasing helium filled party balloons with light sticks attached to test the direction and strength of the wind. But the wind wanted no part of my project. For six days, the answer was 'no go, abort'. Back to our individual beds, we went. This was without a doubt, the worst part of the whole attempt. But as always with ballooning, the weather eventually settled. The winds became friendly, so the decision was made. It's a GO.

Before I left my home, I picked up the phone to call Lismore Police Station.

"Good evening, Ruth Wilson from Bay Balloons here," I said down the line.

"I just want to alert you that I will be flying my balloon in the early hours of the morning and a skydiver will jump out of my basket. We are trying for a World's First and you may get some strange phone calls regarding noise and lights in the night sky."

"Is this a prank?" came the rejoinder from the policeman.

"No, I am serious. Please call me back."

Which he did and I had images of him shaking his head saying, "It's all in a night's work."

The weeks of planning and preparation for this flight had required my focus. My grief at losing Ross from my life appeared in waves, not so totally consuming of my emotions and energy. I now had a huge challenge to draw my attention from my continuing sadness. Other priorities jumped the queue to sit in top place. Complacency around my day to day living frittered away. I questioned the safety of night flying, how I would handle any emergency. For every doubt I raised with myself, I set about finding an answer. It helped that I had total respect for Ron's ability to control his part of the exercise.

My balloon, VH-JLX, was 120,000 cubic foot capable of lifting six average people. I needed weight in the basket for a safer flight, so I asked my son Grant, who was visiting, to join me. As did Shawn.

Ron, in his red and white jumpsuit with a light on the front of his helmet and his wrist altimeter illuminated by a fluro stick, stood in one corner. The balloon basket carried a navigational red light hung five metres below the basket, first aid kit, VHF and UHF radios. I carried a small torch to allow me to check the instruments and the preferred map track. My balloon lifted off at 0339 hrs. Ron jumped at 0344hrs. My eyes followed the diminishing speck of light from his helmet, my heartbeat increasing with each minute.

Ron landed three minutes later with the ground crew confirming by radio to me in the basket he was safe. I hadn't realised I had been holding my breath till I heard air leave my mouth. Now the pressure was on me to fly and land my balloon without incident. As the dark night turned lighter, I could see the outline of roofs of all the houses below. I thought of the inhabitants mostly tucked up in warm beds.

Felt just a little strange floating above the roofs of the houses while folk were most likely asleep unaware of our presence above. I flew on tracking towards the coast with a keen eye on the horizon, waiting for that first glimpse of morning light which sends silvery streaks into the sky. The wind was stable. Flight direction had avoided the mountain range. I had kept my balloon close to the line drawn on my map. Gradually I felt myself relaxing at the burner control, lost in the uniqueness of my flight, had to pull myself back into total concentration mode. Any balloon flight was not over and safe till it was, I reminded myself.

I finally landed at 0505 hrs. Flight time was 86 minutes. An enormous sense of achievement engulfed me. I hugged Shawn. I hugged Grant. My love for Grant had drawn me from Canada to Australia to celebrate his 19th birthday in February. Now, ten months later, Grant was standing beside me in my balloon basket, sharing this first in an aviation world record. There were no shortages of smiles or happy faces. Even more so when Ron hurried towards us, gave me the warmest hug, then yelled, "It was as black as the inside of a horse when I jumped."

The jump itself went without a hitch. Ron exited from 4251 feet, freefalling for around 10 seconds before opening his parachute. He landed at the designated target marked by the lights of two cars.

The records show the first parachute jump from a hot-air balloon at night was made on 20 December 1989 at Bexhill, west of Byron Bay. The record has been acknowledged in the Federation Aeronautique Internationale Parachuting Records as well as at on the Federation Aeronautique Internationale Ballooning web page under "Firsts" http://www.ballong. org/peter/jesper/cia/report17.php.

A week later, I received a marriage proposal.

I had launched from Clunes Oval, flying towards Australia's most easterly point at Byron Bay. The winds played mischievously with me. The territory below offered no space for landing, forcing me to fly on across the Pacific Highway, past my usual point of no return. Huge relief when I spotted a tiny space at the edge of a macadamia plantation close to the coast. My decision was immediate. It was there or the ocean for a landing. After a fast descent, the basket hit the ground, tipped over and the balloon deflated. I left my passengers with the packed-up balloon, walked up the hill to the homestead to knock on the door. An elderly gentleman in his pyjamas, the little hair he had all askew, appeared, looked at me in total surprise. He had not heard the balloon land, but readily agreed for my chase crew to enter his property.

I thanked him, walked back down the hill to the waiting group of passengers, radioed the crew the permission to proceed. As the chase vehicle picked its way towards the balloon and waiting passengers, I noticed an extra person in the cab with my crew, Melinda Smith and Shawn Mackinga. Out climbed our host in his best suit, hair brushed across the top to cover his bald head.

"Did you really fly this balloon and land in my field?" he excitedly asked me.

I reassured him I had.

"Well, I have just come back from down south where I went on this Seniors Blind Date television program, but the woman chose the other guy," he informed us. "I am looking for a strong wife to help me pick the macadamia nuts. You must be strong to fly that thing. Would you like to get married and come and live with me?"

He was definitely not my soul mate. Just one of the numerous interesting people I met through landing on private property in many countries. My crew teased me for weeks about my macadamia farmer.

I was back to occasionally studying the clouds above me, not dancing on them or floating above. My awareness that ballooning offered a meditative state gradually returned to me. Escape from everyday life on the ground was total when I flew. I was missing that total silence I treasured when floating above the clouds. I began to find the urge to fly more regularly.

CHAPTER 41

In 1991, I was contacted from France by the French champagne company, Moet Chandon.

The French 'Flight of the Kangaroo' film had been so well received in Europe Moet Chandon commissioned the French film crew to undertake a similar expedition. To celebrate the company's 250th birthday in 1993, the plan was to capture images for a documentary and book. Two hot air balloons, one shaped like a Moet champagne cork, were being shipped to Australia. French balloonist, Jean-Marie Huttois would pilot one balloon. I was tasked with the responsibility of supplying a second hot-air balloon and to act as pilot of that aerostat. I negotiated a contract, set about gaining the necessary Australian local council and aviation approvals for such an adventure. I looked forward to a reunion with Christian Zuccerelli, film director once more.

Welcomed back by the Severin family at Mt Connor, the expedition's team of balloonists and film crew gathered images of spectacular flights. My second departure from this magical landscape of Australia left me feeling just a little sad, but we were on track for Port Douglas, where everyone boarded zodiacs to cross the water onto Low Isles. To capture unique images of the Barrier Reef, we replicated my 1989 flight crossing the eastern coast at the Daintree River mouth, floating over the Daintree forest. Our flight ended in long grass, a little squashy and wet. The cameraman helped with the balloon's deflation. Jean-Marie landed close by with the stills' photographer. He agreed to stay with the balloons while I searched for a way out.

I stomped through swampy grasslands to find a dirt road. When I did, driving towards me in a beat-up jalopy was an old timer who stopped. He looked at me with raised eyebrows and said, "What you doing Missy, walking through crocodile infested waters?"

Arnaud de Wildenberg, international photographer with the Sigma Agency, captured fantastic images for the company's book.

I returned to life on Coopers Shoot. My adjustment to everyday activities proved difficult. The fridge was continually empty. Skim milk and two bottles of champagne sat in the door along with outdated jars of olives, vegemite and mustard and hibiscus flowers in syrup. Blue cheese and cheese slices plus two aging tomatoes leaned against each other in the main section. I opened the one dozen-egg carton, felt thrilled to find two eggs.

My adrenaline found its pulse once more with a phone call from Japan.

Well-known and respected balloonist, Masashi Kukuda was on the line.

"Are you coming to Saga to compete in the Inaugural Ladies World Cup?" Masashi Kukuda asked.

"The expense to participate is too much for me at this time. I am sorry." I felt sad, even somewhat embarrassed to admit my current financial situation.

"You should be a part of this event, Ruth. If we loan you a balloon, vehicle, crew and airfare, would you please come?"

Two weeks later, I was on a plane to Saga, Japan. Foreign climes were calling once more. I was leaving my unsettlement with loss of loved ones, moving towards my inner warrior once more.

And I learned at the event that Director Masashi Kukuda was the pilot who had destroyed my balloon envelope at the 1983 Worlds in France. He finally apologised in person.

Of the 22 female pilots competing in the 1st Ladies World Cup in November 1990, I placed third. My friend USA pilot Carol Davis 2nd, Lindsay Muir from the United Kingdom overall winner. Nineteen of the other pilots were Japanese. It was always easy to recognise Toshiko Ichiyoshi, the pioneer female pilot in Japan. The local media entourage and television cameras followed her actions constantly. Toshiko invited me to stay with her and her family - her partner Maco Oiwa, her son Shota and daughter Aye in Tokyo after the event.

During that visit, Toshiko, Maco and I joined the expectant crowd at the Yokohama launch site where a Japanese pilot was preparing for a Trans-Pacific Gas Balloon flight. The launch set up, heavily sponsored by Mycal, was impressive. A heavy contingent of media stood by for the final media briefing prior to takeoff.

Niwa-san, the intrepid pilot, had attempted a similar flight the previous year. He had only made a short distance out to sea when he landed in the ocean. This time, he seemed determined to go all the way. I stood on the edge of the crowd watching the pilot closely, sensing an element of fear plus his internal struggle to project confidence and courage to his sponsors, the media and public.

Rugged up against the biting cold in the early morning darkness, I was also wearing my gold ring featuring two dolphins I had made after my rescue in the ocean nineteen months earlier. As Niwa-san walked to the balloon's capsule, I wished him safe flying, spontaneously taking off my dolphin ring to give it to him. He bowed, smiled, put my ring in his flight suit pocket. Dawn broke with the winds gaining strength. The launch was cancelled. At the end of my stay, I flew back to Byron Bay, Australia.

Weeks later, I was in my garden talking with the man who mowed my lawn. My phone rang.

"It's Sabu, Ruth," Sabu Ichiyoshi, my ballooning friend from Japan.

I knew immediately they had found Niwa-san, who had ditched into the Pacific Ocean once again, aborting his flight. I wondered at the time of the proposed launch if he was undertaking the same challenge once more to save 'face' - a strong component of the Japanese DNA. Would he cover the approximately 10,000 kilometres from Japan to the western coast of the United States of America safely? Could he endure somewhere between 136 to 150 hours alone in his helium filled gas balloon, specifically built for long distance ballooning with its capsule full of the latest technology? These must have been the questions playing on his mind as the coast of Japan disappeared and he faced the daunting challenge ahead.

"He has been found and waved to the search plane. We know where he is. A Japanese naval vessel is moving towards him," said a relieved Sabu.

My spirits soared as I thanked Sabu for his call.

Hours later, the news was overwhelmingly sad. Unfortunately, when the rescue vessel finally arrived after many hours, it was too late.

I could identify with his fear in the water, of not being found in such a huge ocean. I wrote a letter expressing admiration to Noriko Niwa, of her husband's need to challenge the ocean and himself. I had not met Noriko, but I hoped my words might ease her pain.

On 31st January 1991, his wife Noriko Niwa, wrote back to me.

"Thank you so much for the letter. We received it 12.1.91. I was very glad to know many other balloonists are respecting my husband's courage. Also, I'm very glad to know what you think about my husband. I want to let you know that my husband took your dolphin ring that you have lent to the flight.

On the flight day, I put your dolphin ring in his bag so when I heard the news, I thought that the dolphin ring has been lost because of the big wave, but when he came back, the police found your ring from his pocket. I think when he was dropped in the ocean, he thought if he loses your ring, he would be lost too, so he held it tightly in his hand and prayed to God. I think he was very scared and cold in the ocean. I think he wanted to come back home and see our faces again.

Even if he was dead, he could have been lost in the huge Pacific Ocean and never be found, but he came back. I could see his face. So, your dolphin ring is 'GOOD LUCK RING'.

If you don't mind, I would like to have your dolphin ring."

"Of course," was my emotional answer.

CHAPTER 42

It was only a matter of months after Niwa-san's fatal flight that Shawn approached me to talk.

"I want to move to Europe to meet up with Gaby again, but I will need to find work. I expect you know many balloonists. Would you be able to introduce me to any?"

My stomach churned. I should have been expecting such a change, but I hadn't. My company, Bay Balloons was struggling financially. The area had a small population with primarily backpackers to draw on as passengers. Most of them could not afford the cost of a balloon flight. In fairness to Shawn, I had no reason to encourage him to stay in Byron Bay. I did find employment for him to fly commercially in France. He married Gaby and settled in Switzerland flying huge commercial balloons.

I began to question my future direction once more, to seek answers for my continued rejection of interested suitors in my life. I had products in my bathroom with a longer shelf life than the time I was prepared to spend working at a potential relationship.

My thoughts often turned to Ross' marriage proposal I had received and not taken seriously at the time. Should I have? Would Ross still be alive today if I had? Why had I denied we could be right for each other? How and why had my relationship with Geoff floundered and died? And then there was Peter.

I had no answers.

I had to find answers to still my financial drain, though. The answer arrived during a phone call from a friend in Sydney.

"Are you interested in doing some PR work that involves magazine editing? I know of a company looking for a consultant," said Barbara.

My prayers had been heard again. My move back to Sydney was somewhat emotionally disturbing, but financially necessary. I was leaving my special place, a place where I believed I was meant to be, having survived the ocean there. I often questioned my choices and events I had attracted over the years. Transplanting from one home to another, choices that kept me with no permanent roots, no committed loving relationship.

As always happens, life settled into a routine again as I embraced both corporate life plus my ballooning world throughout the 1990s. My regular PR salary was boosted when I drew clients from the complementary healthcare industry by introducing the healing modality Reiki to an interested Australia. My investment property rental income, with occasional funds from my ballooning activities, increased my bank account balance as well.

1993 arrived, as did my 50th birthday. I asked myself, "where have those years gone?" Mark and Penny arranged a fabulous surprise birthday party, my first. Birthdays came and went during my childhood. Parties never came.

Also, in 1993 a challenge arose in the ballooning community to be the first to fly non-stop across the Australian continent. Phil Kavanagh and Brian Smith versed Dick Smith and John Wallington. The Kavanagh/Smith team launched first covering around 3000 km, but were forced to land near Windorah in Queensland.

Dick Smith phoned to ask me to manage the media covering his intended Trans-Australia balloon fight with John Wallington. I declined. I had commitments in the United States over that period. On my arrival back in Sydney, Australian television sprouted the news: Dick Smith's delayed balloon flight was planning a departure in the next day or so, depending on weather. I called the expedition Western Australian headquarters to wish the two adventurers a safe, successful flight. Dick called back a few hours later.

"Our PR lady is in the hospital. We need a replacement. Would you be available?"

After settling the terms of engagement, I drove to Terrey Hills to join the team at Command Headquarters.

Dick Smith and John Wallington launched their *Australian Geographic Flyer* balloon from Carnarvon in Western Australia at 10:52am. Over forty hours later, flying non-stop over 4000 kilometres, they touched down near Tabulam in New South Wales.

The following year, Steve Griffin piloted his balloon solo non-stop from west to east, reaching a height during his flight of 25,994ft.

In late 1994, my son Mark married Penny York, who he had met through the 1988 Trans Australia Ballooning Challenge. No person could have felt prouder of that destined and beautiful union.

In 1995, the winds around my life blew through my front door. I was offered the position of Executive Director of the Australian Research Council for Responsible Nutrition. Board members had sought the name of the company or person responsible for increased media coverage on the benefits of antioxidants and omega oils. Once they tracked me down, I was happy to accept their offer. Once again, I worked from my home office with my pioneer spirit endeavouring to encourage key media contacts to cover stories in this area, complementary healthcare. My early approaches to media outlets were met with disinterest. Patience, perseverance and commitment to client eventually won positive responses. The results stand clearly today. The words 'antioxidant' and 'omega oils', so heavily a part of my media campaigns 25 years ago, are currently part of everyday conversation.

In the northern hemisphere's autumn of 1996, I travelled to Zurich for a reunion with Regula Hug-Messner and Shawn Mackinga. Found myself a guest of Regula's standing in a gas balloon basket once more, having flown with her the previous year. Flew for nine hours, covering a distance of 80 kilometres from Bad Zurzach to land at Egerkingen, south of Basel. A few days later, Shawn and I headed to the Chiemsee Balloon Event in Bavaria, my first experience on the Autobahn driving at speeds of 145kmh. Willy Pfeiffer, Event Director, had to cancel the weekend flights due to fog, strong winds and difficult flying directions. While I felt disappointed, I found joy in the scenery, an abundance of autumn leaves, St Anton for lunch. Once back in Zurich, I prepared for my flight to Florida, USA.

It was time for work. I attended the three-day CRN Nutrition Conference held on Amelia Island, Jacksonville, soaking in the latest studies presented on complementary medicines. At the conclusion of this informative gathering, I moved onto New Mexico to fly at the famous Albuquerque Balloon Fiesta in New Mexico where I was welcomed by John and Carol Davis. Their lovely daughter Marne joined us, Heather, her sister, not able to do so. The camaraderie and frivolity of that popular ballooning event is well known internationally among balloonists and public alike.

My highlight during 1997 was the arrival of my first grandchild, Penny and Mark named Tyler Christopher Wilson. My social life mainly moved between my balloon basket and Tyler as I watched him grow into a delightful child.

A personal relationship with an Australian man during the late 1990s led to a proposal of marriage. Emotions floundered. I walked away.

CHAPTER 43

I was seduced by fantasies I created around my birth father. He was a pilot, an American flyer during the war. I imagined him in his cockpit, in the air. Of course, he was tall, handsome, with laughing hazel eyes. To feel closer to him, I decided to fly planes also. I would get my fixed wing license. Consequently, I began flying lessons at the Illawarra Flying School in early 1998 at Sydney's Bankstown Airport, a 45minute drive from my Sydney home.

February 16, 1998: The weather that morning was overcast, slightly raining, when my instructor sent me on my first solo. "It's all yours, Ruth." My heart started hammering in my chest with excitement. Confidence jiggled through my body. Terror had gone on holidays. I had to remember procedures. Down the runway in the Cessna 152, lift off, climb to 500 feet, turn left, climb to 1000 feet, turn left again. On the downward leg do the checks, call the tower.

I glanced momentarily out of the cockpit. In the distance, the outline of downtown Sydney skyline beamed back at me. In that tiny space in the cockpit I yelled to my mystery father, "Yahoo, I'm alone. Flying my plane, Dad."

Turn left on base leg, descend 700 feet, 600 feet and at 500 feet, turn left again on the final leg. Radio the tower for clearance to land. Bring the plane down for final touchdown, back to base. Final radio call to close down operations.

"Well done and congratulations on your solo, Ruth," said the invisible controller. I sat in the plane's seat, momentarily glancing around at the various parked aircraft and felt nothing but jubilation. "Born to fly." The words left my lips resounding around the cockpit.

And what a birthday gift to myself. Tomorrow I would be 55.

Three months later, I achieved my Restricted Fixed Wing Licence. The love of flying, whether it be by hot air or gas balloon, ultralights, hang gliding, gliding or recreational aeroplanes, is a passion that ties folk who chase the aerial magic.

I had been a pilot in command of my balloon for over 23 years. To become a pilot in command of an aeroplane was the most exhilarating feeling. And I dreamed of the day I would meet my birth father. Tell him I was a fixed wing pilot too. I had fulfilled my dream to add another dimension to my Air Affair.

I shared many stories of my air affair with both my sons over the years. I never noticed any obvious concern regarding my flying on their part. It was a different story when each of my sons learned to fly a balloon, taking to the skies in control of my balloon. I remained on the ground, anxious they were up there, anxious until I knew they once again had landed safely. It was a hard lesson for me to let go of my fear for their safety. It took me until my world record attempt went wrong to fully admit to myself chasing my flying challenges might have caused my boys to worry about their mother's safety, that they might lose me. Even though I had heard no such comment from either of them over the years.

The seduction of flight is hard to let go. To experience life suspended from earthly affairs, to move across the sky on fixed wings, or to stand in an open basket soaked in the breath of any wind, moving languorously towards flight's end is a complete joy.

Ballooning allows time to absorb the beauty of nature, to chase adventure, to contour fly only metres above the earth, to feed the competitive side of my personality and the unknown as to what I will find at flight's end thrills me.

Fixed wing flying is structured, with the final landing spot known, the aircraft's motor different. More to learn about and master, rules to observe while flying in and out of airports and the ability to fly greater distances once airborne.

Both forms of flight excited me. The cost to own either aircraft can be similar, but fate put the balloon in front of me first. She remains my master, sucking finances mercilessly.

I strongly believed I had inherited my American father's love of flying. This belief would be smashed in the future.

CHAPTER 44

With some quiet time on my schedule, I gave myself permission to retreat to rest and reflect. To try to find answers to my jumbled thoughts about my life. My continued struggle with the burning urge deep inside my being to look for and chase another adrenalin fix, to explore the extraordinary. My mental dialogue to attempt to quell such urges, to be content with a gentle life, remained a constant.

Armed with three books and my favourite music, I left my computer, locked my house, set the security system, drove out of my garage and waved to my neighbour and friend Lindy Patel. The beach house I rented smelled musty, but soon the chilly sea breezes brought a salty sweetness into the rooms. I made a healthy salad for lunch, sipped green tea, then changed into my comfy blue and white tracksuit, slipped my feet into my favourite mustard-coloured slip-ons and headed to the ocean.

I had the beach to myself. The waves were rhythmically hitting the shore. Sitting on my beach towel, I tuned into the silence around me. Could feel my body responding. Recognised one of the reasons I love my flying. Silence. Often experienced while floating above the clouds in my balloon, especially a hydrogen filled silent balloon, all special times I cherished. It's in such moments of silence I retreat to a more meditative state of being. Such moments where I feel my soul being enriched, feel my uniqueness. A time to feel gratitude, to draw on that deep inner knowingness that drives me throughout my life.

I nodded to the ocean, thanking it for not taking me during the marlin fishing accident. Making a silent promise 'to be kinder to myself'.

The wind increased, whistling gently around me, disturbing my reverie. Thoughts pushed their way back into my rest. Thoughts of Canada; to the family who lost a son at only 15; to Geoff and whether he had married the woman who replaced me; to my close Canadian friend Del Michaud, who bravely faced serious health issues and rose above them; to other joyful times while living in Calgary. Ballooning from the Stampede as the chuckwagons rumbled around the track was definitely one of them. I have been a cowgirl at heart since then.

I reminded myself how precious life is and has been for me with my flying world. My logbooks with recorded flights as dawn broke against the morning sky, offering a pallet of colours mostly enjoyed by early risers, definitely by balloon pilots. Flights skimming above all nature could offer – lakes, forests, vineyards, hills, rural towns, even city skylines. Flights that had been easy, fun, brought joy and smiles to my life, to my passengers' faces each time. To the numerous student pilots I had taught the skill of inflating, flying and landing a balloon. A promise to myself never to forget the many chasers who had retrieved my balloon and self from paddocks with locked gates, successfully cleared bogged vehicles from wet, muddy fields, dealt with numerous landowners seeking permission to enter their properties. Crew who became good friends like Adrian Cole and his wife Dianne. On a flight from Canowindra towards Parkes I had chosen a field for landing, descended quickly, balloon hit the ground tipped over and dragged in the wind. Adrian was sitting with his brother-in-law Ian on the homestead's verandah when he heard the swooshing noise of my balloon's burners for the first time. In a matter of moments balloon basket with pilot and one passenger was dragging across his paddock, paddy melons filling the basket. I eventually climbed out of the basket, shook hands with Adrian as Ian also hurried to the scene. Over 46 years later, Adrian and Dianne remain lovely friends.

Witnessing the joy on a couple's face when a marriage proposal was accepted while airborne, standing in my wicker basket. And most importantly, using my balloon to support others – Rotary, Birthright Orphans, Autistic Children, Lion Clubs, many others and more recently Beyond Blue with balloon flights offered for charity fund raisers. And I asked myself two important questions – Have you brought joy to others during this lifetime? Have you found joy, Ruth E? I can honestly say YES. Through my magical ballooning world.

And I marvel at how my respect and admiration for all the Australian males in my favoured sport have flourished. Those early day attitudes towards a female pilot had disappeared, as had those early day male pilots, no longer involved in the sport.

Replaced by family succession with youngsters following in or sharing their parents' love of ballooning. The Saunders family Patterson, Edward,

Scarlett (Women's Altitude Record holder at 23,714ft on July 4, 2019) sharing the sky with their father Kiff, in their individual colourful balloons; Graeme Scaife actively ballooning since the mid-80s in the United Kingdom and Australia, his son Matthew, popular and a champion in competition ballooning. Martin Tregale, ABF President, his wife Jodi and their two Ella and David all taking a turn at the burner tap of their balloon VH-THZ lovingly called *Terra Hertz*.

Danny Galbraith with son and daughter, Justin and Amanda, both pilots; Nikki Coleman and her daughter Alana Kohl; Rob Robertson, his son Andrew; David Parkes, his son Ben; Paul Gianniotis, his son Stephen; Graham Kerr, his son Anton; John Stein, his son Justin; Peter Dutneall, his son Matthew; Steve Buckley, his daughter Tash; Richard Gillespie, his son Dan; Kay Turnbull with Richard and John; Mark Fraser's two, Harry and Mia; Jared Shore, son of Alan Shore and Jacky Jansse, both pilots also. Early pioneering pilot Adrian Clements now retired, his sons Mick, Peter and Andrew; Lauren Allen whose father Dale, one of the early Australian pilots, retired but administered our sport after hanging up his flying gloves; Jason Livingston flying in outback Alice Springs, having grown up in New Zealand, watching his father Andrew fly commercially. Also, but not least, Phil Kavanagh & sons, Sean & Paul.

My thoughts also turned to a man who had not proposed, but left an imprint in my life's tapestry. We were both participating at a World Ballooning Rally when we first met in Europe. Being aware of Alexandre's good looks and gentle, sensuous essence distracted me from my total concentration to flying tasks. My scores were lower than expected. We shared the odd drink or two and more personal conversation at each social activity during the week. He was an airline captain in everyday life, in the middle of a divorce, living in Europe. My home was Sydney, on the other side of the planet. After the final awards dinner, we committed to staying in touch with letters to each other, postcards from the various cities he flew in and out of over the next ten months. A time way before the internet and social media. A reunion in Sydney was magical, if only for five days. Then he was gone. Gone from Sydney; gone from my romantic life.

Gradually and gently, my thoughts acknowledged the behaviours the journey of life attracts are reflected worldwide. The sky fills and empties with clouds and stars, birds fly, animals prowl, people sleep, dress, eat, work and some even kill. In my small world, comparatively speaking, I was doing well, accepting responsibility for my decisions and actions, always with the hope

I was profoundly walking in the 'light'. Accepting the continuously evolving spirit of who I am will be my legacy.

I returned home feeling renewed from my ocean sojourn. I fell asleep nightly, my last thought - how could I afford my challenge in the upcoming 1999 Gordon Bennett Gas Balloon Race? My desire to feel the thrill of long-distance gas ballooning had resurfaced.

Gordon James Bennett (1841 – 1918) was the American newspaper proprietor of the New York Herald. After 1877, he lived mostly in Paris. Fond of sport, he established the Gordon Bennett trophy for long distance international yacht, balloon and airplane races. His rules for the gas balloon race were that a maximum of three balloons per country were allowed. Each balloon must carry two pilots of that country's nationality. The pilot in charge had to hold a gas balloon licence. The second person did not need to do so, but had to be of the same nationality. The balloon that flew the longest distance from launch site to landing position was the winner. In 1906, the first Gordon Bennett gas balloon race lifted off from the Tuileries Gardens in Paris before a crowd of over 200,000 spectators. The American pilots Frank P. Lahm and Henry Hersey won by flying a distance of 402 miles. Each year, pilots bitten by the bug of endurance ballooning would continue their struggles to stretch their journey's distance to claim the famous Gordon Bennett trophy.

Sitting on the balcony of my home, I recalled a comment from Carl Jung, Swiss Founder of Analytical Psychology, 1875 – 1961.

"Anyone with a vocation hears the voice of the inner man."

I had heard that voice in my past. It was no longer whispering to me. I would be one of the pilots competing in the prestigious 43rd Coupe Aèronautique Gordon Bennett, the only Australian female gas balloon rated pilot to ever do so over the past 93 years. And I hoped my parents in the afterlife would feel proud of their daughter.

Before that, I attended the wedding of my younger son Grant to his gorgeous bride, Sharlene McIllvenna. And in May that same year, I became a grandmother to Mark and Penny's second child, Josephine Mae, who has brought me infinite joy over the ensuing years.

CHAPTER 45

"It's truly elite ballooning. The America's Cup of ballooning," said my gas ballooning mentor and friend Regula Hug-Messner down the phone from her home in Switzerland. "Go for it," she enthused.

"I really want to, but I have more experience with hot air ballooning than gas ballooning," I countered. "It's years now since I had the opportunity to fly a gas balloon."

"Remember Ruth E, the gas balloon knows where it wants to go. Just let it find its equilibrium. You can do it," said Regula. Words she had shared with me during my first gas balloon flight in July 1985. I had not an inkling who the older woman sitting next to me at a hot-air balloonists' dinner in Zurich was. I knew most of the other people, but not that grey-haired lady. We chatted easily throughout the night. Unexpectedly, she turned to me and asked, "Would you like to go for a gas balloon flight?" My answer was immediate, with huge enthusiasm. "I would love to." And with those words, the famous Swiss gas balloon pilot Regula Hug-Messner became a gas ballooning mentor in my life.

Only three days after our dinner meeting, I stood with Regula and two other passengers as we lifted off on an early Swiss morning from Attiswil in her gas balloon filled with hydrogen. I had my passport tucked securely in my bag. My fantasies of floating over the border of various countries, landing who knows where, being met by local police with my final grand flourish of presenting my Australian passport, were about to be fulfilled. I felt the luckiest lady on earth. This was an experience that could never happen in my country, an island. After nearly all day in the air, we landed near Lohn, still in Switzerland, crossed no borders and no person of authority saw my passport. The winds had been light and variable all day, taking the balloon in circles. Even though I was a little disappointed that my flight over country borders was unfilled, I was sufficiently captivated to return for my second flight in September. The following year, I flew three more gas balloon flights under instruction from Regula and US pilot, David Levin.

Now, 10 years after my marlin fishing near death experience in the ocean, I had finally reconnected with my inner warrior. I was ready to challenge myself at endurance ballooning. It took me a few years to realise the ocean had been kind to me. It could have taken my life, but didn't. And once more I looked at the ocean with pleasure instead of bad memories. I can paddle about in the ocean, a pool, a river or lake, but hesitate to submerge my head totally under water.

I signed the entry form as the Australian pilot/competitor in the Gordon Bennett Gas Balloon race, also recognised as the World Gas Ballooning Championship. I intended to soar high and long.

Non-stop gas balloon flight time has been recorded up to 92 hours, with distance records set at over 3000 kilometres. Picture the round gas balloon filled with helium or hydrogen gas, high above the 1.5 metre square wicker basket, 50 sandbags hooked around the outside edge of the basket, instruments, radios, cold weather gear, food, water and toilet facilities all packed inside the basket for the long haul. The excitement of adventure this form of ballooning presented, thrilled me.

In comparison, distances travelled and flight times in a hot-air balloon were much less. The hot-air balloon comprised of a wicker basket holding four gas tanks, one in each corner filled with LPG for fuel. Pilot lights lit the LPG supplied to the burner above the pilot's head. The resultant flame poured into the balloon's envelope caused rise and flight. Flights lasted up to two hours in general. Loved cutting ties with my earthly life to float above or dance on clouds with this form of ballooning. I had owned seven hot-air balloons. I had to admit I was definitely addicted to both forms of flight, gas and hot air.

One of my biggest challenges for the 1999 gas balloon race in Albuquerque was to find an Australian co-pilot to meet the race rules that required two people of the same nationality to share the basket. I contacted Jenny Houghton, a hot air balloonist and fixed wing pilot who lived in Victoria. Jenny had no gas ballooning experience, but the co-pilot was not required to hold that category licence. Jenny accepted the challenge.

One of twenty pilots from ten different countries, I had to go to America for my support to locate a gas balloon with associated equipment. Jim Herschend loaned his balloon *Jazz Bird*. David Levin and Mark Sullivan, champion gas balloon pilots, assisted with night-lights, a transponder and other essential gear while Roberta Levin and Irene Sullivan were my girlfriend support. George Hahn, an Albuquerque balloonist, thoroughly checked *Jazz Bird* for gas leaks prior to the flight.

The day prior to the race, my experienced American crew arrived in Albuquerque. Don Weeks, a Texan from Amarillo with a huge personality and heart, was responsible for inflating *Jazz Bird.* His wife, Becky assisted. The official observer was Rick Hughlett from Missouri.

Saturday, October 2nd, 1999. 1330hrs: D-Day:

Over ninety sandbags for *Jazz Bird* were filled in the heat of the day. Eight huge helium trucks moved into place to commence filling the balloons over a period of several hours. Jenny helped me load all the necessities for the flight around and in the basket. Our home for the next day or so was ready.

An hour before launch I used a phone in the Event Headquarters to call my sons, Mark and Grant, in Sydney, Australia. "I will call you once we have landed, my loves." My emotions were spilling over from toe to head and back as the first balloon launched at 10pm.

Balloon number 10, the Japanese team of Sabu Ichiyoshi and Maco Oiwa departed, heading to the east towards the mountains. Our launch position was number 11. I clearly heard a male voice amongst the huge crowd yell out, "Let's hear it for the Aussie gals," as our crew walked the balloon to the official launch platform. The crowd erupted with clapping and yelling.

My excitement gave way to steely calm. Intensely focused, I gave the command.

"Stand clear."

Jazz Bird climbed at 300 feet a minute, leaving behind the floodlights, cheers from the crowd and officials waving to the Australian team. I tipped a little ballast water over the basket's edge to maintain the balloon's climb. Jenny trailed the transponder, night-lights and strobes to drop below the basket.

"They are playing Waltzing Matilda," Jenny yelled. "What happened to our national anthem?" I was too concentrated on our flight to notice.

Floating through the starry night sky, I counted six sets of strobe lights in the distance. I was sharing the space with a select group of pilots who understood the desire to challenge their personal horizons.

Jazz Bird drifted towards the mountains. At 13,900 feet, we passed over the mountain crest, secured our oxygen masks, glanced at the GPS and glanced again. 33 knots. We had found a fast wind stream heading due east. We were unaware we were leading the pack. The balloon settled into equilibrium, maintaining her altitude just as Regula had reassured me. I turned off some of the lights to conserve their batteries for our planned second night of flight.

Sitting on the floor in the basket's corner, I felt overcome by a sense of sadness that there were insufficient words to describe to my loved ones this beautiful moment of my being embraced by the night sky. I glanced across at Jenny sitting opposite, head bent over the map. We had worked extremely well as a team to this moment. I reached for the camera and photographed the balloon above the basket in the night sky. The toy kangaroo and Australian flag remained attached to the balloon's netting.

Our track followed the Interstate 40 East. From 12,000 feet, the cars and trucks moved like illuminated ants rushing to their destination. At 0410hrs Sunday, the strobe lights of six gas balloons could be counted south of our position. As our balloon drifted over Tucumcari, New Mexico, Jenny radioed our chase crew.

"We have just driven into a service station for gas at Tucumcari." I heard the reply, liked that Texan drawl.

"Look south at about 10,000 feet. I will flash you six times," I said, grabbing the 500,000-candlepower searchlight.

"We see you," the guys yelled excitedly down the radio.

Regular contact was made with the crew ten minutes past the hour to report the balloon's position off the GPS. Our projected track was passed also to the crew, who relayed this information to the Albuquerque Command Centre. I had no appreciation that our balloon was in front of all the others, but rushing towards bad weather.

Jenny and I were dressed in layered warm clothing, down jackets, wrapped in warm sleeping bags bunkered down in opposite corners of the basket to rest. My feet in ski socks and fur-lined boots remained warm. My black woollen beanie pulled down over my ears, kept the heat in my body. Jenny dozed a little. I closed my eyes, but sleep stayed on the outside of our basket. Our portable toilet called to me, but I crossed my legs until I could wait no longer. Difficult removing so much heavy clothing, cold too. So much easier for the men who pee into a bottle.

As dawn broke, the balloon floated over the Texas panhandle, inhospitable, rough terrain. Because of the extreme cold temperatures at height, my camera's battery had frozen. No photographs could be taken. 0710hrs we drifted over Dumas, Texas at an altitude of 6145 feet, the lowest during our flight. Our speed was still 34 knots. One hour later, the sun warmed the helium. *Jazz Bird* climbed to 10,300 feet. We were literally dancing on the clouds. The GPS had us over Borger, Texas. Noise from pumping oil wells rose up to greet two hungry women in a balloon basket.

Breakfast. Jenny set about preparing Granola in our tin cups. Warmth from the sun increased. We removed our headlamps, down jackets and sleeping bags. Our bodies screamed for stretch and bend. We had now been in the small basket for ten hours. A little housekeeping was necessary to find space. Our communication with the crew worked perfectly. It was not the same with our vital meteorologist who was supposed to present us with a current weather update of wind direction, speed and more importantly, what the weather was, we were heading for in our balloon. We flew on unaware an 80-mile long cold front was speeding towards us. We were on a collision course with black clouds and electrical storm activity. Three separate telephone numbers were called. Contact was never made.

I had no way of handling my frustration. We were flying blind. I went looking for Confidence. She had not totally left me. I continued with my pilot responsibilities.

My focus was on the flight's journey log: every 30 minutes recording the balloon's position, our wind speed and direction plus height. On a separate document, I kept a tally of our important bags of sand, our necessary ballast: how much used, what amount remained. Airspace radio calls to alert other aircraft to our position were made.

I missed my face moisturiser I religiously used morning and night since I was 30 years old. It was more important to keep items on board to the absolute minimum so we could carry more sand for ballast. A small roll of dental floss and comb were my only nod to a daily beauty routine.

We shared the one and only small navy folding stool when either of us needed to sit awhile.

Gas ballooning is totally silent. The drone of a light aircraft invaded our quiet just after breakfast time. Jim Herschend, the owner of *Jazz Bird*, had invited a television crew to fly in his Cessna 182 to film. He flew five or six passes around *Jazz Bird*. The excitement at sharing that space of sky with others had me waving enthusiastically, yelling 'thank you'. In the meantime, the ground crew was singing "Deep in the Heart of Texas" as they crossed the Texas line. After 400 kilometres, they were only 15 kilometres behind the balloon.

"We're parked on the bend in the road," Don called down the radio.

"Which bend?" I replied, scanning the countryside below. I counted 11 from our height of 10,000 feet.

The role of the ground crew, that essential other part of any balloon flight, is to chase their balloon to arrive at or soon after the landing, to pack the equipment, load onto a trailer, then drive the complete team home. Our American crew was amazing. Swapping drivers so one would drive, the other sleep, kept a steady course driving north-east chasing *Jazz Bird* with the two Australian gals. Stops for coffee and doughnuts were many while driving through the night to stay close to their balloon.

At 10am *Jazz Bird* was in the lead by 233 kilometres. At 4pm we were still leading with a distance of 458 kilometres. Thirty minutes later, we were staring at threatening cumulus clouds rolling towards our balloon. The pie wedge shaped clouds were black from 12,000 feet to close to ground level. An extra squall line of angry black clouds scudded across the darkened sky in support. My heart jumped into my mouth. I couldn't talk. For minutes I felt mesmerised, couldn't move. This was a first for me. My previous gas balloon flights in Switzerland with Regula, thirty years ago, were flown in stable gentle skies.

I bit my bottom lip. I had to act quickly to get the balloon on the ground. We could be sucked up into the violent clouds racing towards us. We needed to get out of the sky immediately. The race to descend was on. I opened the valve to allow helium to escape from the top of the balloon. *Jazz Bird* began her descent: 400 feet, 500 feet, 600 feet per minute. We were falling too fast, would lose the balloon's shape. Would plummet, smash into the ground. I grabbed two full sandbags, heaved them towards earth. Jenny stood with her hand on the dropline. All gas balloons carry one very thick rope rolled into a ball, encased in a bag attached to the outside of the basket. Once released to hit the ground, this single rope acts as a brake against any forward drag. Causes the balloon to stop. Our balloon had two thinner ropes, released at the same time were meant to act similarly to one thick rope.

Don's Texan drawl came over the radio. "You gals should get that thing on the ground. Quickly. It's black on the ground where we are. It will only get worse."

"I've already made that decision, Don," was my hurried reply. I juggled our rate of descent with correction by throwing out sand.

Huge relief once I had *Jazz Bird* under control, levelling out at 1900 feet AGL.

Relief that disappeared quickly as I noticed *Jazz Bird* had changed flight direction. I turned to Jenny and asked, "Are we losing ground?"

"Yes, we are drifting back to Albuquerque," I heard her reply.

I wanted every kilometre we could get for our final distance result. All hopes of capturing favourable winds to further our distance were dashed. I had not lost my competitive urge amongst the danger. My decision was immediate.

"The wind has deserted us. We're landing as soon as we can get down," I said to Jenny.

We had crossed the Oklahoma border. Now flying above open countryside, moving away from the storm's path. Large power lines ran through the first and second fields. I kept flying. I could see no power lines or major obstacles, just rough grass and small bushes in the third field. I vented helium and shovelled sand to maintain as smooth an approach as possible in the conditions.

Jenny stood by at the back of the basket, ready to drop the drag rope. The wind gusting from the disappearing storm was about 15 knots. *Jazz Bird's* basket clipped the top of an old, barbed wire rusted fence post as we sped towards touchdown.

"Release the drop line Jenny," I yelled.

She pulled the pin on only one of the two thin lines. With the release of only one thin line instead of the two, the normal braking power was halved. The balloon's forward momentum remained fast. Hardly a slowing.

"Did you drop both lines?" I yelled with increased concern.

"You did not say drop both lines," Jenny screamed back.

She set the second rope free. Too late to be effective. If both drop lines had hit the ground simultaneously, acting as a stronger brake, the balloon drag would have been far less with a more controlled finish. The impact of the balloon's basket on the earth was hard, dragging with the wind, skidding over rough grass. The basket hit a berm or large dirt contour covered in grass and weed, tipped to its right side, then dog housed. Both pilots lay underneath. I was still holding the rip line, firmly spilling the helium into the atmosphere. Jenny was on her back. The wind gusted.

The envelope rolled from side to side. I handed Jenny the rip line, reached up, tipped the basket back, climbed out. Ran to the top of the balloon to untangle the vent to empty any remaining helium. Back to the basket.

Finally, *Jazz Bird* sank to the ground, totally deflated. Our landing place was 32 kilometres northeast of the town, Canadian in Oklahoma.

Not long after we exited the basket, two trucks drove up. Aussie pilots met Okie farmers in the fields of Oklahoma. We exchanged names and addresses. Jenny nursed her ribs, hurt as she fell against the basket edge on landing. Our crew arrived within twenty minutes. I thought of my sons, Mark and Grant, in Australia. The cell phone could not raise their numbers. I was nowhere near any other telephone. After much persuasion, Jenny agreed to go to the nearest hospital to check her ribs. Meanwhile, *Jazz Bird* was packed away, ready for her next flight.

Jenny and I were unaware information on the progress of our flight was on the Internet, early days of this facility in 1999. Back in Australia, my family, friends and the ballooning community were following our progress with great excitement. "Australian female pilots lead the race,"… "Australian female pilots maintain their lead." Troy Bradley, American pilot, is closing on the Australian female team. Australian female pilots have landed." Mark and Grant knew the balloon was down. Did not know for many hours why. With mounting concern, they phoned Albuquerque Balloon Headquarters. There was great relief when they finally heard from their mother and that she was safe.

The majority of the Gordon Bennett teams had finished in Texas or Oklahoma.

The winning team from Belgium funnelled through good weather with guidance from their professional meteorologist to reach Amory, Mississippi. The Aussies had finished in 15th place, with our Japanese friends in 16th. Mark Sullivan and David Levin, both so supportive of the Aussie team's participation, finished 7th.

It had not occurred to me Jenny was unaware of the fundamental role of the dropline, its behaviour during a landing, that she had to drop the two lines simultaneously from this particular basket. I acknowledged later as pilot-in-command I should have checked that important action with her. Additionally, I was dismayed to learn the coverage from the mobile phone on board only had a limited distance from our launch site. The US coverage only spread locally, different from the Australian national coverage for all cell phones. Hence no contact with our meteorologist consequently being unaware of the dangerous weather we were flying towards. The black pie shaped cloud reaching from 12,000 feet to ground is permanently stamped on my brain.

On arrival back in Albuquerque on the Monday evening, stories of the pilots who flew on the second night were shared. A British pilot had broken his back when he fell from his balloon on collision with a barn during the night. A German pilot lost skin from his face as his basket ripped across the ground in the dark in fierce winds. Two American balloons had been torn on landing and a Canadian pilot was traumatised after having spent the night in a gas balloon with a fierce thunderstorm in the distance.

Long distance gas ballooning is definitely not for the fainthearted. I was emotionally and physically exhausted. Jenny had to cope with her painful ribs. Both of us joined the social activities throughout the remainder of the week. At the formal black-tie Gordon Bennett Gas Race Awards ceremony on October 9, all pilots and crews were acknowledged for their achievements and advised their names would be recorded in aviation history.

As pilot of *Jazz Bird,* a solid red netted gas balloon almost twenty years old kindly loaned for the flight, I had flown this lady of the air non-stop from Albuquerque, New Mexico to Canadian, Oklahoma, covering 602 kilometres in nearly fourteen hours. I had fulfilled my enduring desire for long distance ballooning. Was privileged to join a small number of international pilots who could claim to be a member of this elite ballooning group of the Coupe Aéronautique Gordon Bennett, the most prestigious aviation event in the world.

Gas ballooning does not exist in Australia. It is a sport of the northern hemisphere. Only three Australian males at that time held a gas balloon pilot certificate – Peter Vizzard, John Wallington and Steve Griffin, while I was the only female. The following year, the Australian Women's Pilots' Association presented me with the prestigious Mrs. Harry (Lores) Bonney Award for an outstanding aviation achievement. Jenny Houghton, my co-pilot during the flight, accepted the award with me. I felt proud to hold the trophy.

History is swamped with stories now shared over the internet of human ingenuity and courage, of Gordon Bennett race competitors. I had no answers whether I would enter the Gordon Bennett Race in future years.

I had no answers also to the final loss of my darling brother, Ronnie.

CHAPTER 46

I boarded a plane in Broken Hill, having worked on the launch of 2002 Year of the Outback. On arrival in Brisbane where I was living at the time, I caught a taxi to my Kangaroo Point home. I heard my younger brother's voice among my mobile phone messages.

"It's Keith, Ruth. Ronnie has killed himself."

A loud, wailing scream left my throat. Sobs wracked my body.

"I'm sorry," I said, looking at the taxi driver. "My brother has killed himself."

The driver kept his eyes on the road until we arrived at my destination. I rushed into the lift to take me to the top floor, put the key in the front door, pushed into the living room, conscious I was still sobbing out aloud. The Brisbane River shimmered below as I leaned on the large glass plate windows attempting to contain my distress.

On December 4, 2001, my darling brother ended his life by hanging. Ron and his wife, Margaret had moved interstate for her work. Consequently, Ron needed to find a new doctor when he ran out of his medication. He had gone to a local doctor for his medication on Friday. Tuesday, he was dead. And the tragic thing was on the day he died, he seemed okay when Margaret left for work. About 2pm he knocked on the door of the adjacent flat and said, "I'm going to kill myself". The neighbour's response was to close the door. At 4pm, Ron climbed onto the furniture, tied the noose around his neck and jumped. When Margaret returned from work and found him, his neck on the right side was deeply gouged from his struggle in an attempt to undo the knot.

There was only a 14-month age difference between brother and sister. I was always the older, protective sister. My brother's life's journey had not been easy, had not been helped by his joining the Army at seventeen to escape a dysfunctional home life.

At 18, he was based in the jungles of Borneo and Malaysia with the Third

Battalion. In 1966, at only 22, he was in the thick of the war in Vietnam, an infantryman in the 7 R&R Battalion. He was one of the numerous Australian soldiers taken from the jungle, put on a plane for Darwin and flown back to his homeland. Days later, he was being abused by those who did not support the war. He came back a scarred human being. He struggled to find the young man who grew up in Australia in the 50s and 60s.

But the fear that stalked his mind and body in the blackness of the Vietnam jungles while on patrol, night after night, never fully receded. I was always there at the end of the phone to listen to his comments on his life, his continual conversations about his difficult childhood, his troubled relationship with our parents, his own family problems.

"It will be alright. Try to find someone who needs some help and do something for them. Ring the Salvation Army. See if you can become a volunteer," was my advice to my troubled brother. It was a time when so little support existed for loved ones to cope with a family member or friend who was lost in their mental turmoil.

Many young Australians who went to the Vietnam War in their early 20s had hit a life-crises point. Media stories appeared of men shooting their families, themselves, but still society and the Government remained silent. I had contacted the Vietnam Veterans Association when Ron had shot himself years earlier. They were so supportive over the phone. Ineffective because they could do nothing unless Ron admitted himself to hospital and/or personally requested assistance for his condition. That he would not consider.

The eulogy was profound and emotionally stated at my brother's funeral in Bowen, attended by local Vietnam Veterans.

"Ronald Owen Lawson was born in Rockhampton, June 8, 1944, three months premature, weighing just over three pounds. Those early months were a struggle to survive, but his spirit was strong. He was born with a gift. A natural golf swing, the envy of many of his young peers. At 16, he was invited to study with golf professionals in Townsville. For family reasons, that did not eventuate, so at 17 he joined the Army. He served his country for almost seven years, nearly three of them in overseas combat. The young man who went away was not the young man who returned. His experiences had cut deep into his soul.

"There is a tear being shed around this country today by other men who served in Vietnam, who are searching for inner peace and who can identify

with Ron's *struggle. We honour and salute these men today. We also honour and salute our loving brother, Ron,"* I said as grown men wiped tears from their eyes in the church.

Ron's other siblings Glenda, Keith and Jeffrey hugged each other as my son, Mark, helped me into the car to follow the hearse to the cemetery, to Ron's final resting place. His three grown children from his first marriage to Carol; Gary, David and Amanda had flown from New Zealand to join his family and friends for the final farewell. His coffin was slowly lowered into his grave to the sounds of the Last Post.

If we should be born with a definitive number of tears throughout our lifetime, then I spent the majority of mine between the ages of 3 to 18. At the age of 58, I was crying buckets of those remaining tears for both myself and Ronnie.

A few months later, I was inducted into the Australian Ballooning Federation's Hall of Fame.

Five years later, I would take on a World Record attempt to promote the work of *Beyond Blue*, to try to find an avenue to help mentally troubled males.

CHAPTER 47

During 2000 and 2001, I worked as Chief Executive Officer, setting up the 2002 Year of the Outback. My grief from Ron's suicide drove me to move away from Brisbane early 2002 to settle close to my circle of dear friends in Canberra. Floating down Lake Burley Griffin in my balloon basket, looking at the distant blue Brindabella Mountains, I felt I would be more at peace in our nation's capital. My next home was found that same afternoon. Within a short time, I was making friends in my new neighbourhood.

My initial intense grief for my brother dominated my days and often throughout my nights. Pain was all-consuming. Flooding my thoughts, followed by my incessant crying. Life did not feel fair. Had not been fair for Ronnie. I prayed each day he had found some peace, was even happy in the afterlife. Gradually my grief eased. Days without crying. Nights sleeping better. Gaining an awareness of my new home and Canberra community.

Six months after my Canberra arrival, I faced my financial situation. I needed to find work, income. It was one of my immediate neighbours who rescued me.

"My friend at the University has received a government grant to set up a new Centre of Excellence. He is looking for a person to manage that," Brian mentioned casually.

I asked for a favour from him. "Would you introduce me, please?"

At our first informal meeting, Professor Hans Bachor said, "Tell me about yourself".

I did. His reply was disappointing.

"I don't think the job will be interesting enough for you. Also, the university won't meet your salary expectations. The job will be advertised in the national paper next week. You are welcome to apply, of course."

I did. One of 20 applicants, I was selected as one of the final four to be interviewed.

I had asked to see a copy of the Centre's proposed budget. All four final applicants were sent the budget prior to being interviewed. Interview day arrived. I was a little anxious walking into the interview room to see five people behind the desk. Before the interview could end, I spoke up.

"Your budget has a mistake that involves a large amount," and duly explained.

I got the job. Not because I had university qualifications. I was the only applicant to find the financial mistake. There may have been other reasons, but I was only told of that one.

Monday to Friday was spent at the Australian National University working as Chief Operations Officer for the Australian Research Council Centre of Excellence for Quantum-Atom Optics. Managing a $15m budget, working to support a large number of physicists researching the physics of the future, was stimulating.

Weekend social ballooning was fun. Most evenings I spent alone. I missed hugs. How I loved to feel arms hold me from behind, pull me close to a warm, caring body, with light kisses on the back of my neck. Touch. True intimacy. How could I find that? Would a dating site solve my dilemma? I doubted it would. Threw the idea out the window.

My salary was sufficient to cover my living costs, to support any expenses with flying my old balloon, *VAMP*. The LPG gas for a flight cost around $50, with an annual insurance bill of $1200. My other indulgence was to have a supply of inexpensive champagne for after-flight celebration.

In 2004 the World Hot Air Ballooning Championship came to Mildura, Victoria. International pilots and crews blended with Australian balloon teams to chase the esteemed title of World Champion. German pilot Markus Piper took that home. Australian pilot Paul Gibbs kept the Bronze medal locally. I took on the role of Worlds' Fiesta Director planning and managing the flights for the Fiesta pilots.

Spending my annual leave ballooning – what else?

Working during the years 2002 through 2008 with such brilliant minds, including a Nobel Prize winner, proved a wonder. When Government funds for the Centre were stopped and no other University positions were available, I retired.

CHAPTER 48

Before my retirement from the University, I attempted a world ballooning record in 2006. Almost died.

A group of my friends sat on a tartan blanket near the sailing club on the southern side of the lake in Canberra. Discussions centred around ways to contribute to society. To help those who needed support. Later that night in bed, I pondered on my journey over the past thirty years of ballooning, travel, work and family.

I had won the first Australian Ballooning Championship, competed at four world major championships, in the elite Gordon Bennett Gas Balloon Race, flown over alps, deserts, the ocean, raised funds for charities, been an essential part of a team who achieved a world first with the night parachute drop. Introduced hundreds of people to the joy of floating above the earth, either as student pilots or passengers.

The only thing I had not achieved was a personal world record in the sport I loved.

The thought took wings and grew. Why not try for a world record, a 15-hour non-stop flight over 750 kilometres. Use the flight to gain publicity for a good cause?

I found the missing link for my challenge. *Beyond Blue* was introducing a new phone service in July 2006 to assist those struggling with depression and suicide. I would use my world record attempt to promote the new phone number. Someone, somewhere, would benefit. I could only hope.

I designed and purchased a new red, royal blue and golden yellow balloon, eating into what savings I had. Chose my support team. I would not have contemplated such a challenge without Retired Lieutenant Colonel Dennis Collins as my Ground Crew Chief with support from his lovely wife, Margaret.

Team meetings for the record attempt were held regularly. Maps, helium, satellite phones, VHF & UHF radios, cold weather gear and oxygen purchased. Chase and retrieve plans drawn up and studied. Jody Hammond donated her time to promote my endeavour. Karin Bergseng and Peter McCrohon set up legal papers to support the attempt. Well-known and respected media interviewer, Andrew Denton talked with me on his ABC program, 'Enough Rope' The feedback to my office from men with depression was overwhelming.

It was essential I find a capable meteorologist who could guide my flight with weather updates for a safe and successful flight. I did not want a repeat of my previous experience with my USA long distance gas ballooning. Had no desire to stare at a 12,000-foot black angry thunderstorm. Don Whitford, with over thirty years of experience with the Bureau of Meteorology, joined my team. Began studying weather models, patiently listened to my repeated statement. My flight could only succeed with clear knowledge of what weather I was flying towards.

Late July 2006, my team headed for our base in Mildura. Most importantly for my emotional support, my elder son Mark drove from Sydney to act as stills photographer. His brother Grant was commissioned to shoot a documentary of the record attempt. Don Whitford flew in from Melbourne. Mick and Margaret Toller offered aerial support and arrived in their plane. Flying Doctor pilot Cameron Gibbs and his wife Kate joined Mike Kelaher and Susan Merrill. I was surrounded by the best support team.

On July 31st, the team departed for Waikerie Airfield in South Australia, the chosen launch site for the attempt. Headquarters was set up in the airport briefing room. Dennis had the responsibility of securing 13 tanks of LPG inside and around the outside of the basket. Grant quietly filmed the whole exercise.

A group of men stood near a hangar watching the activity. I eventually walked over to introduce myself.

"I saw you on the Andrew Denton Show," said one of the men. "My father committed suicide. Just disappeared on Christmas Eve one year. We found his body a couple of days later. I suffer depression. My teenage son also is not well."

"Good luck," he said as I headed back to the action on the edge of the airfield. I felt even more committed to the flight. To my endeavour to help troubled males.

At 2000hrs, heads were laid on pillows for a short sleep. Flight-briefing time was at 2330 hrs.

I walked into the briefing room well rugged up in my cold weather flying gear, ready for flight. Don was already at the computer interpreting the weather.

"You have clear skies from 5000 to 15,000 feet, 30 kilometres westerly all the way to Canberra," he said. I leaned towards the weather map on his computer. These were the conditions I had prayed for, had dreamed of for months. I silently thanked God.

"And if I wait, what is the weather pattern doing over the next few days?" I asked.

"The winds will swing around to the northwest. Your flight path will take you to Melbourne. You won't get the distance required for the record."

I called the flight. The local SES volunteers set up lights to assist Michael Kelaher with the inflation of *Aurora* as I checked my flight gear nearby. Both my sons were separately filming. Waikerie Gliding Club members helped my team with various jobs. Other locals stood by, the children in their pyjamas. At 0110 hrs, I lifted off in *Aurora* into a black night sky. Extra burns were needed to lift *Aurora* as we drifted level just above ground down the airfield runway. Light, misty rain began falling on the launch site. *Aurora* and pilot disappeared into the distance, unaware with the black night sky that light raindrops were falling on the crown of the balloon. Also covering Mark's camera lens back at the airfield.

"What's happening with the weather, Don?" a concerned Mark asked.

"She should be fine. She's flying in front of the weather pattern," was Don's reply.

With maximum load, I used the burner consistently climbing to level out at 3000 feet on track with my flight plan. I looked again for the horizon. None to see. Thoughts of Ron Llewellyn and his comment about jumping from my balloon into a sky that was as black as the inside of a horse flashed through my mind. All my previous night balloon flights had been done with a full moon and stars. I had seen the horizon clearly. As well as the outline of trees and rooftops, but on this occasion, there was no moon, no light at all. I had neglected to consider the moon phase.

My last altitude check showed 3500 feet. Next time I checked the instrument pack to record data, it was completely black. The back-up instruments were not operating either. The separate temperature gauge was changing numbers erratically. 45 degrees, 78 degrees, 128 degrees. My GPS blank also. I had lost all instrumentation.

"What's happening here?" I said aloud, "You learned to fly a balloon without any instruments. Stay calm Ruth E. Fly the aircraft till dawn, then assess the situation and land. You can do this," I told myself. I flew on in pitch black, alone in my wicker basket. Out of nowhere came a loud bang. A crashing sound, at what height above ground, I had no idea. What could I possibly hit while airborne?

I immediately turned out the pilot lights. Did not want a potential fire. Had a horrible dread of being burned. The balloon moving at 30 kilometres had crashed through the tops of tall trees. The basket finally thumping into the ground. I clung to the sides of the basket. Frozen. I could see nothing.

I reached down, picked up the candlepower torch I had specifically placed on my right side for easy retrieval. Turned it on. Swung it around. *Aurora* and I were encased in a forest of tall trees. The balloon's envelope draped over a few of those large, high trees. Rain was filling the envelope. A thick tree stump had penetrated the middle of the basket's floor, just missing my stomach. Shock and disbelief raged through me. I searched for my satellite phone. Called Dennis.

"I am on the ground and my balloon is in trees. I am so sorry. I have let you all down." My emotional pain was all-consuming as I stood there amongst the wreckage. My strongest thought was I had let everybody down. My feelings strongly echoed that disappointment. I felt shattered.

"Are you okay?" Dennis asked. "Where are you? Are you near a road? Are there any cars on it?"

I swung the torch around to find a bitumen road just a couple of metres behind my landing position. Relief, I was close to a road and not splattered on it, surged through me.

"I am next to a road, but there are no cars," I answered. And then I saw the headlights approaching. I exited the broken basket. Ran onto the road waving the torch at the oncoming vehicle. It stopped.

Three men returning from a three-day fishing expedition sat in the front cab of their camper van. Their boat on a trailer was attached. All three heads turned to the right, looking at me with amazement through the driver's window. It was 0245hrs in the middle of nowhere, pitch black.

"I have just landed my balloon in the trees," I said. "Can you give Dennis directions on how to find me, please?" I was definitely in shock. I handed the stunned driver the satellite phone. The rain fell heavily, drenching me.

All three heads turned in unison towards the trees, then back to look at the woman who had stopped their van, then back at the trees. Disbelief registered on their faces.

"Get out of the rain," said the driver. "Climb up into the back of the camper van. I will make you a coffee," said another.

As I did, I felt the pain in my ribs. I was hurt.

"Sorry about the state we are in. We've been away fishing for three days," I heard. I was whimpering out loud to myself. "What have you done, Ruth E? What just happened?" Someone handed me a cup of coffee. Another male voice said, "Just be pleased you are still alive!".

About an hour later, all my team members arrived.

Mark and Grant climbed up into the camper van. Their concern was reflected in their faces. I did not want an ambulance. Did not want to go to any hospital. My sons convinced me to go to Berri hospital. Everyone else worked to retrieve the balloon basket. The gas tanks had stayed attached to the outside of the basket. Dennis had secured those tanks well. The rain continued. I departed the accident scene with my sons for Berri, nursing my ribs. The ache in my heart and the shock in my mind were all-consuming. The decision was made to leave the wet balloon envelope stranded over the trees till next morning. Then it was pulled free by team members without further damage.

"We usually get motorbike accidents at this time of the night," said the doctor. "Never had a balloon pilot before," as he began examining my ribs. "You have probably just bruised your ribs. If they are still painful in a couple of weeks, go get an x-ray." Armed with some painkillers, I set off with my sons to drive to Mildura for a reunion with all team members. Five kilometres west of Mildura, Mark stopped the car. Climbed out to set up his tripod and camera. Huge black, angry clouds screamed across the sky, heavy rain falling.

I heard the deep concern and anger in his voice.

"Mum, you would have been flying right into those at this time."

I had taken off on my flight, completely unaware of the horrific weather conditions in the area. Would not happen currently with the available weather information from Weather Apps on our mobile phones. Another instance of my missing out on modern technology.

Sitting in Mark's passenger car seat August 1st 2006, I closed my eyes. My realisation that my need to chase the aerial challenge had caused great pain and concern to my sons hit me hard. My heart felt very heavy. I had also come close to killing myself. I had cheated death by just missing the nearby powerful electrical hummer lines in the dark. Smashing onto the bitumen road would have ended my life. How did I not fall forwards in the pitch black onto that large tree branch jutting through my basket's floor on landing?

All team members returned to our Mildura base. August 1st late in the afternoon, stories were shared from each person's perspective. Once Dennis had received my message, the ground team headed off in tandem in three different vehicles. Dennis and Margaret with the official observer, Scobie Peart in one; Mark with Grant in the second; Mike Kelaher and Susan Merrill in the third. After 35 minutes driving, Michael and Grant got out of their cars, walked towards the gate. The sign 'private property trespassers will be prosecuted' did not deter them. Just as Michael raised his hand to knock on the door, it swung open. A naked man putting on a dressing gown stood in front of them.

"We are looking for a lady who has landed her balloon somewhere near here," said Michael.

"There's no f...ing lady here. Do you know what time it is?" he shouted as he slammed the door closed in their faces.

At that point, my other son Mark rushed up to the scene. "Is Mum here?" he anxiously enquired

"Apparently, the gentleman doesn't think so," answered Michael. All three turned and walked back to their respective cars.

Don Whitford's answer to the weather I confronted was I had flown into a rogue rain cell that had not shown on his computer modules. Today I would have my own weather app on my wrist with my Apple watch backed up by my Apple phone meteorological apps. My July 2006 flight was another instance of being a pioneer, too early for modern technological support, ahead of the curve, as one says.

Phones were running hot with calls from the media. Jody Hammond, Mark Wilson and my Canberra ballooning friend, Jacky Jansse, took over one hundred requests for interviews about the flight and landing. Through it all, the *Beyond Blue* phone number gained exposure. I was told later the organisation had received over 500 phone calls seeking help and advice around that same period. As I tried to sleep through the pain of my broken ribs over the next few weeks, I consoled myself that maybe my attempt had saved at least one man's life as he struggled with depression or mental illness.

It was not difficult to repair *Aurora*. The eight torn panels were replaced with new ones, the basket repaired. She was ready to fly once more. It took weeks to repair my three broken ribs. Months to repair my mental state. Even longer to rebuild the finances I had invested in the attempt.

Would I do it again? The memory of the emotional distress I caused my family and loyal team won't leave me. As does the fact, I have faced my mortality five times and survived. First the family house bombing; my near drowning in the local swimming pool; falling towards high tension power lines just missing electrocution; the wreck of Innovator leaving me fighting the ocean for my life, saved by dolphins and finally my world record attempt destroyed by wild weather? I find it hard to say "yes".

The day came when I returned to my work as Chief Operations Officer at the ARC Centre of Excellence for Quantum-Atom Optics at the Australian National University in Canberra. Horrid memories of my record attempt slowly began to fade. Working with renowned Professor Hans Bachor and his team of physicists, I found a world of people drowned in their passion around their scientific research. I appreciated their commitment, not dissimilar to mine with my flying.

When questioned about the science, I would quote my Professor, "Quantum-Atom Optics has become a driving force behind the development of future technologies. In a similar way that optics in lasers, semiconductors in computers have both shaped the way we live and work today, so too have quantum concepts. Within the next few decades, these concepts will influence and improve communication, sensing and meteorology, navigation and computing devices and other yet unknown areas."

I contributed six years of my corporate skills to this amazing pioneering work, unaware that quantum physics could illuminate the mysteries of the mystical. Had been explored enthusiastically by various international physicists many years earlier.

CHAPTER 49

I discovered my birth father's name two months after my fateful balloon record attempt. To my dismay and disappointment, no American serviceman featured.

An envelope arrived in the mail from the Queensland Department of Families in response to a formal application I made to check out my birth records months earlier.

Edward J. Lee from Rockhampton, Queensland, had signed official documents when I was four months old agreeing to pay 13 pounds, two shillings for confinement expenses plus 12 shillings and six pence per week maintenance. All information regarding my father's life was blackened out – for privacy laws. Except that he was an Australian. The above bit of information was all that was cleared for reading. Anger and disappointment raged in equal amounts through my body.

As my tears fell, I read the words written so many years ago. The story of my mother's life when she gave birth to me. Finally, at the age of 63, I knew her story.

Twenty years old and pregnant, Joyce Thorne needed her parents' written approval to marry because she was under 21. Edward Lee was a Catholic. Joyce's father was a Grand Mason in the Masonic Temple. He strongly disapproved of the union on religious grounds.

Five days after my birth in 1943, my mother signed the following statement for the District Registrar's Office of the State Children Department. *"I have this day received notice under the 17th Section of 'The Infants Life Protection Act of 1905' of the birth of an illegitimate child under the age of five years."*

The Sergeant of Police interviewed my mother one week later. His report for his superiors stated, *"I saw the child that appears to be healthy and strong and is being nursed by the mother, who on her discharge from hospital intends to take the child with her to her parents' home and with their assistance intends to care for the child herself. The requirements of the 'Infant Life Protections Act of 1905' have been complied with and no breaches of the act have been committed."*

My years of yearning to know the name of my birth father fell away. I tried to create an image of this man. He must have been a decent person to offer to look after me financially. How tragic it would have been for Joyce and Edward – star-crossed lovers. My poor mother, pregnant and in love with my imagined, handsome Irish father. Yes, he was Catholic, so he must have been Irish. My imagination could not be contained. But stronger than my imagination was my determination to find the man who had loved my mother, who had fathered me.

The documents showed two months before her 21st birthday, my mother gave birth on June 8, 1944, to her second child, a son she christened Gene Owen. His father was an American serviceman stationed in Rockhampton but was fighting in New Guinea at the baby's premature birth. My mother now had two young babies, no money or financial support.

On March 14, 1945 and in desperate circumstances, she applied for financial assistance to the State Children Department. A record of her interview on the situation surrounding my birth father states, *"He offered to marry me, but my parents would not consent to it because he was a Catholic. When I did attain age (21) and was in a position to marry him, he had gone away".*

Memo in response to the request for financial assistance for both children was sent to The Office in Charge of Police.

"Is she receiving any payments from the fathers of these children and if not, what steps has she taken to compel them to support the children?"

March 19, Constable Armanasco called on my mother to conduct a personal interview. His assessment follows:

"From the result of my inquiries I am satisfied, that applicant is a woman of good character, in very poor circumstances and in my opinion, I consider this a deserving case for some assistance by the State Children Department, until such times as some financial assistance is received from the putative fathers of her children."

Five days later, her request for financial assistance was denied. Three days later, she made the decision to apply to have her children admitted as State Wards.

The application form carried the words *"state children are liable at any time to be boarded out, hired out, adopted, or apprenticed to a trade in any part of the State; without reference to their parents or relatives, and without information to them of what has been done. Only children under the age of fourteen years can be admitted as State children. The children named in this application must not be forwarded to an Institution until the applicant has received notice that they may be sent."*

I sat in my comfortable Canberra home while I attempted to move into my mother's skin during the 1940s. How emotionally drained and abandoned she must have felt. I wished she had shared all this with me so I could have hugged her, thanked her for not aborting my baby self. Educated myself further on how life was for unwed pregnant women during years past.

During the 1940s, society shunned such mothers. The terminology 'love child' was nowhere to be heard. 'Bastard' was more prevalent. Society has now become accepting of mothers with children born out of wedlock. In fact, it is more than acceptable. It is a way of life for many.

My grandparents took me as a ward of the State but would not take Gene. At nine months of age, he went into foster care. He was moved between families for another thirteen months.

It was still wartime where women were drawn into the workforce learning new industrial skills in steel plants, shipyards and lumber mills. After the birth of her second child, my mother moved to work at the Rockhampton Meatworks.

When I was three years old and Gene nearly two, Joyce and George Edward Lawson applied to adopt both of us under the Adoption of Children Act. This was granted in March 1946. My life took a new direction when the family moved to live in a North Queensland coal-mining village.

I sat staring at the thick file of paper outlining a part of life in the 1940s I had not known. I had my birth father's name. I felt an unusual feeling of belonging to a person I had never met. I had to find him. Fell asleep in the early hours after my plan for a father search became clearer to me. In the first instance, I went to the national electoral role. I copied the addresses of every E Lee throughout Australia, then wrote to each one. Many I telephoned after finding their numbers through the Internet. I contacted the Salvation Army Family Search office, giving them details. His name, his address in Rockhampton around the time of my birth, my mother's maiden name and of course, my birth date. I also continued my father's search through Army records.

I felt a powerful responsibility to find out my father's story of his journey. Had he gone through life observing my personal journey from afar while hiding his secret? Was I a secret daughter he had hidden from others during his lifetime? Had he comfortably forgotten my existence?

And then the letter from the Salvation Army Search office arrived.

"We have not been successful in locating Mr. Lee even though we have contacted numerous persons. We suspect that he may be denying his existence, most likely because he believes you may be seeking maintenance payment."

That thought had never crossed my mind. Yet again, I was reduced to the pain of disappointment with my father's search. The hunger of my hope remained unfed.

I asked myself, "What now?"

CHAPTER 50

I asked myself that question interminably over many months. What now? My core belief in the power of spirit, of positive thinking, was slowly being squashed. Then the golden light appeared.

Lights out, curtains drawn so tightly the room was in total blackness, I snuggled into my pillow, ready for sleep. My eyes were drawn to the corner of the room's ceiling on the left-hand side of the door. A bright golden light the shape of a rock melon was blinking rhythmically. I jumped out of bed, turned on the light to check the ceiling. Nothing was there at all, no smoke alarm, just a painted ceiling. I opened the curtains, but the world outside was settled. No pulsing lights that could penetrate my bedroom.

"Who are you? What do you want of me?" Curiosity was beaming out of my pores.

The only reply to my questions was the continual pulse of the golden flashing light. Eventually I settled. Drifted off to sleep. The date was May 25th, my sister's birthday.

There was no light the following night. The next night, the light returned to my bedroom. I shared this experience by phone with my daughter-in-law Penny, who listened to the story without much comment. After our phone conversation, I squeezed oranges for my fresh juice, spread strawberry jam over two pieces of toast, then moved to my study to continue writing.

A couple of months later, Penny saw my golden light.

She was visiting with her family for holidays. I had to leave them for an overnight trip away. Turning up the car volume on my Troy Cassar-Daley CD, I drove out the gate. My meeting with my accountant in Sydney went well. I enjoyed a tasty dinner with my younger son, Grant and his lovely wife, Sharlene. On arrival home the next day close to noon, I found Penny propped up on the white leather lounge with the cream and navy cushions behind her, reading a novel. A large glass of water sat on the coffee table. The home was quiet.

"Mark has taken the children to the beach," she said as I entered the room further. "How was your trip?"

I filled her in on news as I unloaded fresh fruit and vegetables from my shopping on the kitchen bench.

"I saw your golden light last night," Penny said without warning. "The mattress in your guest room was quite hard. I could not get to sleep, so I moved into your room and your bed. I hope you don't mind. I was lying there in the dark, staring at the ceiling, trying to go to sleep. The golden light appeared rhythmically flashing. You had mentioned it a few months back, so I was not shocked. I did get up to check if it could be coming from any outside lights, but at 2am everything was black," she explained.

"I did not feel any fear. After about ten minutes, I rolled onto my side and eventually went to sleep."

I had a witness, a second person who had seen the golden light. I felt ecstatic. The Moet champagne I had been saving for a special moment had found that moment.

"Have you googled 'golden light'?" my friend Margaret T asked when I told her both Penny and I had seen it. I hadn't, so I promised I would. I researched 'golden light' on the internet, overwhelmed at the available information. There were Christian, Budda and Tao references to Golden Light. Now I was more confused than ever, so I poured another glass of champagne.

Yet it has been faith that has driven me forward; not a structured religious faith, but my strong personal connection to the 'other' world I believe has supported me with my life goals. It does appear though I have been left on my own to attract a life partner and successfully trace my birth father. I must painfully say I ache to at least find one before I die.

I have to accept my search for my birth father has been thorough, having searched through a professional agency plus my personal endeavours. My birth father remains a ghost. Even today when I see the surname 'Lee', I wonder if we could be related.

My adoptive father gave me a name, a childhood home, until I moved out at nearly 18. He was of an era where it was not usual for the Australian male to show familial affection, physical touch or an obvious show of love. His love came from doing things for me and I thank him for that. I ask myself at various times what would a loving, interactive father/daughter relationship have been like? I will never know.

CHAPTER 51

I received an invitation to Sheikh Majid Bin Mohammed Bin Makhtoum's birthday celebrations in Dubai three months after my disappointing world record attempt.

"You are invited to be the sole Australian pilot at the first Dubai International Ballooning Festival to be held in December this year to celebrate our Sheik's birthday. Your expenses will be paid."

I was still disillusioned with my world record attempt outcome. I continually reminded myself I should be thankful I had not died. Travel to the United Arab Emirates for ballooning offered an adventure I had not anticipated. And to fly my balloon in the Arab world, a culture so foreign to me, also raised my spirits.

I began educating myself on my upcoming destination. Dubai's earliest history was first recorded in 1095, with the first settlement dated from 1799. Oil was discovered in 1966, leading to a huge influx of foreign workers. Modern Dubai was created in 1971 when, together with Abu Dhabi and five other emirates, the United Arab Emirates was formed. Today Dubai's main revenues as the oil diminishes come from tourism, property and financial services.

Dennis and Margaret Collins joined me on this adventure. We departed Sydney December 18, 2006. My balloon, *Aurora* (VH-BJF) left a day earlier by air freight as one large package. Quite a demanding exercise to ship a hot-air balloon internationally.

Three gas tanks emptied and purged, signed off by an approved company, were positioned in the basket. Ropes, gloves, instruments turned off, all packed into one large satchel placed in the middle between the tanks. The balloon itself, the envelope rolled tightly, packed into its own protective bag, was placed on top of the basket. Rolls of clear plastic covered the whole package, holding it all together safely. The paperwork required by the Department of Customs proved more demanding than any other.

At breakfast on the first morning in Dubai, I picked up the local paper. The headline:

Australian businessman was jailed for 3 months while his Executive Assistant from the Philippines sentence is for one month.

Their crime: Being affectionate in public that offended a local. A powerful 'open your eyes' call to me. My usual hugs with my fellow ballooning peers would not happen on this expedition, of that I was sure.

All 75 balloon teams representing 18 countries were accommodated at the Al Bustan Residences not far from the Dubai international airport. Local law allowed no alcohol for sale on our premises. All teams had been warned beforehand, so it was not unusual to observe the foreigners checking in at reception with duty-free bags laden with their preferred choice of drink.

On our first day, teams were bussed to Global Village, a 30-minute drive south of the city. A mad scramble ensued as pilots attempted to locate their balloons, to select a chase vehicle with driver for the event. We were directed to a specific desert destination. A huge white marquee perched in the desert. Inside, Sheikh Majid Bin Mohammed Bin Makhtoum, his bodyguards and entourage were sitting on red and gold ornate chairs on colourful rugs.

All balloons were inflated. Fireworks exploded nearby. Arabian music filled the air around us. The sun was at 30 degrees to the horizon as balloons were finally deflated. Work completed. Teams were invited to the marquee for food and drinks. The birthday entourage had departed well earlier.

Tahir, my team's Pakistani truck driver assigned to my balloon, was uncomfortable with taking directions from a woman. Ignored that I was the pilot. He made it clear he would not take his truck off-road into the desert sands to retrieve my balloon. I withdrew. Asked Dennis to communicate our needs. That situation worked better.

An excited enthusiasm to fly from the Burj Al Arab at Jumeirah permeated our social catch ups. The iconic sail shaped hotel rose from the water, a spectacular backdrop for any ballooning images.

"Will we fly from the Palm?" a question asked at each pre-flight briefing.

"Don't have permission yet," was the regular reply.

After eight days of desert ballooning, all teams piled onto buses headed in a different direction from our hotel.

"Where are we going?" yelled one of the Brits to the driver. "To the Burj Al Arab," was all he said. Loud clapping filled the bus.

We drove through downtown Dubai to Jumeirah Beach Road. On arrival, the famous 6-star hotel, shaped like a sail, surrounded by the most azure coloured ocean stood waiting for us. The flag on top of the Burj Al Arab was not fluttering. It was blowing, waving crazily. There was a strong wind, but everyone was keen to fly.

The flight briefing was specific. Initial height must be maintained at 500 feet AMSL. At the approved flying area to the southeast, balloons could climb to 1500 feet AMSL. All balloon inflations were hectic, even dangerous. *Aurora* was rolling to one side, back to the other. The inflation fan was blowing sand into the belly of my balloon. Still, I persisted with the flame. I would not be denied this flight. The basket was straining against the launch rope. I yelled amongst the craziness to Dennis and Margaret. "Jump in!". We were gone, airborne in minutes.

The Emirates Mall, famous for housing an indoor ski run of 600 to 800 metres was now below my balloon basket. Only 30 feet of clean air to the mall roof. Looking back, I felt in awe of that spectacular hotel. The mass of colourful balloons at various heights with the hotel as a background completed the scene.

After the flight, teams prepared for a special dinner in the desert. Driven over numerous sand dunes through the black night. A light appeared in the distance. On arrival, we entered a compound, low tables with cushions on the sand. A stage stood in the middle. In the far corner was the bar. The majority of balloonists had dressed in Arabian outfits. The belly dancer was popular. Dennis, Margaret and I arrived back at our apartment well after midnight after an action filled 21-hour day.

The demands from the organisers were tough. Fuel tanks had to be removed, carried to a refuelling spot, filled, then replaced in the balloon basket. Twice daily. Dennis Collins never demurred. There was little time to socialise with other teams, to form new friendships. This adventure had been so totally different from my previous ballooning trips throughout Europe, Canada, Japan and the USA. I did not feel completely comfortable with the local culture. Been there. Done that. Will not return.

CHAPTER 52

Retirement from my University work and colleagues had left a huge emotional gap I had not anticipated feeling. My life felt adrift. I had left my dear Canberra friends to settle temporarily in Sydney with Mark and Penny. It was time to find my forever home, my retirement gem. Sadly, I did not know where I wanted to settle, only that I had to see water. Water view homes in Sydney cost into the millions of dollars, funds I did not have. But I clung to my desire to find a house with water views. Meanwhile, in an attempt to stall my diminished love affair with the air, I went searching for an adrenaline fix over the Austrian Alps.

Filzmoos, 55 kilometres southeast from Salzburg, sits in a snow pocket at the foot of the spectacular Bischofsmütze Mountain. Famous for its winter skiing and summer hiking, this quaint Austrian village has hosted an international balloon festival since 1979. Excited to be part of the 31st Alpine ballooning event in 2010, I could now cross this off my bucket list.

Sliding and slipping on the icy snow-covered launch site, I worked with David Levin, Ron Martin, Michael Stein and others to prepare our balloon for flight. After a couple of days of snow flurries, we launched into a welcoming, cold sky. Flew just over 40 kilometres north-west to land near the village of Abtenau. The following day, our flight path moved almost due north over Grosse Bischofsmütze (known as the Bishop's Hat due to the shape of the mountains). We passed over Grosser Schwarzkogel. Our balloon drifted down to land on a sporting field on the edge of Gosau. A horse-drawn winter sleigh with tourists, their knees covered with blankets, trotted past – a picture card perfect scene burned in my memory forever.

The headaches started February 1st, the day I returned from Filzmoos alpine flying. My personal diagnosis was they were a result of my neck being out of alignment. Made an appointment with my chiropractor.

In April, the opportunity came for me to discover if I had lost my competitive ballooning skills. The inaugural 2010 Canowindra Balloon

Challenge was well attended. Pilots were keen for competition. I was not feeling confident. Competition ballooning had changed enormously since my earlier days of chasing targets. The younger pilots, armed with the latest electronic equipment in their baskets, flew a clear track shown on their computer. Their onboard GPS was of great assist with wind speed and direction to ensure their success.

Balloons inflated around me as I poured heat into my *Aurora*. I stood in my basket with a paper map, ruler and compass, feeling outdated and the oldest pilot competing. My friend and pilot, Kevin Cooper, who I had taught to fly, stood beside me. My form of navigation was to draw a line from launch to goal on my paper map before my balloon left the ground. In addition, I would circle ground highlights along the track, such as dams, farmhouses or outbuildings, tree clumps. Once airborne, I flew in short increments - aiming for my first map mark, then onto the next, flying so I stayed on or as close to my paper map track as I could by finding the different wind direction at various heights.

After a weekend of flying, my score was higher than the younger competitors. The event's trophy was presented to me, along with congratulations from most of my peers. At 67 years of age, I had not lost my competitive streak or flying skills.

Six weeks after that challenge, I was rushed into Sydney's Royal North Shore Hospital Emergency. My head felt it was about to burst open. The arteries of my brain were florid with inflammation. Surgery showed I was minutes or hours away from going permanently blind. After seven days in intensive care, I emerged into the light, the daylight. Fear had darkened my inner light. Initially, after returning home from hospital, my days were speckled with fearful thoughts. Fear the condition would return. Fear I would go blind. Fear I would never meet a special man to spend the rest of my life with. Fear my savings might run out before I died. Fear my ballooning days would soon end. And with a huge shock, I had to accept swallowing a pill daily would be needed to control further brain inflammation. But hopefully, would release me from fear.

I was not the woman who previously had lived a life from a basis of passion, one that underpinned my need for adventure and fed my sense of self. I loved that I was ready to go where the Universe needed me to go. I never consciously put up barriers.

Months later, devastating news hit me harder than my health issue. My close friend, American balloon pilot Carol Davis, was missing. September 29, 2010 the gas balloon Carol and Richard Abruzzo were flying was lost from Italian air traffic control (ATC) radar over the international waters of the Adriatic Sea.

Four days earlier, as the sun set over the English city of Bristol, 20 balloons were prepared for competition – the 54th Coupe Aeronautique Gordon Bennett Race. Each balloon entered into the race was provided with a GPS tracking device, which transmitted the position, altitude, speed and direction of each balloon back to race control. Team USA2's balloon was also equipped with a satellite telephone, VHF radios, radar transponder and two mobiles, as well as survival suits, lifejackets and two single-person life rafts. Some of their equipment was found to be faulty, needed fixing. Carol and Richard (Team USA2) missed their scheduled departure slot. They eventually launched at 11.29pm to the sounds of 'The Star-Spangled Banner'. For the next four days, Team USA2 drifted more than 1000 miles (1610 kilometres) first south over France, then east over the Mediterranean and across Italy. Their skill at finding the optimum wind direction had moved them into 6th place.

Morning broke on September 29. Team USA2 vanished.

Countries united in the search for the missing pilots. Search aircraft, fast patrol boats and all shipping in the area found no trace. Family, friends and the ballooning community eventually returned to their daily lives.

An Italian fishing boat pulled Carol and Richard's remains from the Adriatic Sea. The boat hauled in the balloon basket with their bodies still inside just before dawn, while fishing 11 miles north of Vieste on Italy's eastern Adriatic coast in the southern Puglia region, which makes up the 'heel' of boot-shaped Italy.

Clarity of what caused their balloon to fall into the sea remains blurred, but severe thunderstorms picketed the skies at the time the balloon disappeared. One of the sport's darkest chapters had ended.

Six weeks before Carol's death, I opened a small parcel sent from her Denver home in Colorado. Carol had made a beautiful necklace of pearls with a blue glass dolphin hanging from its centre for me. It's a piece I treasure.

Tears dropped on my computer as I wrote the following piece for ballooning magazines.

I lost a close friend and the world lost an amazing woman when Carol Rymer Davis disappeared over the Adriatic Sea while competing in the prestigious 2010 Gordon Bennett Gas Balloon Race with her ballooning peer and pilot, Richard Abruzzo from Albuquerque, New Mexico.

Carol began hot air ballooning in 1973. We met at the US Nationals in 1980, where I was involved as an Official Observer. We connected immediately and that was also the year she took out both the AX5 Duration (6hours 34 minutes) and AX5 Distance (143 miles) World Records. The following year, she was awarded the Diplome Montgolfier for her record achievements.

We dreamed of undertaking quite a few amazing ballooning adventures together, especially on my annual trips to the States and visits to their Denver home. Her lovely daughters, Heather and Marne, would listen to our schemes with a smile on their faces.

In 1990, the inaugural Ladies World Cup was held in Saga, Japan. Both Carol and I were competitors with 17and 15 years' experience, respectively. But it was a fresh new UK pilot called Lindsay Muir who pipped us at the post with Carol finishing 2nd, me third. But we had lots of laughs, too much sake and food over that week in the Land of the Rising Sun. Her husband, John, was never too far away from our merriment also.

Both Carol and John were passionate about long distance gas ballooning, but it was with Richard Abruzzo, a well-known and respected balloonist from Albuquerque that she formed a formidable flying team. I met Richard while competing in the 1999 Gordon Bennett Race from Albuquerque. He was charming and walked with an inner quiet strength of 'knowing'.

Together they won the 2004 Gordon Bennett Race. The following year, during a gas balloon race, violent thermals pushed their balloon onto power lines. Richard was thrown out of the basket and the balloon with only Carol on board, ascended very fast to a height of 14000 feet. She eventually landed after 10 miles near Kendal, Kansas coping with strong winds. Richard was taken to the hospital for treatment. Carol was not injured.

Her achievements in life were many. She was a trained doctor and worked as a radiologist, spent 22 years in the US Army Reserve as a flight surgeon, retiring as a colonel in 2001. In her younger days, it was climbing mountains that challenged her, but her love of ballooning and competition hugged her heart and soul.

It's what finally took her from us.

I thought of my years of ballooning. How many times had I escaped potential hurt or death? I felt blessed, even protected by angels in those instances. I could identify with Richard and Carol's belief they would win the race if they stayed the course. A sense of hopelessness engulfed me each time I thought of their accident. Surely, with her experience, she had assessed all possible danger remaining airborne. Her thoughts and beliefs on that last morning of her life will never be known.

CHAPTER 53

I have found my latest home. A charming pale blue and white coastal retreat with water views, a few minutes to the beach. Fifty-six indoor potted plants, some large, others smaller, surround me in my attempt to remain closer to nature, bringing warmth, colour and energy into my home. It is a one-hour drive to wine country where I can fly when the desire hits. I joined a croquet club, began to contribute to local charities and committed to my writing. But essentially, I have settled well into a less frenetic lifestyle.

I write briefly of my ballooning activities. More and more, I am being invited to fill the role of an official at ballooning events, to call upon my experience gained over such a long journey. The number of female balloon pilots in Australia continues to grow. Georgia Croft, Tash Buckley, Mia Fraser, Alana Kahl, Scarlett Saunders and Ella Tregale lead the charge amongst the younger women. Nicola Scaife held the Women's World Champion title in 2014 and 2016. Kay Turnbull also a pioneer balloon pilot and Canberra-based pilot Suze McKenzie remain actively flying after many years. The male pilots plus those who give of their time as officials, Marc Andre, Gary Lacey, Steve Ireland, John Wallington, Don Whitford and Ian Benning are absolutely professional, charming and remain friends.

The phone call from David Levin, Competition Director at the 2012 World Championship in Battle Creek, Michigan, caught me by surprise. One of his officials had died suddenly. Would I come as a replacement to complete his team? I was there two days later. Moving amongst the colourful balloons and even more colourful characters – pilots and crews from a variety of countries.

The following year, I celebrated my 70th birthday. 'Where have the years gone?'

I remembered asking myself that same question on my 50th. My family arranged a professionally catered lunch to celebrate in Sydney.

Later that year, Paris was my destination. I had dreamed for years of visiting Paris, preferably with a loving partner. That wasn't going to happen. So, I took myself off on my own. To experience Paris. Had to visit the Eiffel Tower, but the queues were so long I turned away to seek pleasure elsewhere. Strolling along the Champs-Élysées, I was just another face among many, mostly tourists. And I found more tourists as I joined the line to inspect the Musée de Louvre with its amazing artworks. Tired after a few hours, I ventured across a bridge over the Seine to a quaint café to join others chatting and eating outside, watching folk stroll past. Felt totally seduced by the fashion and shoe variety in the stained-glass domed Galeries Lafayette. Shoes, one of my weaknesses, won and I came home with my Parisian collection as a special memento of my visit. Wandered the River Seine bank at night as the cruise boats drifted by full of couples – how romantic, was all I could think.

After six days, I boarded a train to travel to the city of Nancy for the launch of the 2013 61st Gordon Bennett Gas Balloon Race. From there, another train trip took me to a pretty French village, Brissac-Quince. My work as a Juror at the French and UK National Championships followed. I left Europe buoyed by the interaction with my fellow aeronauts and my gorgeous shoes from Paris.

November 2014 Tochigi, Japan came calling. I flew to the Land of the Rising Sun. As a Juror for the International Tochigi Fiesta, I worked with Tomek Kuchcinski (Poland) & John Davis (USA), the other Jurors. Loved being back in Japan testing myself with speaking Nihongo (the local language). The city of Tochigi had survived damage during the war years. Historical temples plus typical Japanese shopfronts dotted the city centre, adding to that mystery of the East I still felt. Once home, it was soon Christmas celebrations with my fabulous family. What would 2015 bring?

I was off to Northam, approximately one-hour drive north east of Perth in Western Australia. An official at the Australian Ballooning Championships, with my painful memories of my 1981 Northam ballooning experience trying to sabotage my current visit. I returned to Northam in 2017 once again an event official but found time to enjoy a fun balloon flight sharing a basket with pilot and owner Curtis Greenwood, also an established hang glider pilot renowned for dare and dashing glider flights.

My years of ballooning have rushed by like water trickling through my fingers, accumulating thousands of hours as pilot-in-command, thousands of hours of magnificent mixed memories. More recently my flights have become fewer and fewer. Now that I was flying less, my time alone increased substantially. Moments when I felt lonely intruded into my nights. My thoughts that I might attract or meet a special person as a companion, a lover, grew more insistent. Yes, I recognised my strong streak of independence had supported me so well, but I also recalled my friend Ross' last comment to me before he died.

"Ruth, you have such a strong sense of self that you will never surrender to any man."

That was a challenge I was ready to embrace. But where to start?

"Join an online dating site," my friends repeatedly suggested. After months of urging me towards that track, I relented.

CHAPTER 54

Brett and Paul were now on my radar.

My toothbrush swirled around my teeth as I stared at my vision in the bathroom mirror. Who was this predatory female running around this morning taking the initiative, contacting the opposite sex? She's not anyone I had met before.

After an initial comfortable and fun coffee date with Brett, we agreed on a golf game together. I chose my favourite golfing outfit, took extra care with my hair and make-up. Drove to the golf club. The sky was crystal blue with a few friendly clouds. Not much wind, but plenty of heat in the sun.

I tried to look relaxed when I noticed Brett wearing a black golf shirt with white trousers. His golf shoes white trimmed with red.

I shaped up to my golf ball in a sky-blue top and white knee-length skirt, my Albuquerque ballooning cap on my head. White and blue golf shoes on my feet.

"Just hit the ball down the middle of the course," I silently repeated to myself. I swung at the pink golf ball. It flew through the air, settled about 110 metres just off centre of the course.

It was obvious from Brett's swing he had been playing for years. His golf ball disappeared in the distance. The two-some was off. For a round of golf, for a definite friendship, possibly a few passionate times together, or even a relationship. Nothing was clear on this day. Over drinks at the bar after the game, Brett suggested dinner the following week. Later he cancelled.

A message from Paul pinged on my computer. We would meet for a coffee date.

I was embracing my personal search for what I had not yet found - a life partner to share true intimacy in an equitable relationship, with whom I could feel safe, could share all aspects of who I am.

The paint on the outside windowsill of the coffee shop was starting to chip. The plants around the doorway added life and a welcoming feeling to the environment. As I moved through the doorway, I noticed Paul from his photo, already waiting, dressed in a Hawaiian shirt. He stood to greet me with a handshake. After moments of no conversation, I broke the silence, sharing just a couple of stories about my ballooning world. It was a struggle to even talk with each other. Within the next ten minutes we were farewelling each other with the "will be in touch" which neither were. I wasn't disappointed. There was no spark of humour between us. Laughter and a sense of humour were of paramount importance to me if I was to develop any relationship with a partner.

My third attempt to find a partner might prove more productive, I told myself as I waited in my car. The black BMW drove up and parked a couple of cars away from my car. After a short time, the driver hobbled into the café using a cane. I soon followed dressed in jeans, boots, white linen shirt, red sweater, my leather flying jacket and a multi-coloured silk scarf.

"Hello, Brian."

He attempted to stand, but sat back resignedly into his chair.

"Not long out of hip surgery, Ruth," he casually stated.

We ordered sandwiches and coffee. Jumped into a two-way communication scurry. There were no long silences at all.

"I was a Qantas pilot for many years till I retired due to age. I was ready to go as I had started having a lot of pain with my hips, which I had to live with when flying."

"The air has been my playground for years, too. Since 1975, in fact," I told him.

"What are some of your special memories?" He asked me with honest interest.

"I was hired by Fontana Films to shoot a television commercial near Ayers Rock. In 1980, it was not necessary to fill out forms or seek permission to fly around the Rock. We were required to consult with the local park rangers who were most helpful. Such balloon flights around the Rock are forbidden now. The advertising agency staff member assigned to accompany me in the balloon chase vehicle to Ayers Rock had arrived from England two weeks earlier. Twenty minutes after our first meeting, we left Alice Springs in tandem with two other vehicles with crew and filming gear. The road from the main highway between Alice and Adelaide into the Rock was along primitive dirt tracks with no lighting. As daylight faded, the car lights grew further apart, becoming separated from each other.

"I found myself in the centre of Australia under a starry sky with a man I had just met that day. In the stillness and to the hum of the motor vehicle, I heard him say, 'I must be mad. In a car with a woman I have just met in the middle of Australia without a clue where I am or where we are headed.' I could have felt the same way, in a car with a man I did not know at all, alone, but the difference was I knew where we were."

Not sure why I told Brian that story, but he had listened attentively. As we left the cafe, Brian put his hand on the middle of my back. Suggested we meet again. We never did.

After many coffee meetings that went nowhere, I gradually lost interest with the internet dating process.

The months ticked by. One evening I was sitting in my kitchen reading 'The Celestine Prophecy', a glass of red wine in one hand, a bowl of nibbles on the table nearby. Keith Urban's music drifted across the room. As midnight approached, I headed to bed to sleep.

In the early hours of predawn, my astral body went flying again. I passed through various previous centuries commenting on a beautiful 'timepiece', a clock I had never ever seen. I smiled at a little old granny character. Ended my journey at the feet of a Christ-like being, kissing the tops of his feet. As a non-active Christian, (I had been christened a Methodist at birth) I had no preconceived beliefs about Jesus. The powerful light that flowed from his being caused me to consider I may be interacting with Jesus. But I had no way of definitely knowing that was so. On waking that morning, I remained suffused with love and light.

And the months rolled on. I began to accept I would live alone into my older years. My drive to find an authentic, loving partner remained an unfulfilled fantasy, but choosing a mediocre partnership definitely held no stronger appeal.

I suspect discovering my birth father's life story will be a mystery I will take to my grave.

CHAPTER 55

I hurried to answer my phone. Voices from my past. Tanys and John McCarron, keen aviators each with their personal Spitfires. We first met through aviation in the early 1990s. Over ensuing years Tanys shared my balloon basket and I listened to her pioneering stores of her ultralight flights. Out of our reconnection came a plan. John and Tanys would support my participation in the 2018 Gordon Bennett Gas Balloon Race from Bern, Switzerland. Tanys would join me in the basket as co-pilot.

I became more alive. Any thoughts of yearning for a male partner in my life disappeared. Any thought other than Tanys and myself in a balloon basket floating through the night sky had to fight its way into my mind. Moved through my daily chores with increased enthusiasm. In my calmer moments, I made lists. Entry form registered and accepted. Team Australia 1 prepared for our challenge. I had flown the 1999 Gas Race with a co-pilot with no gas ballooning experience. I would not do that again. It was imperative Tanys gain gas ballooning experience, even if limited.

Consequently, in April 2018, Tanys and I travelled to Germany. Who better for Tanys to learn the essence of gas ballooning and for a refresher flight for myself than with renowned and popular pilot Wilheim (Willi) Eimers? His knowledge and passion allowed him to claim the duration record of 92 hours' flight in the 1995 Gordon Bennett race from Switzerland to Latvia with his co-pilot, Bernd Landsmann.

Our phones were set for a 3am wake up call for our first flight. Once on the Gladbeck site, Willi began studying area maps, completing flight planning. Tanys assisted other crew members with the preparation of the layout of the envelope, securing tie downs, getting it ready for hydrogen filling. I sorted out the basket and ropes. Finally, we launched into the night sky. City lights twinkled below. The absolute quietness surprised Tanys. The three of us in the basket soaked in the silence that comes with a gas balloon flight. A magnificent sunrise drenched us. Our gas balloon drifted lazily on its path till we caught thick smog, difficult to see far ahead. I thought of our Australian blue skies. Appreciated my country that has not totally succumbed to such visible pollution.

We went 22, 25, 30 kilometres per hour – the balloon drifted northeast, moving over a huge forest. "That's a chemical plant," said Willi, breaking the silence as the balloon took a slight turn to the right. A relief to move away from the white painted buildings with their chimneys pointed skyward. A church spire in the distance dominated our view from the balloon basket. The decision was made to land just before, basically on the edge of the village.

Tanys and I began our agreed landing procedures. She read out loud the metres per second descent. I worked the release of gas (just a small amount) and shovelled sand at the same moment to manage the balloon's downward trajectory. At tree top level, the wind dropped to 12 kilometres per hour. Over the trees, down into a slower speed. The descent continued. Back to earth once more. Willi congratulated us both on our landing procedures. And I had not appreciated the local with an iPad filming our landing. The Australian pilots practising for the popular gas balloon race in Switzerland appeared on the local German news channel that evening.

We flew three fantastic gas balloon flights, taking off in the early hours of the morning, landing later that day to be retrieved by Axel Krischbach. Tanys was hooked, her eyes shining with exhilaration as Willi endorsed her ballooning logbook. I felt so proud of my friend. Admiration for her attention to detail was profound. I had no doubts we would work extremely well together. We had four months to finalise our participation in the 62nd Gordon Bennett race and World Gas Ballooning Championship. Rent a gas balloon, flight equipment, rescue gear, find experienced European crew for support, arrange travel and accommodation – the myriad of jobs necessary for this mammoth adventure.

CHAPTER 56

And what an adventure! Taking on the Swiss Alps and the Italian Dolomites in our rented old balloon and basket, representing our country, only registered female pilot team, a virgin support crew who had never seen a gas balloon in person before 2018. I recall clearly my initial statement to Tanys prior to the race commencement.

"We will have to fly over those snow covered 15,000-foot mountains if we want Italy as our target". Tanys offered no objection, only support. And it was total support all the way from our 'Australian' team: my family Mark, Penny and Josie Wilson from Australia, John McCarron's grandson Mason from Sweden while Tanys had invited her close friend Becca Wilhelm from the USA as essential crew. We had secured Detlef Göcke, Balloon Meister for Gas Inflation, Axel Krischbach, an experienced gas balloon chase driver, while an offer of support from Dutch meteorologist Ab Maas was accepted with pleasure.

First job of the day for the ground team at the launch site was to fill 56 lightweight bags with sand, each bag to weigh 9 kilos. During flight, one sandbag had to be lifted from its moorings on the outside of the basket, then tipped into the sand hopper, the central point from where I would shovel out sand to throw towards earth. Mostly small amounts just to keep our balloon flying level. Large amounts of sand scattered from the basket's hopper would cause the balloon to climb to a different flight level. Sand our important ballast required to gain flight distance.

Our rented 20-year-old basket had none of the comforts of the modern gas balloons on the launch site. It did have our Australian flag draped from the balloon. Other teams were blessed with a bed in each basket so one pilot could sleep, catch up on rest while the second pilot remained in control of the balloon. Then swap positions. Tanys and I did not have such luxury. We bought two small folding chairs on which to sit to rest our bodies.

I was feeling confident, excited to test myself in the air once more, to share this magnificent challenge with Tanys, an ultralight pilot who also had flown her own spitfire aircraft, a true aviator. Now a gas balloon endorsed pilot who worked with Becca on navigation possibilities pre-race.

Twenty balloons representing 12 countries stood inflated on the official launch site in Bern, Switzerland. Enthusiastic crowd numbers grew. Shawn Mackinga with his Swiss friends arrived to cheer us on while my dear friends Jean Michel and Francine Hieber had driven to our launch site from France to offer support. Teams completed last-minute jobs as countdown to lift off approached. Our personal met advice was the balloons heading to France would fly into wind conditions that might swirl them back to Germany, resulting in shorter final distances. And distance from take-off was the goal to win the race. Taking on the Alps to fly to either Italy or Slovenia would be a mammoth challenge but should give us a longer flight distance. My competitive streak was pumping through me.

The Flight Director Markus Haggeney, called a final pilots' briefing at 6pm. The Swiss night vibrated around me. "Who's going to Italy?" Markus asked the assembled group. "We are," was my answer. Decision made. Only two other pilots spoke up. The other seventeen had plans to fly anywhere but over the Alps to Italy. I eagerly checked the briefing paper Markus handed me - the final advice from the Italian Air Traffic Controllers. The Padova Airspace north of Milan and Venice looked like a cobweb of varying heights for approved flight altitudes. I thought of venomous spiders. Had only one reaction. Horror!

"We're not going there," I said with great authority to Tanys, standing quietly beside me. The instructions were even more complicated than those received from the French. I now faced my main insecurity about our flight. My concern I had felt for months. Working with the myriad of Air Traffic Controllers throughout Europe with my lack of languages, the stress of ensuring we did not infringe airspace, or cause the Gordon Bennett Race organisers problems. The majority of the pilots, except the Americans, were in reality flying in their European backyard.

Light was fading fast. Last minute thoughts danced around inside my brain. Should I have chosen the French direction? What if our projected winds changed and we found ourselves flying through the demanding Italian air space? I lent on my belief that had served me well over my forty-four years of aviation experience. Lift off with strong clear decisions for flight would be far safer than the possible confusion of last minute changes. Even if my initial decision would demand increased attention.

Once *Bernadette* sat on the launch podium, Detlef Göcke removed the weighted sandbags to allow the balloon to find lift. I turned to wave farewell to my loved ones and fabulous crew. Yelled to Detlef. "Final bag count?"

"42."

Had I heard correctly? 42! I had calculated we could depart with 48, maybe 50 bags of sand. Our old basket with all our gear weighed so heavily more sandbags had to be removed to get the lift to leave the podium, to be able to fly. I swore deeply into my core. We now faced a huger challenge with reduced sand, reduced ballast.

42. I thought of Douglas Adams, author of The Hitchhiker's Guide to the Galaxy. His writing that 42 was the 'Answer to the Ultimate Question of Life, the Universe and Everything'. All I knew now was 42 was insufficient sandbags for us to fly for a race podium finish, but hopefully sufficient to get us over the Alps.

Bernadette was airborne into the night sky, with the lights from the city of Bern twinkling below us. There was no time to relax or take photos.

Nightlights dropped over the side. Tanys ensured our transponder and radios were working perfectly. Bern Air Traffic Control had our balloon on their radar and cleared us to 16,000 feet. We were on our way, at this point, into the unknown.

We were not getting the wind speeds I had expected to clear the Alps. Our flight would keep us above the jagged tops of the mountains for a much longer time. There was nowhere safe to go if the balloon developed any problem. I knew I would not sleep, even doze until *Bernadette* was clear of the threatening snow-covered peaks below us, that I could see open ground for a landing, even an emergency one. I remained mentally alert to recognise as pilot in command I had to concentrate on keeping the balloon flying level to conserve the sand plus our hydrogen gas. We needed it all to get us off the Alps and over open ground.

In the early hours of the morning, we talked with our ground team. Ab Maas, along with Mark Wilson and Becca Wilhelm, had little sleep too. Both Ab and Becca checked the weather while Mark kept an eye on our flight path and altitudes. Experienced Dutch pilot, Rien Jurg, was on standby in The Netherlands for emergency assistance if required.

Finally, the full moon snuck from behind thick clouds, throwing shafts of moonbeams disappearing into the mountains below. Snow-covered mountains forming a magnificent carpet of images, rippling towards and disappearing over the horizon. A most fantastic image melted into my brain forever. My whole essence full of gratitude. I could feel myself consciously relaxing to allow myself to take time to absorb the beauty of what was before my eyes. Would I ever be so fortunate to encounter such magical, ethereal beauty in my future? I had to ask myself also would I ever be so exposed to such cold again. The moon finally joined us permanently. *Bernadette* floating through the illuminated sky, Tanys sitting in her corner of the basket, her iPad clearly featuring our digital map with track beside her. I stood leaning over the edge, right hand on the sand shovel, ready to drop sand from the hopper should the balloon plummet without warning towards mountain darkness below.

The all-important count of our sandbags continued. We commenced with only 42 x 9 kilo bags, a total of 378 kilos of sand. Twenty bags ballasted to climb to 14,000 feet. Twenty-two bags or 198 kilos of sand left to control our balloon's ascent and descent to fly to safety once off the Alps. In other words, only 22 bags to use until we reached the coastal plain of Italy. The eventual medal holders flew with double the amount of sand, or ballast, that we launched with for our flight. Can't fly a gas balloon for long distances without sand for ballast.

Another area we needed support with was the supply of sufficient oxygen for the flight's duration. Nicolas Tièche, a Team Swiss 2 pilot, stepped up, renting three cylinders of oxygen on our behalf. He then gave us both a quick lesson just prior to launch on how to use this equipment. After seven hours of alpine flying, we had used the first cylinder. The red line showed empty. It was close to 0300hrs. Tanys and I looked at each other. We had to change to the new cylinder in the dark at 14,000 feet. Tanys had her headlamp pointed at her notebook where she had diligently written Nicolas' directions for use. With serious attention to detail, we did it correctly. The alternative being passed out through lack of oxygen at our altitude did not bear thinking. We felt each other's huge sense of relief once we found ourselves breathing a new supply of oxygen. Our relieved smiles said it all.

The cold felt indeterminable. I continued to count the number of sandbags remaining hooked in their original spot - 17. I had used only five bags of sand to cover approximately 10 hours of flying. I silently congratulated myself on such control of the balloon's passage to that point. We had those remaining

17 sandbags or 146 kilos of sand with still a final two mountain ranges to cross before Tanys and I could assess our next options.

Try to track south through Italy or head east to Slovenia?

We were staying on a track north of the dreaded Italian Padova airspace. I did not want to confront the Italian airspace cobweb. We were flying close to the section that required altitude between 16 and 19,000 feet. Did not want to climb to those altitudes with a limited amount of ballast onboard. But our goal was to stay on track at 14,000 feet to benefit from the wind speed and direction.

"The wind will come around to 345 degrees," Advice from our experienced meteorologist Ab Maas noted. Tanys and I checked our map. That direction would take the balloon through Padova. My nerves began chattering to each other. Did not want to interact with the Italians who only a couple of years earlier denied the race pilots Italian airspace. Could we outrun the direction change? Absolute quiet existed in our balloon basket. Both pilots scanned the horizon for that first light that would grant us increased visibility. Both pilots dealt with their own thoughts, possible fears. Mine was interacting with the Italian Air Space Controllers. The weather beat us. The wind change arrived, taking *Bernadette* towards less than friendly airspace. I was forced to face my fears. Firstly, I checked twice to make sure I understood clearly which part of the airspace we were flying in; then the correct airspace we needed to seek permission to transverse. Reluctantly I called Italian Air Traffic Control. Briefly the interchange went like this:

"Delta Oscar Whiskey Mike Lima, permission to transverse airspace at 14,000 feet."

"Delta Oscar Whiskey Mike Lima. Descend to 9000 feet to be out of controlled airspace."

They did not want us in their controlled airspace. Not what we wanted to hear. We wanted to stay at 14,000 feet to hold our tracking speed to the east and retain our precious sand. With limited resources of ballast, I succumbed. Did what we were directed to do. Vented a small amount of gas till *Bernadette* descended to settle at 9000 feet. Our speed dropped dramatically. Drifted along at a snail's pace – 3 to 4kph.

After another close to eight hours of flying, our second oxygen cylinder moved to the red line, empty. At this time, we had commenced flying along the Italian Alps at 9000 feet. I made the decision not to open the third oxygen cylinder, to save money on the rental, yet to be paid. Not a wise decision, I was told by the more experienced alpine pilots after the flight. Some of those pilots continued to use oxygen at 6000 feet to keep their brain clearer. And the older the age, the more one required oxygen supply to make safer decisions. How had I gotten away with this? Flying at 9000 feet for many hours without sleep or oxygen. Do not have a sensible answer.

In that final valley to cross surrounded by alpine peaks, Tanys and I found hell.

The wind died, causing our balloon to hover other than fly. The heat of the midday sun stirred alpine thermals that buffeted *Bernadette* and its two Aussie pilots around the sky. At one point, I turned in the basket. The ragged, rocky cliff sides of a mountain loomed. *Bernadette* was in a nasty thermal, rushing for a sideways collision we would not survive. Images of the impact, the balloon destroyed, Tanys and I falling, flashed across my mind. My initial impulse was to lean out of the basket to push the balloon off the cliff face. I had to do so to save us. A ridiculous thought. Instead.

"Two bags out," I yelled to Tanys as I also furiously shovelled sand from the control sand hopper.

In response *Bernadette* shot up perpendicularly to the mountain edge, just averting a collision. A quick pull of the line to release a little hydrogen to stop the climb. Huge relief we had not crashed into the mountain. I felt my breath rush from my chest while my legs shook. We had survived possible death. But soon the balloon was in a rapid descent again. The unstable air mass was not finished with us. Balloon and pilots were bouncing around the alpine air like an out-of-control ping-pong ball. This erratic balloon behaviour carried on for too long. I shovelled sand with no sense of logic, only intuition, searching for control. I continued working diligently to maintain control of my emotions. The responsibility I felt for Tanys' safety was all-consuming. I could feel her discomfort even though only silence came from her.

Moments later, the largest, whitest cloud formed in our flight path at 9000 feet. I felt stunned when I saw the large doughnut shaped hole in the middle of the top of the bulbous cloud. All the cloud shapes I had studied had not included this one. I had no experience or knowledge of what could happen to a hydrogen-filled balloon inside the belly of such a cloud. Would the balloon explode? Would two female pilots plummet to the earth? Would we survive? At that point, fear took over. Terror jiggled up my legs. My heart was pounding in my chest. I had lost my breath, went searching for that gasp of air to fill a stunned chest. Such a relief once I felt my lungs fill. Total silence existed in our basket. Total stillness also as both Tanys and I confronted the force, moving to smother us. I had no answer other than surrender to our fate and pray earnestly.

It seemed an eternity, but it was most likely only a matter of seconds. The cloud wrapped itself around us, then gently dissipated behind us. I felt angels had protected us. I stood drenched in profound relief and gratitude that both of us were safe - for now. Gradually, the wind increased. I was able to find sufficient movement to fly the balloon over the last mountain peak. I had used 15 of our 17 bags of sand to survive those three hours of hell compared to using only five bags of sand during our earlier 10 hours of flying. I would never forget the turbulence *Bernadette* experienced. The necessity for me to control the erratic behaviour of the balloon leaving us with only two bags to control our final landing. Only two bags of sand as we came off the Alps. By all accounts in any gas ballooning training manual, five bags were deemed essential for a safe landing. I recognised we would have to defy the odds once a landing site was found, but after what I had faced in the Alps, anything else would be easier.

But challenge had not left us. The mountains were behind us. The might of the American military stood in front of us. The Aviano Air Base. Restricted. The Italian Air Force controlled the base as hosts of the US Air Force's 31st Fighter Wing. Their mission – *Lethal Rapidly Ready.*

Was the base ready for the two Aussie gals, one 75 the other 55, in their gas balloon? I radioed for permission to cross their runway at 6000 feet. I could feel myself searching my mind for our aircraft call sign. I grasped it, but slowly. Was the lack of sleep, possibly lack of oxygen to my brain catching up with me? Yes. Definitely.

The response I heard was, "What are your intentions?"

"To land as soon as we can find a suitable spot," I advised.

"Will you land in the next five miles?"

"We will land where it will be safe," was all I could tell him. It was now nearly 32 hours since I had slept. No water, little to eat, as my mouth was too dry to chew or swallow. I recognised clearly it was my responsibility to get our balloon and both of us safely on the ground. My shoulders were buckling with the pressure I was now carrying.

"Advise when you descend through 2500 feet," clear instructions I heard.

"Affirmative. Thank you. Delta Oscar Whiskey Mike Lima."

Beyond the Air Base lay Italian villages, fields of vineyards, mud flats and in the distance, the Adriatic Sea.

Bernadette moved a fraction forward, then completely stopped. Hovered on the edge of the airfield. The wind had left, just disappeared. I glanced down the runway, taking in the military aircraft poised ready to attack or defend when required. As weary as I felt, I had not lost my need for calm. We were not close to the possibility of a safe, easy landing, but my competitive streak battled to push through my heightened emotions. I still wanted to fly to the coast to gain those additional kilometres for our final score. More prayer asking for wind – please – imploring nature to help move our gas balloon over the runway then on towards the coastal plain. We started to move. Huge relief as the Air Base stood behind us. My attention was transfixed on trying to find space to land our balloon.

Tanys stood in the basket, holding a bag of sand in each arm. Our final two bags we would need to control a safe landing. I could feel her eyes watching, taking in my concentration on decision making.

"We need to land, Ruth."

My mind raced with the various challenging situations we would confront below – houses, vineyards, vehicular traffic with the airbase behind us should the wind at the lower levels take us back there. It could be confronting, even dangerous to land. I looked at Tanys. Could feel her concern at what might lie in front of us if we didn't get on the ground. I didn't hesitate. It was a moment of surrender on my part. Dropping my need to chase more distance to achieve a better race placement.

My words rang out loud and strong. "We're landing."

"Whatever happens, we are in this together," I heard the words of my co-pilot clearly.

I heard no fearful expectations in her comment. What I did hear was the voice of true friendship, a true aviator, words from a courageous woman of integrity, Tanys McCarron.

I vented just a small amount of hydrogen from the top of the balloon. Our descent from 6000 feet began. Radioed the Air Base passing through 2500 feet to clear their air space. Our downward track was taking the balloon towards a final landing spot in the middle of a roundabout covered with moving cars. My heart was racing. We had to avoid crashing into the local vehicular traffic.

"Half a bag out," Tanys heard my command, reacted accordingly and dropped sand.

I held my nerve till we were within 200 metres of the roundabout at a height of 180 feet. "Half a bag out," my voice seemed higher in octave. Earlier, I had observed a flag flapping atop a building and knew there was a wind change of direction at ground level. We got it. The balloon turned 160 degrees and floated towards the fields of grapevines. The local traffic on the roundabout was left behind us, along with a loud sigh of relief from me.

"Half a bag out," I called as our balloon scooted a metre above the grapes at 10kph. My hand was on the red line, ready for a fast deflation. "All sand out," my final command to my co-pilot. The basket was within breathing distance of crashing into the final vine. "Anything out," I yelled loudly. Tanys dropped the large red bag holding our immersion suits, plus the food bag between the two rows of vines.

I mustered every ounce of strength I could find. Pulled the red line as the basket hit the ground. The balloon's envelope tipped over on the grass track between the vines. The hydrogen spilled into the early afternoon. *Bernadette* settled on the grass. Died a peaceful death. This lady of the air had flown close to 410 kilometres over 18 hours. She had earned her rest. Even in my exhausted state, I knew I had just performed the best and smoothest balloon descent from altitude and landing of my 43 year long aviation career.

While I felt mentally elated, Tanys and I were safely back on solid ground, I also felt physically shattered. Peeled off my thermal jacket. Sat on the hard ground. Tanys retrieved the last two bags dropped seconds before landing. After sorting all our bits and pieces into a few piles, two exhausted Aussie pilots threw out sleeping bags on the earth near the basket. Sleep came instantly. Meanwhile, Axel Krischbach, with Mark and Penny in chase vehicle #1 was leading our second vehicle with John, Becca and Mason, driving through the Italian countryside with the sole aim of rescuing us.

I woke first. Sitting up with Tanys following soon after. Contact was made with our ground team. They were moments away. What joy to watch their vehicles arrive, to hug our loved ones. Excited chatter bounced from one to another. Tanys' husband John showed huge relief as he exited the chase vehicle to see his wife so vital and smiling as she welcomed him along with her American friend Becca.

Penny filmed the landing site reunion and that pleased me. I could invite my younger son, Grant watching from Sydney, Australia, to use his editing skills to pull together the various videos and photos of our Gordon Bennett adventure to complete a video of worth.

Mark opened the magnum of champagne. Sergio Gelisi, the owner of the vineyard, finally arrived as pink streaks coloured the evening sky. The level of excitement in the group climbed as our host shared his story in Italian over his phone with the local media. "Australian ladies landed in my vineyard."

And yes, I felt proud to be Australian. Proud and relieved Team Australia had conquered threatening clouds plus those potentially perilous peaks. But most of all, I felt proud I was 75 years old and had given myself permission to chase such a daunting life challenge.

CHAPTER 57

At the beginning of my story, I asked myself in an open balloon basket on top of the snow-covered Swiss Alps at night – "What am I doing? How did I get here? Would I survive? And to remind myself, 'Ruth you are 75 years old'."

I have attempted to share various stories of my personal journey, some challenging, some joyful and others borne of pain that may have forged my evolving spirit. A spirit and mind that allowed me to embrace with great passion and commitment my 2018 Gordon Bennett adventure.

Clouds have featured strongly throughout my life.

Personal clouds, both mental and emotional, I have had to rise above, often through pain and tears.

Physical clouds throughout the sky over numerous countries where I danced upon, floated above or fell through in my colourful, magical balloons.

All clouds to date that I have conquered.

With ballooning, I found a love not merely a passing infatuation, but one that has stood the test of time. Sure, my fascination for the sky has brought me much pain and loss of all kinds - personal, financial, physical. But what it's given me is power, self-knowledge, independence, and above all...... freedom.

FOOTNOTE

Carl Jung
1875 – 1961
A man with a vocation will hear his inner voice.

As recorded in this memoir, Ruth Wilson heard her inner voice. Always listened with intent. She was born with a vocation and is one of those fortunate souls who found her tribe during her lifetime: Aviators, particularly balloonists. She has been quoted,

"My happy place is my balloon basket. My happiest place is my gas balloon basket in the night sky."

Other members of that ballooning tribe have shared with Ruth over their years of flying together what ballooning meant to them. Enjoy.

Ballooning offers the opportunity of being totally away from it all –
a concentrated experience of freedom and tranquillity.
Del Michaud, Pilot Canada

The beauty of ballooning is that, like life, it is truly multidimensional.
I feel the sky and make a plan, then I get to go and experience it.
Ballooning makes me feel totally alive and in harmony with nature.
Shawn Mackinga, Pilot Switzerland

Ballooning is a quiet and momentary intrusion into God's space.
I continually wish I could share the intensity of feeling each balloon stirs in
me but that's not possible because it's such a private experience.
Bill Bussey, Pilot USA

I love to fly – passionately.
Nicolas Tièche, Pilot Switzerland

Ballooning is like daydreaming. It's a moment in time of freedom. When I'm in the air, I'm immersed in my flight. Anything that was occupying my mind on the ground disappears. It's just the wind, my balloon and me. I love that.
Nicola Scaife, Pilot Australia

Ballooning - to be at peace with oneself, to be as far away from reality in a laundry basket without going to the moon.
Kevin Cooper, Pilot Australia

Ballooning – A way to escape, please and achieve.
Graeme Scaife, Pilot United Kingdom

Ballooning is important in my life because I love to do it. Besides it's the next best sensation to falling in love.
David Levin, Pilot USA

Going Ballooning is living the life of childhood dreams – it is so random and fanciful - it makes people smile. It is my happy place filled with light, nature and eclectic people.
Kiff Saunders, Pilot Australia

Ballooning to me is about working with the powers of nature to escape the usual constraints which keep us on the earth, giving me a feeling of delight, accomplishment and an unusual freedom.
Maaike Bierma, Pilot Australia

Ballooning? It is simply an armchair in the sky.
Tom Donnelly, Pilot United Kingdom

In a balloon, it doesn't matter where you are going, as long as you are on your way. It resembles a life path, not the destination, it is the journey.
Judy Lynne, Pilot Australia

Ballooning creates an indescribable feeling of being separate and apart, calm and beautiful – all at the same time.
Bill Cunningham, Pilot USA

Ballooning is a unique form of aviation. It is not like any other forms of flying. To hang in the sky and look at the world moving by provides a perspective that never ceases to fascinate me.
Peter Vizzard, Pilot Australia

Ballooning is a great lesson for life. I start each flight not knowing what will happen along the way or where it will end. The challenge is to make the most of every minute and every opportunity.
Simon Fisher, Pilot Australia

During three quarters of a lifetime in Aerostation, I have amassed a mental scrapbook of times, people, places, faces and includes some spectacular parts of this planet that can only be seen with the aid of a balloon. The 'scrapbook' is my most prized possession.
Gren Putland, Pilot Australia

Ballooning is being at one with the wind. It is a great reason to get up in the morning.
Jacky Jansse, Pilot Australia.

It has been always important to me to share my ballooning. I do not enjoy flying alone because I like to observe and enjoy the feelings of my passengers.
Willy Pfeiffer, Pilot Germany

Ballooning has been a life encompassing pursuit. Hard, rewarding, full of great experiences - I look forward to it every day!
Paul Gibbs, Pilot Australia

Ballooning - a life full of friendship and wonder.
Laurent Sciboz, Pilot Switzerland

Touching the leaves at the top of trees,
gently brushing the heads of flowers in the fields, rising
gracefully over hills and fences, feeling the coolness of rivers,
the warmth of ripened wheat, the softness of mist –
it is like breathing nature from my basket suspended in the sky.
Carolinda Witt, Pilot Australia

Ballooning is my superpower.
Matthew Scaife, Pilot Australia

My adult siblings TOP Glenda Jeffrey Self Ronnie (Below) Keith & wife Kerri, self with Glenda

Grant & Sharlene Wilson

Mark & Penny Wilson

Tyler Wilson with partner Emily Hazell

Josie Wilson hugs her grandmother Ruth   *2018 Launch of my first book non-fiction*

The Wilson Gals - Josie Ruth Penny Sharlene Ute

EPILOGUE

In the 1960s, a group of university students designed and built a few experimental balloons and formed the Aerostat Society. Phil Kavanagh and Peter Vizzard were two of the pioneers of the sport. They remain the only members of that early ballooning scene who are currently still actively involved with the sport.

In 1978, a small group of balloonists, including Ruth Wilson, formed the now controlling body of the sport in Australia, the Australian Ballooning Federation (ABF) with Ruth as the first secretary. Over the ensuing years, she has held the position of President, Vice President, FAI Ballooning Commission Delegate, ASAC Delegate and Vice President of the National Aero Club of Australia. She is currently the ABF Secretary.

In 2002 Ruth Wilson was inducted in the Australian Ballooning Hall of Fame.

In 2008 the prestigious William Deane Award in recognition of excellence in contributing to the sport of Ballooning was presented to her.

In 2017 Ruth Wilson was nominated to the Fédération Aéronautique Internationale Ballooning Commission Hall of Fame in Switzerland.

In 2021 Ruth Wilson was awarded the Federation Aeronautique Internationale Paul Tissandier Trophy for serving the cause of Aviation in general and Sporting Aviation in particular, by her work, initiative, devotion and in other ways.

RUTH E WILSON

ACKNOWLEDGEMENTS

I would like to begin by acknowledging the Darumbai people, Traditional Custodians of the land on which I was born and pay my respect to their Elders past, present and future.

Most importantly, I want to thank my mother, who chose to give birth to me against all that society embraced in 1943. And to my Pop Lawson, who treated me as his daughter even though I was not – thank you from my heart.

To my unknown biological father – my wish for you is that life has been kind to you. My wish for me is that I will find someone who can enlighten me on as to the kind of man you were throughout your life.

And to my Grandparents Bill and Lilian Thorne - you nurtured me for those precious first three years of my life. Blessed with your love.

My siblings: Ronnie, Glenda, Keith and Jeffrey – thank you for sharing most of my journey with me. I love you.

My goddaughter, Tanya Matheson, I feel so proud of the woman you have become.

My former husband Kevin Wilson, who shared with me the journey of parents to our sons Mark and Grant.

To Tanys & John McCarron – your friendship and generosity allowed me to find my inner warrior. I remain eternally grateful.

My Editors – Bella Pollen & Kristen Cosby, who believed in my story initially and encouraged me to dig deeper into my emotions to share my truth. Finally, Shawline's Senior Editor Samantha Elley who polished my writing to its finished form.

My Agent/Publisher – Bradley Shaw, who accepted I had a story to tell.

To the Australian and international ballooning community – my life has been enriched each time we spent together, sharing airspace, sharing champagne or supporting each other. To my differing chase crews over 45 years - I truly valued each and every person.

To my girlfriends who were there when I needed to be held up, encouraged: all pillars of strength. Wende Anstruther, Julia Atkinson, Connie Bachor, Alison Batty, Margaret Collins, Anne Crick, Jan Edwards, Kris Galbraith, Anne Hansen, Jacky Jansse, Wendy Kavanagh, Jan Kenny, Kerri Lawson, Judy Lynne, Susan Merrill, Julie Molloy, Lorraine Parkes, Lindy Patel, Helen Patfield, Jan Puckeridge, Margie Putland, Judy Scaife, Martina Schmidt,

Margaret Toller, Fay Turnbull, Joanne Windeyer, Carolinda Witt and many others. Those who are based overseas, whose homes are a home away from home when I travel: Judy Scaife, United Kingdom, Wende Anstruther, Canada, Roberta Levin, USA, Francine Hieber, France, Marialucia Luongo, Italy, Toshiko Oiwa, Japan, the Tièche family in Switzerland – Léa, Patricia and Yvonne. Thank you. All these lovely women, my friendship warriors.

And long after I have flown to the 'Other Side', I promise to be close in spirit enjoying any balloon flight that appeals – and that definitely will be gas balloon adventures.

Finally, I want to thank my 'Angels' who kept me alive and safe when the opposite loomed.

www.ruthwilson.net

Shawline Publishing Group Pty Ltd
www.shawlinepublishing.com.au

SHAWLINE
PUBLISHING
GROUP